101 SPORTS CARD INVESTMENTS

Best Buys From $5 To $500

Edited by
MARK K. LARSON

©1993 by Krause Publications, Inc.

Published by

**krause
publications**

700 E. State Street • Iola, WI 54990-0001
Telephone: 715/445-2214

Library of Congress Catalog Number: 93-77546
ISBN: 0-87341-259-1
Printed in the United States of America

CONTENTS

INTRODUCTION

In today's society of mass-produced sports cards, most of them aren't scarce, which is one of the factors related to value. Nor are they in great demand, yet.

So the first question for someone looking to invest in cards becomes what to buy. With so many cards, sets and players to choose from, it's hard to decide what to pursue. Sometimes it's just too confusing.

This book concentrates on the who-to-buy part of the question and offers 101 recommendations of players whose cards generally have a steady track record of rising in value. It's a case of tried and true versus speculating on a rookie, who could be the next Willie Mays, or but another flash in the pan. The maxim that applies here is that the margin of profit on a card rises as the margin of chance decreases through perpetual, solid seasons.

A Hall-of-Famer's card is a secure investment, because there is usually some demand, but in varying degrees per player. The players recommended in this book are either Hall of Famers, soon-to-be Hall of Famers, or have been in the league long enough to have compiled numbers which can be projected towards Hall-of-Fame caliber numbers, barring an injury to the player.

So think long-term career, instead of one-year wonders. Generally sluggers and RBI men should be taken over singles hitters, batting average leaders and pitchers. Stick with the scorers in basketball and hockey.

In football, always think offense over defense; stick to the quarterbacks, who have the highest profile and are generally the highest prices. Then look at the running backs, then the wide receivers. Offensive and defensive linemen don't get the ink, so they generally aren't wise investments. But pick up a rookie card of Minnesota Vikings defensive lineman Carl Eller, based on his six Pro Bowl selections and his four Super Bowl appearances. Those two factors — all-star recognition and playoff exposure — are key factors when it comes time to decide who goes into a Hall of Fame and who doesn't.

Football presents a unique situation — only one kicker (Jan Stenerud) and two tight ends (Mike Ditka and John Mackey) have been elected, so steer clear of these positions, except for tight ends Kellen Winslow and Ozzie Newsome. They're Hall of Famers in this book.

In most cases, the recommendations in this book are for a player's rookie card — it's the first year a player's card has appeared in a nationally-distributed set, but doesn't always coincide with the year of his first appearance in the big leagues or in a Traded or Update set.

Like first-edition books, rookie cards are generally considered to be a player's most valuable card and generally climb at a faster rate than the other cards. They offer the highest rate of return.

If you want to speculate on the rookie cards of players who are playing their first year in the big leagues, it's a good idea to have tracked a player's progress through the minor leagues, so you can get a jump on other collectors, scooping them before the player goes on to win the Rookie of the Year award.

Learn about the player. Watch batting average, potential power, age, ERA, strikeout ability, years in the minors, major league city affiliation (cards of major league players on the coasts have bigger population bases, and more media exposure, thus generally have more demand) and supply of rookie cards.

Buy those rookie cards early while they are still cheap; hot rookies rise quickly before the price guides can catch up, so shop around for the best price. Watch for opportune buy/sell periods.

For the short-term investment, if a rookie comes out and tears up the league in his first season, you're in the money if you have 100 of his rookie cards. But the rookie card phenomenon of a what-have-you-done-for-me-lately? is driven by speculators and investors. And fame is often fleeting...

Often, you'll see 100-count lots for sale, but we're not suggesting that you go out and buy monster 1,000-card lots. The result could be a financial disaster if the guy throws his arm out.

Plus, remember, there are more buyers for the fewer cards you have, as opposed to only a half dozen who may want the entire 1,000-card lot. Finding someone to buy the cards at a higher price than what you paid for them is difficult. So think quality, too, when making a purchase, not necessarily quantity.

Beginning sports card collectors are often advised to collect anything they like, since the cards only have intrinsic value, a value derived from the enjoyment behind collecting and the memories triggered by the players depicted.

But if you want to make some money, you can't become too attached to your cards; as the value goes up, and a decision to sell has to be made, the sentimental value has to be set aside, for a paper profit is just that. It's not cold hard cash in hand. You have to be willing to sell at the right price at any time.

National media coverage regarding the boom in the card collecting hobby and skyrocketing dollar values the last few years has caused people to think that the values can only go up. But they can sink, too.

David S. Krause, an assistant professor of finance at Marquette University in Milwaukee, studied the baseball card market from 1978-87. He concluded in a *Sports Collectors Digest* article that baseball cards had risen approximately 32 percent per year; rookie cards were at 45 percent.

That doesn't mean you'll make money on every investment, anymore than someone playing the stock market. If it were easy, then you wouldn't need the advice. Cards can sink, as some of them in this book have done over the last two years.

But they can rebound, too, as we're projecting the cards to do when the Hall of Fame beckons. We're going to help you make some money, or at least not lose a lot of it. You'll win some, and you'll lose some. But when it comes time to cash in your cards, you'll have more money than when you started.

1) Getting started

Shop around. In addition to card shows, shops and retail outlets, check out rummage sales, auctions and antique stores. One suggestion is to arrive at card shows toward the end of the show. Some dealers, who might not have made much money during the show, are more hopeful in making a quick sale. They will drop prices so they can cover expenses and so they don't have to lug so much home with them; cash is lighter than their inventory. Remember, they need to turn their inventory over so they can move on to newer, faster-selling material, and generate profits.

However, arriving early may help you get a card before a dealer can determine what the buyer demand is. So try that method, too, because oftentimes your offer might be the best offer the dealer receives.

Let store owners know you're interested in baseball cards; give them your name and number so they can contact you if additional items come in. Flea markets are a good source for cards, too, where the dealer's idea is to unload something quickly while turning a small profit. Look for discounts and bargain rates. Stores which may have recently gone out of business might offer blow-out rates, too.

Footwork and network. Ask around if anyone you know might have a hidden treasure chest of cards in the attic. Also, establish a relationship with the dealer; he wants a steady customer, and will keep you in mind. A good, honest dealer should be willing to buy back cards at the same grade, provided it still is the same, and he should have a return policy if you are not satisfied.

Be willing to negotiate, because a dealer, looking for the quick profit in turning over the card immediately, may have already lined up another buyer. Those other buyers may be a potential source for cards, too; maybe you'll be able to buy and sell with them. And don't forget the lost art of trading.

2) Keeping current

Do your homework. Know the basics. Learn what is available and what you should pay for it. Someone somewhere has probably got what you want at a lower price. Or perhaps there's something else which you later decide you like much better.

To make money, you can't only invest your money; you've got to invest in the time necessary to become knowledgeable and to acquire the foresight needed to reap the cash rewards later on.

Keep informed and current. Krause Publications offers three publications (*Sports Card Magazine*, *Sports Collectors Digest* and *Sports Card Price Guide*) for collectors to keep up with their hobby. These publications contain price guides which provide starting points for purchases. Dealers often refer to price guides when they are selling newer cards which they haven't priced. Be prepared; you'll make better transactions. Spend not only dollars, but spend time doing research and reading.

3) Establish a grading scale

Condition generally regards the wear and tear of a card, while characteristics are imperfections which occurred during the printing process, such as centering, smudges and dots, photo quality and quality of printing. Centering regards how even the card's borders are and how well the picture fits on the card.

Off-grade cards do not sell as quickly as top-grade material, nor does it increase in value at the same rate. If you expect to resell a card, only buy Near Mint or Mint cards; that leaves you with only one thing to argue about — price, not condition.

Krause Publications' periodicals offer a standard grading scale (found immediately after the Introduction) which can facilitate buying and trading between two people. Although no one is required to adhere to these condition standards, the *Sports Collectors Digest/Baseball Cards Magazine* scale, created in 1981, is an attempt to bring some consistency in grading and to allow for an informed agreement between buyer/seller. If you feel you need a second opinion, get one.

Ultimately, the collector himself must formulate his own personal grading standards for deciding whether cards available for purchase meet the needs of his own collection. The condition of your card is the primary factor in determining its worth when you sell it to a dealer. Remember, too, that a card's condition will never improve with age; it can only deteriorate.

Before buying a card, examine it; have it taken out of its holder, which could be hiding defects or imperfections. Watch, too, to see if the holder has been tightened too much; it could crush the card. Look at both sides of the card, bottom to top, side to side. Inspect.

4) Buying cards

The first thing one must do when investing in cards is to get over the initial sticker shock. Yes, these pieces of cardboard are worth something today. And they might be worth even more tomorrow...

Usually, the best time to buy a player's card is in the off season, when the hype and media attention he's generated during the season, which helps drive prices up, has died down. When the baseball card market is slow, compared to the basketball, football and hockey markets, stock up on your 1988 Mark Grace Score Traded cards.

As a rule, stay away from boxed sets, reprints and commons. They just don't sell. And don't have the player autograph the card, either; it decreases the value. Have the player sign a photo or a baseball if you want his autograph.

Error cards are not worth pursuing, either; they do not command more than normal prices unless the card has been corrected, thus making one scarcer than the other. But still, they don't sell too well.

No 1980s card will ever be scarce; companies withhold print numbers, so it's impossible to gauge current scarcity. It doesn't pay to try to guess those numbers. Instead, buy an older card or two. Because of its scarcity, there's almost no chance that a pre-1970s card will drop in value; it can only go up.

When buying cards from wax boxes, picking several from the same box instead of one or two from each different box gives you a better chance at getting stars and having fewer duplicates. But there's nothing wrong with building up a stockpile of doubles, as long as they aren't all commons.

Be alert for cherry picking — when packs are resealed after having been opened and the stars have been taken out and replaced with commons. When you open the packs, do so carefully; be gentle so you don't affect the cards condition.

If you've found the major stars inside a few of the packs, save a few unopened wax packs, too; you'll be able to sell them for more than what you paid for them, because they potentially could have a player in demand who has made it big since the cards were issued.

Everyone wants wax packs year round; they're in constant demand. Buying a few boxes is a wise choice, because dealers, who are now flooded with so many card company offerings, have to decide what gets shelf space. They may cut back on their inventory of certain items, so wax boxes will retain a strong trade value over the years.

As newcomers enter the hobby and work backward in completing sets, the older material's demand increases. Someone will always be willing to pay the price.

However, the older the material is, the more careful you should be regarding possible tampering. But as long as it's unopened, chances are you can't quibble on condition. And, since it's increasingly difficult to find unopened older material, all you'll have to settle on is a price.

Finally, buy the best quality you can afford. And buy good values, not just good prices. But buyer beware — if a deal seems to good to be true, then more often than not it probably is. It could be a counterfeit, too.

5) Storing your collection

Take an inventory: Make a list of your cards, by year, number and condition. Compile a want list, too, indicating the highest price you'd be willing to pay. If you've got doubles, keep them handy, too, for trade or sale if the price shoots up. But remember to get a fair price for your double — you have two of it; your transaction partner either has none or wants an extra.

Establish a budget and don't spend any more than you have planned to spend; you will act more prudently.

When it comes time to store your cards, keep them out of the hot, stuffy attic or the cold, damp, leaky basement. A cool, dry place is the most suitable environment. Keeping the cards in binders works the best, with top-loading plastic sheets so the cards don't fall out as easily. But be careful not to overload the binders, or stack them too high so as to crush the cards inside.

The standard 220- to 800-count boxes are made especially for large quantities to keep the movement inside to a minimum, thereby preventing corner dings. No movement means no wear. Don't over-handle your cards too much, and take them out of binders as little as possible, preferably only when being sold; it's easy to ding the cards when they are being put back into sheets.

When buying a card that is in a holder, ask the owner to take it out of its case. The case could be hiding creases, or scratches, which may appear to be on the case but are really on the card.

6) Selling your collection

Baseball cards are sometimes compared to penny stocks. But, while the percentages on returns have been greater than those for stocks, bonds and coins in recent years, it's easier to find a stock broker to buy your stock than it is to find someone to buy your cards.

If you're going to make money after you've bought a card, there has to be a two-way market — you must be able to sell your cards. The demand for the card by other collectors is what sets the value.

Basically, to make a profit your cards must at least double in value from what you paid for them. But there's a potential 50 percent difference between retail value and the dealer's actual buying price; thus, it may take a few years to gain the values needed to gain the value back. Dealers will generally take 60 to 70 percent of book value.

But remember, the higher the price goes, the fewer collectors there are who can afford it or want it. Sometimes it's wise to sell off half of your cards for profits now, and save the others for potential increases. That's your call.

Pay attention to the buy ad prices; you'll get an idea of what you can sell your cards for. Continually monitor the ads to see if the dealers are still looking for the cards and to see if the prices are still going up. The price will go up until the demand is met.

Also, watch the sell ads to see which cards are scarcer than others. Scarcity pertains to how many were actually made; rarity means how many still exist and have survived.

Regionalism affects values, too. Any card is worth more in the player's home city than in other locations.

The popularity of a card can also influence its price; the greater the popularity, the greater the liquidity of your investment. But remember, you don't want to get stuck with 1,000 cards of one player. Where can you go to sell them?

The last, but not the least, important factor to remember if you're going to sell a card is to keep it in Mint condition. That means you can't use it in your bike spokes, like kids did in the good old days. Just a little difference in quality can mean a huge difference in price. The better the eye appeal, the greater the value.

ACKNOWLEDGEMENTS

In addition to bringing in many of his own cards to be photographed for this book, Tony Prudom, the assistant editor of Krause Kublications' *Sports Card Price Guide*, was a "ghostwriter" on this project, providing tidbits and reassurances as this project was underway. He, and Krause Publications sports staff members Shawn Riley, Tom Hultman and Rick Hines assisted in selecting the players and ranking them. Don Butler, former football/basketball/hockey price guide editor for *Sports Collectors Digest*, also assisted in the non-baseball card rankings.

Robert "Red" Wimmer supplied several photographs which were used in this book. The public relations department for the National Basketball Association and John Chymczuk from Elias Sports Bureau provided statistical information. The July 1991 issue of *Baseball Cards Price Guide* was used for pricing information from that period.

Mary Lou Marshall designed the cover of this book; Tom Nelsen designed the inside pages. Dawn Van Epern entered in data for the players' card checklists, while Jeanette Sawall helped proof pages.

GRADING

It is necessary that some sort of card grading standard be used so that buyer and seller (especially when dealing by mail) may reach an informed agreement on the value of a card.

Each card set's listings are generally priced in Krause Publications' price guides in the three grades of preservation in which those cards are most commonly encountered in the daily buying and selling of the hobby marketplace.

Older cards (pre-1981) are listed in grades of Near Mint (NR MT), Excellent (EX) and Very Good (VG), reflecting the basic fact that few cards were able to survive for 25, 50 or even 100 years in close semblance to the condition of their issue.

The pricing of cards in these three conditions will allow readers to accurately price cards which fall in intermediate grades, such as EX-MT, or VG-EX.

More recent issues, which have been preserved in top condition in considerable number, are listed in the grades of Mint (MT), Near Mint and Excellent, reflective of the fact that there exists in the current market little or no demand for cards of the recent past in grades below Excellent.

In general, although grades below Very Good are not generally priced in price guides, close approximations of low-grade card values may be figured on the following formula: Good condition cards are valued at about 50 percent of VG price, with Fair cards about 50 percent of Good.

Cards in Poor condition have no market value except in the cases of the rarest and most expensive cards. In such cases, value has to be negotiated individually.

For the benefit of the reader, we present herewith the grading guide which was originally formulated by *Baseball Cards* magazine and *Sports Collectors Digest* in 1981, and has been continually refined since that time.

These grading definitions have been used in the pricing of cards in this book, but they are by no means a universally accepted grading standard.

The potential buyer of a baseball card should keep that in mind when encountering cards of nominally the same grade, but at a price which differs widely from that quoted in this book.

Ultimately, the collector himself must formulate his own personal grading standards in deciding whether cards available for purchase meet the needs of his own collection.

No collector is required to adhere to the grading standards presented herewith — or to any other published grading standards — but all are invited to do so. The editors of Krause Publications' sports books and price guides are eager to work toward the development of a standardized system of card grading that will be consistent with the realities of the hobby marketplace. Contact the editors.

Mint (MT): A perfect card. Well-centered, with parallel borders which appear equal to the naked eye. Four sharp, square corners. No creases, edge dents, surface scratches, paper flaws, loss of luster, yellowing or fading, regardless of age. No imperfectly printed card — out of register, badly cut or ink flawed — or card stained by contact with gum, wax or other substances can be considered truly Mint, even if new out of the pack.

Near Mint (NR MT): A nearly perfect card. At first glance, a Near Mint card appears perfect; upon closer examination, however, a minor flaw will be discovered. On well-centered cards, three of the four corners must be perfectly sharp; only one corner shows a minor imperfection upon close inspection. A slightly off-center card with one or more borders being noticeably unequal — but still present — would also fit this grade.

Excellent (EX): Corners are still fairly sharp with only moderate wear. Card borders may be off center. No creases. May have very minor gum, wax or product stains, front or back. Surfaces may show slight loss of luster from rubbing across other cards.

Very Good (VG): Shows obvious handling. Corners rounded and/or perhaps showing minor creases. Other minor creases may be visible. Surfaces may exhibit loss of luster, but all printing is intact. May show major gum creases, tape marks or extraneous markings or writing. Exhibit honest wear.

Good (G): A well-worn card, but exhibits no intentional damage or abuse. May have major or multiple creases. Corners rounded well beyond the border.

Fair (F): Shows excessive wear, along with damage or abuse. Will show all the wear characteristics of a Good card, along with such damage as thumb tack holes in or near margins, evidence of having been taped or pasted, perhaps small tears around the edges, or creases so heavy as to break the cardboard. Backs may show minor added pen or pencil writing, or be missing small bits of paper. Still, a basically complete card.

Poor (P): A card that has been tortured to death. Corners or other areas may be torn off. Card may have been trimmed, show holes from paper punch or have been used for BB gun practice. Front may have extraneous pen or pencil writing, or other defacement. Major portions of front or back design may be missing. Not a pretty sight.

In addition to these seven widely-used terms, collectors will often encounter intermediate grades, such as VG-EX (Very Good to Excellent), EX-MT (Excellent to Mint), or NR MT-MT (Near Mint to Mint).

Persons who describe a card with such grades are usually trying to convey that the card has all the characteristics of the lower grade, with enough of the higher grade to merit mention. Such cards are usually priced at a point midway between the two grades.

VALUATIONS

Values quoted in this book represent the current retail market and are compiled from recommendations provided and verified through the authors' daily involvement in the publication of the hobby's leading advertising periodicals, as well as the input of specialized consultants.

It should be stressed, however, that this book is intended to serve only as an aid in evaluating cards; actual market conditions are constantly changing. This is especially true of the cards of current players, whose on-field performance during the course of a season can greatly affect the value of their cards — upwards or downwards.

Publication of this book is not intended as a solicitation to buy or sell the listed cards by the editors, publishers or contributors.

Again, the values here are retail prices — what a collector can expect to pay when buying a card from a dealer. The wholesale price, that which a collector can expect to receive from a dealer when selling cards, will be significantly lower.

Most dealers operate on a 100 percent mark-up, generally paying about 50 percent of a card's retail value. On some high-demand cards, dealers will pay up to 75 percent or even 100 percent or more of retail value, anticipating continued price increases. Conversely, for many low-demand cards, such as common players' cards of recent years, dealers may pay 25 percent or even less of retail.

BASEBALL

 Gary Carter

Gary Carter: 1975 Topps #620, $50; $35 in July 1991.

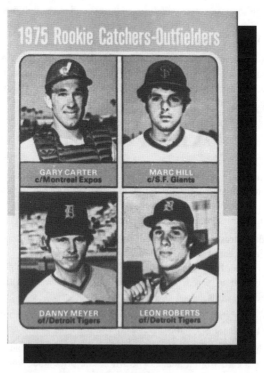

Gary Carter

April 8, 1954; 6-2, 214; throws and bats right; catcher and first baseman; retired; 19 seasons (Montreal 1974-84, New York Mets 1985-89, San Francisco 1990, Los Angeles 1991, Montreal 1992).
G: 2,296 (70th); AB: 7,971 (92nd); R: 1,025; H: 2,092; 2B: 371;
3B: 31; HR: 324 (54th); RBI: 1,225 (85th); TB: 3,497 (93rd);
Ave.: .262; SB: 37.

Holds major league career record for putouts for a catcher (11,785) and most chances (12,988); holds record for fewest passed balls, playing 150+ games in a season (1, in 1978); holds major league record for most years leading the league in chances accepted by a catcher (8); holds N.L. records for most seasons leading the league in games by a catcher (6), most years leading the league in putouts by a catcher (8) and most years leading the league in chances accepted by a catcher (8); holds N.L. record for most games by a catcher (2,056); led N.L. catchers in putouts and double plays five times and in total chances seven times; led N.L. catchers in fielding percentage and assists once; won Gold Glove Awards in 1980-82; shares major league record for most home runs in two consecutive games (5, Sept. 3-4, 1985); tied for N.L. lead in RBI in 1984 (106); hit three home runs in one game twice; shares career record for most game-winning RBI in championship series play (3), and most in a single-series (2, 1986); shares single-game record for most home runs in an All-Star game (2, Aug. 9, 1981); led the N.L. in sacrifice flies in 1986 (15); named to the All-Star team 11 times; All-Star game MVP in 1981 and 1984.

He's always seemed to be in the shadow of future Hall-of-Famer Carlton Fisk. But compare Gary Carter's lifetime statistics with Fisk's, and you'll see why Carter deserves more respect.

During his 19-year career, Carter hit 324 home runs, had 1,225 RBI, 2,092 hits and a .262 batting average. Fisk, entering the 1993 season, has hit 375 home runs, has 1,326 RBI and 2,346 hits, and owns a .270 lifetime batting average. But Fisk has played for 23 seasons.

Like Fisk, Carter has been an ironman; he holds the National League record for games played by a catcher, trailing only Bob Boone and Fisk. The wear and tear has taken its toll; Carter only played in 338 games his last four seasons. Some even say he held on just to surpass Al Lopez's National League record for games caught. Not so. Carter's a gamer.

But that's enough negativism about a player who was a throwback to the 1950s era of baseball. The hard-nosed Carter was always hustling, always in the game. And he was always grinning and smiling; he loved playing baseball.

Although Carter, who one reporter described as having a "lumberjack swing," is fourth all-time for home runs by a catcher, he was also a top-notch defensive catcher, and holds several major league defensive records.

"The Kid" is eligible for induction in 1998. Depending on who doesn't make it in some of the preceding ballots, Carter might not make it on the first ballot, but he should be inducted. He's one of the top six or seven catchers of all time.

Since Carter shares it with three other players, his 1975 Topps rookie card might not be the most appealing to Carter collectors, who may want to pick up his 1976 card instead ($12; that's a bargain). But his 1975 card is the most valuable of the 11 "Rookie"-designated cards in the set (which also includes the high-demand Robin Yount and George Brett rookie cards) and should hold at $50, then rise after he's inducted.

Gary Carter Checklist

Year	Company	No.	Price
1975	O-Pee-Chee/Topps	620	35.00/50.00
1975	Topps Mini	620	50.00
1976	O-Pee-Chee/Topps	441	15.00/12.00
1977	O-Pee-Chee	45	8.00
1977	Topps	295	6.00
1978	O-Pee-Chee	135	5.00
1978	Topps	120	4.00
1979	O-Pee-Chee	270	4.00
1979	Topps	520	3.00
1980	O-Pee-Chee	37	2.00
1980	Topps	70	2.25
1981	Donruss	90	.50
1981	Fleer	142	.70
1981	O-Pee-Chee	6	1.00
1981	Topps	660	1.00
1982	Donruss	2/114	.50/.35
1982	Fleer	185	.35
1982	O-Pee-Chee	244	.75
1982	O-Pee-Chee/Topps	344	.30/.35
1982	Topps	730	.80
1983	Donruss	340	.40
1983	Fleer	278/637/638	.35/.15/.20
1983	O-Pee-Chee	314	.30
1983	O-Pee-Chee/Topps	370	.50/.50
1983	Topps	404	.35
1984	Donruss	55	1.00
1984	Fleer	271	.40
1984	O-Pee-Chee	366	.70
1984	O-Pee-Chee/Topps	393	.40/.30
1984	Topps	450	.40
1985	Donruss	55	.40
1985	Fleer	393/631	.35/.30
1985	Fleer Update	U21	1.00
1985	O-Pee-Chee/Topps	230	.30/.35
1985	Topps	719	.20
1985	Topps Traded	17T	1.00
1986	Donruss	68	.35
1986	Fleer	76	.25
1986	Leaf	63	1.00
1986	O-Pee-Chee/Topps	170	.25/.25
1986	Topps	708	.20
1987	Donruss	69	.30
1987	Fleer	4/629/634	.25/.60/.25
1987	Leaf	109	.60
1987	O-Pee-Chee/Topps	20	.20/.20
1987	Topps	602	.15
1988	Donruss	199	.25
1988	Fleer	130/636	.25/.20
1988	Leaf	156	.40
1988	O-Pee-Chee	157	.15
1988	Score	325	.15
1988	Topps	530	.15
1989	Bowman	379	.03
1989	Donruss	53	.20
1989	Fleer	30	.20
1989	O-Pee-Chee	324	.12
1989	Score	240	.15
1989	Topps	3/393/680	.10/.10/.15
1989	Upper Deck	390	.25
1990	Bowman	236	.05

14

Gary Carter Checklist

Year	Company	No.	Price
1990	Donruss	147	.06
1990	Fleer	199	.06
1990	Fleer Update	U62	.10
1990	Leaf	134	.35
1990	O-Pee-Chee/Topps	790	.10/.07
1990	Score	416	.07
1990	Score Traded	35T	.10
1990	Topps Traded	19T	.10
1990	Upper Deck	168	.10
1990	Upper Deck Extended	774	.15
1991	Bowman	598	.06
1991	Donruss	151	.08
1991	Donruss Studio	182	.15
1991	Fleer	258	.08
1991	Fleer Ultra Update	86	.15
1991	Fleer Update	U93	.08
1991	Leaf	457	.15
1991	O-Pee-Chee/Topps	310	.07/.08
1991	Score	215	.08
1991	Topps Traded	19T	.08
1991	Topps Stadium Club	424	.30
1991	Upper Deck	176	.10
1991	Upper Deck Extended	758	.12
1992	Donruss	36	.08
1992	Fleer	450	.08
1992	Fleer Ultra	514	.25
1992	Leaf	442	.15
1992	Leaf Studio	53	.15
1992	Score	489	.08
1992	Score Pinnacle	321	.15
1992	Score Traded	59	.12
1992	Topps	45	.08
1992	Topps Stadium Club	845	.20
1992	Upper Deck	267	.10

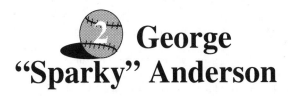

George "Sparky" Anderson

George "Sparky" Anderson: 1959 Topps #338, $45; $20 in July 1991.

Feb. 22, 1934; 5-9, 168; throws right, bats right; second base; retired; one year (Philadelphia 1959); currently manager of the Detroit Tigers.

Major League hitting totals
G: 152; AB: 477; R: 42; H: 104; 2B: 9; 3B: 3; HR: 0; TB: 122; RBI: 34; Ave.: .218; SB: 6.

Managerial record entering the 1993 season: active; 23 seasons (Cincinnati 1970-78, Detroit 1979-92).

PHILADELPHIA PHILLIES
SECOND BASE

Sparky Anderson

Regular season — W: 1,996 (7th); L: 1,611; Pct.: .553; Post season (championship series) — W: 18; L: 9; World Series — W: 16; L: 12; All-Star games — W: 3; L: 2.

Named A.L. Manager of the Year by the Baseball Writers' Association of America in 1984 and 1987; led the Cincinnati Reds to five divisional titles in nine years; lost in World Series appearances in 1970 and 1972 but defeated the Boston Red Sox to win the World Series in 1975 and the New York Yankees to win the title in 1976; lost to the New York Mets in the N.L. Championship Series in 1973; led the Detroit Tigers to two divisional titles in 14 seasons; lost the Championship Series in 1987 to the Minnesota Twins, but led the Tigers to a World Series title in 1984 over the San Diego Padres.

Sparky Anderson certainly isn't going to be inducted into the Hall of Fame based on his lifetime .218 batting average. His three World Series titles and more than 2,000 wins as a manager are what will put him alongside baseball's other immortals, including 10 other managers.

Heading into the 1993 season, Anderson, starting his 15th season as the

16

Tigers' manager, was 15 victories behind Leo Durocher for sixth on baseball's all-time wins list. His first nine years were spent as the manager of Cincinnati's "Big Red Machine," the Reds, who won two World Series titles.

Granted, Anderson has had some talent to work with during his 23-year career. He's managed four Hall of Famers (including Johnny Bench, Joe Morgan, Tom Seaver and Pete Rose, who's a Hall of Famer in this book), and three future Hall of Famers (Jack Morris, Lou Whitaker and Alan Trammell). But he's been able to survive a revolving-door position for 23 seasons, with but two teams.

Anderson has a .553 lifetime winning percentage. He just knows how to get his teams to win; he's only had four losing seasons, which are offset by his four 100-win seasons. Although he's not going to top Connie Mack's all-time record of 53 years or 3,776 wins as a major league manager, Anderson, with 164 more wins, could finish third on the all-time list for wins (passing Bucky Harris, 2,159).

Considering Tommy Lasorda's 1954 Topps rookie card is $175 and Whitey Herzog's 1957 Topps is $30, Anderson's 1959 Topps card, which has jumped $25 in the last two years, is still a steal at $45, with plenty of room for growth.

George (Sparky) Anderson Checklist

Year	Company	No.	Price
1959	Topps	338	45.00
1960	Leaf	125	40.00
1960	Topps	34	2.50
1970	O-Pee-Chee/Topps	181	1.25/1.75
1971	O-Pee-Chee/Topps	688	2.50/3.50
1972	O-Pee-Chee/Topps	358	.75/1.00
1973	O-Pee-Chee/Topps	296	.50/.90
1974	O-Pee-Chee/Topps	326	.40/.50
1975	O-Pee-Chee/Topps	531	.75/.90
1975	Topps Mini	531	1.25
1976	Topps	104	.90
1977	Topps	287	.80
1978	Topps	401	.30
1979	Topps	259	.60
1981	Donruss	370	.10
1981	Fleer	460	.10
1981	Topps	666	.30
1982	Donruss	29	.10
1983	Donruss	533	.10
1983	Topps	666	.12
1984	Topps	259	.12
1985	Fleer	628	.08
1985	Topps	307	.08
1986	Topps	411	.07
1987	Topps	218	.07
1988	Topps	14	.06
1989	Topps	193	.06
1990	O-Pee-Chee/Topps	609	.25/.03
1991	O-Pee-Chee/Topps	519	.25/.04
1992	Topps	381	.03

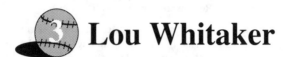 **Lou Whitaker**

Lou Whitaker: 1978 Topps #704, $20; $12 in July 1991.

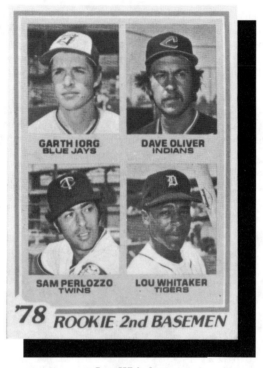

Lou Whitaker

May 12, 1957; 5-11, 180; throws right, bats left; second baseman; active; 16 seasons (all with Detroit).

Career statistics entering the 1993 season
G: 2,095; AB: 7,616; R: 1,211; H: 2,088; 2B: 353; 3B: 62; HR: 209;
TB: 3,192; RBI: 930; Ave.: .274; SB: 134.

Named A.L. Rookie of the Year in 1978; won Gold Glove Awards in 1983-85; led A.L. second basemen in total chances (811) and double plays (120) in

1982; has played in two championship series and one World Series; has been selected for the All-Star game five times.

Lou Whitaker has had 11 consecutive seasons in which he's played at least 100 games and hit 10 or more home runs. It might seem like an insignificant feat, until you realize only one other second baseman in major league history has compiled a longer streak — Hall of Famer Bobby Doerr, at 12.

But then again "Sweet Lou" Whitaker has been so consistent for 16 seasons, he, even though he's a five-time All-Star, has been almost unnoticed, and certainly underrated. As a result, his 1978 Topps card, at $20, is undervalued, considering he's compiling Hall-of-Fame-caliber numbers.

Whitaker has more hits and runs than Doerr (2,042 and 1,094), but entering the 1993 season trails him by 14 home runs and 317 RBI. Each has made a World Series appearance.

A first-rate defensive second baseman, he can turn the double play as well as anyone. His partner for 16 seasons has been shortstop Alan Trammell, who broke into the big leagues along with Whitaker during the second game of a September 1977 double-header. Their careers have paralleled each other; Trammell was the sixth player in Tiger history to collect 2,000 hits, while Whitaker was the seventh.

Whitaker shares his 1978 rookie card with three other players. If it isn't as attractive for that reason, you can't go wrong with an $8 second-year 1979 Topps card. But, considering Eddie Murray's 1978 Topps rookie is $75, and Trammell's from the same set is $60, Whitaker's is a steal at $20.

Lou Whitaker Checklist

Year	Company	No.	Price
1978	Topps	704	20.00
1979	O-Pee-Chee	55	1.75
1979	Topps	123	8.00
1980	O-Pee-Chee	187	.75
1980	Topps	358	1.25
1981	Donruss	365	.40
1981	Fleer	463	.40
1981	O-Pee-Chee/Topps	234	.40/.60
1982	Donruss	454	.40
1982	Fleer	284	.40
1982	O-Pee-Chee/Topps	39	.25/.40
1983	Donruss	333	.40
1983	Fleer	348	.40
1983	O-Pee-Chee	66	.30
1983	Topps	509	.40
1984	Donruss	227	.60
1984	Fleer	92	.40
1984	O-Pee-Chee	181/211	.50/.25
1984	Topps	398/666/695	.20/.15/.40
1985	Donruss	5/293	.30/.40
1985	Fleer	24	.35
1985	Leaf	5	.20
1985	O-Pee-Chee	108	.20
1985	Topps	480	.30
1986	Donruss	49	.30

Lou Whitaker Checklist

Year	Company	No.	Price
1986	Fleer	242	.30
1986	Leaf	33	.15
1986	O-Pee-Chee/Topps	20	.15/.25
1987	Donruss	107	.25
1987	Fleer	168	.25
1987	Leaf	78	.15
1987	O-Pee-Chee	106	.15
1987	Topps	661	.15
1988	Donruss	173	.25
1988	Fleer	75	.25
1988	Leaf	169	.12
1988	O-Pee-Chee	179	.09
1988	Score	56	.20
1988	Topps	770	.20
1989	Bowman	103	.08
1989	Donruss	298	.20
1989	Fleer	151	.20
1989	O-Pee-Chee/Topps	320	.12/.15
1989	Score	230	.15
1989	Upper Deck	451	.15
1990	Bowman	356	.08
1990	Donruss	16/298	.08/.08
1990	Fleer	619	.09
1990	Leaf	34	.35
1990	O-Pee-Chee/Topps	280	.10/.07
1990	Score	75	.09
1990	Upper Deck	41/327	.06/.10
1991	Bowman	150	.06
1991	Donruss	174	.08
1991	Donruss Studio	60	.20
1991	Fleer	357	.08
1991	Fleer Ultra	130	.08
1991	Leaf	120	.10
1991	O-Pee-Chee	145	.07
1991	Score	297	.08
1991	Topps	145	.08
1991	Topps Stadium Club	101	.25
1991	Upper Deck	367	.10
1992	Donruss	285	.08
1992	Fleer	149	.08
1992	Fleer Ultra	65	.15
1992	Leaf	391	.12
1992	Leaf Studio	180	.15
1992	Score	255	.08
1992	Score Pinnacle	29	.10
1992	Topps	570	.06
1992	Topps Stadium Club	550	.15
1992	Upper Deck	516	.08

 # Tim Raines

Tim Raines: 1981 Topps #479, $7; $9 in July 1991.

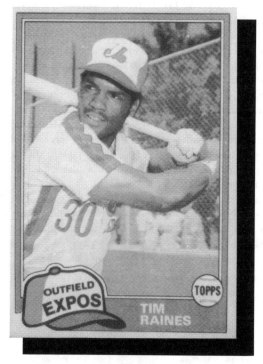

Tim Raines

Sept. 16, 1959; 5-8, 186; throws right and switch hits; outfielder, active; 14 seasons (Montreal 1979-90; Chicago White Sox 1991-92).

Career statistics entering the 1993 season
G: 1,704; AB: 6,465; R: 1,138; H: 1,923; 2B: 315; 3B: 96; HR: 108;
TB: 2,754; RBI: 656; Ave.: .297; SB: 730 (8th).

Holds major league single-season record for most intentional walks in a season by a switch hitter (26, in 1987); led the N.L. in on base percentage in 1986

(.413); led the N.L. in runs in 1983 (133) and 1987 (123); tied in the N.L. with 38 doubles in 1984; led the N.L. in batting average in 1986 (.334); led the N.L. in stolen bases in 1981 (71), 1982 (78); 1983 (90) and 1984 (75); hit for the cycle Aug. 16, 1987; switch-hit home runs in one game on July 16, 1988; led N.L. outfielders in assists in 1983 (21); has played in one championship series, in 1981; has been selected to the All-Star team seven times.

He's been called a "poor man's" Rickey Henderson, but Tim "Rock" Raines has career statistics which are quite comparable to Henderson's, considering he's played in 155 fewer games. Although Henderson holds the edge in runs (1,472-1,138), hits (2,000-1,923), doubles (329-315), home runs (199-108) and stolen bases (1,042-730), the multi-faceted Raines leads in triples (96-54) and batting average (.297-.291), with one batting championship.

Although he had enough power to sometimes hit third while with Montreal, Raines has always been one of the game's best leadoff men, blending his speed with his higher batting average. As a table-setter in Chicago for the big bats (Frank Thomas and Robin Ventura) behind him, Raines, a switch-hitter, adds an extra dimension to his game that Henderson doesn't have.

Raines hasn't had the World Series exposure that Henderson has had, but he's on a White Sox team which appears to be a more serious contender over the next few seasons than the Oakland A's do. That, coupled with a few more solid seasons before he retires, could generate the extra attention Raines needs to pull closer to Henderson's card value.

At $7 each, you can get 11 of Raines' first Topps card for the price of one $80 1980 Topps Rickey Henderson rookie card. Considering they are only one year apart, Raines' card is a steal. And you'd still have three bucks left over to buy some plastic holders.

Tim Raines Checklist

Year	Company	No.	Price
1981	Donruss	538	5.00
1981	O-Pee-Chee	136	10.00
1981	Topps	479	7.00
1981	Topps Traded	816	12.00
1982	Donruss	214	1.50
1982	Fleer	202	1.50
1982	O-Pee-Chee/Topps	70	1.50/2.00
1982	Topps	3/164	.30/.35
1983	Donruss	540	.35
1983	Fleer	292	.35
1983	O-Pee-Chee	227/352	.40/.30
1983	Topps	403/595/704	.35/1.00/.35
1984	Donruss	299	.80
1984	Fleer	281/631	.70/.20
1984	O-Pee-Chee/Topps	370	.60/.50
1984	O-Pee-Chee/Topps	390	.40/.25
1984	Topps	134	.30
1985	Donruss	299	.50
1985	Fleer	405	.35
1985	Leaf	218/252	.35/.80

Tim Raines Checklist

Year	Company	No.	Price
1985	O-Pee-Chee	277	.30
1985	Topps	630	.35
1986	Donruss	177	.40
1986	Fleer	256/632	.30/.30
1986	Leaf	108	1.00
1986	O-Pee-Chee/Topps	280	.25/.30
1987	Donruss	56	.30
1987	Fleer	328/642	.30/.12
1987	Leaf	149	.50
1987	O-Pee-Chee/Topps	30	.20/.25
1988	Donruss	345	.25
1988	Fleer	193/631	.25/.15
1988	Leaf	2/114/211	.20/.20/.50
1988	O-Pee-Chee	243	.20
1988	Score	3/649	.20/.25
1988	Topps	403/720	.12/.20
1989	Bowman	369	.08
1989	Donruss	97	.25
1989	Fleer	391	.25
1989	O-Pee-Chee	87	.15
1989	Score	40	.25
1989	Topps	81/560	.08/.15
1989	Upper Deck	402	.25
1990	Bowman	118	.08
1990	Donruss	216	.09
1990	Fleer	359	.10
1990	Leaf	212	.35
1990	O-Pee-Chee	180	.12
1990	Score	409	.10
1990	Topps	180	.10
1990	Upper Deck	29/177	.06/.12
1991	Bowman	362	.08
1991	Donruss	457	.08
1991	Donruss Studio	37	.25
1991	Fleer	244	.08
1991	Fleer Ultra	81	.10
1991	Fleer Update	U15	.15
1991	Leaf	413	.15
1991	O-Pee-Chee/Topps	360	.10/.15
1991	Score	35	.12
1991	Score Traded	10T	.15
1991	Topps Traded	94T	.12
1991	Upper Deck	143	.15
1991	Upper Deck Extended	773	.15
1992	Donruss	312	.10
1992	Fleer	97	.10
1992	Fleer Ultra	43	.15
1992	Leaf	37	.15
1992	Leaf Studio	156	.15
1992	Score	635	.06
1992	Score Pinnacle	178	.15
1992	Topps	426	.10
1992	Topps Stadium Club	426	.20
1992	Upper Deck	575	.10

Wade Boggs

Wade Boggs: 1983 Topps #498, $35; $35 in July 1991.

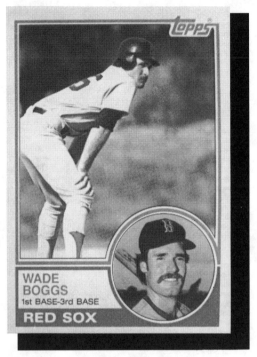

Wade Boggs

June 15, 1958; 6-2, 197; throws right, bats left; third base; active; 11 seasons (Boston 1982-92, New York Yankees 1993).

Career statistics entering the 1993 season

G: 1,625; AB: 6,213; R: 1,067; H: 2,098; 2B: 422 (77th); 3B: 47; HR: 85; TB: 2,869; RBI: 687; Ave.: .338 (16th); SB: 16.

Holds A.L. record for most consecutive seasons with 200+ hits (7, 1983-89); holds A.L. record for highest batting average for a rookie, 100 or more games

(.349 in 1982); holds major league record for most seasons and most consecutive seasons leading the league in intentional walks (6, 1987-92); shares major league single-season record for most games with one or more hits (135 in 1985); holds A.L. record for most singles in a season (187 in 1985); led the A.L. in on base percentage in 1983 (.449), 1985 (.450), 1986 (.453), 1987 (.461), 1988 (.476) and 1989 (.430); led the A.L. in hitting in 1983 (.361), 1985 (.368), 1986 (.357), 1987 (.363) and 1988 (.366); led A.L. third basemen with 486 total chances in 1985; led A.L. third basemen in double plays in 1984 (30), 1987 (37) and 1989 (29); has played in eight All-Star games; tied the championship series record for most sacrifice flies in 1988 (2).

For most hitters, a .300 batting average at the end of the season would be a satisfactory result. But if Wade Boggs hit .300, he'd be 38 points below his career average. He hasn't hit .300 just once; he did it in each of his first 10 seasons, tying him for the third longest streak to start a career.

Although Boggs tailed off dramatically in his 11th season in 1992 (.259), a change of scenery might do wonders for him, as he takes his classic swing from Fenway Park to Yankee Stadium, where he's joining the third leading hitter over the last 10 years, Don Mattingly (.311). Expect Boggs, a five-time batting champion, to rebound.

Boggs, who fills 8.5 pages in the Yankees' 292-page 1993 media guide, ranks 16th all-time in career batting average. Although he doesn't have as much playoff and World Series exposure as George Brett or Brooks Robinson, he holds the distinction of equalling their five consecutive All-Star game starts.

The classic contact hitter has had multi-hit games in 38 percent of the games he's played in. His 135 games in which he collected one or more hits during the 1985 season is a record. Boggs ranks high in several all-time offensive categories, including a record seven straight 200+ hit seasons, and holds the sixth (342) and eighth (340) spots for most total bases in a season (Babe Ruth is first with 379).

He's been considered to be a one-dimensional player, hitting for a high average but supplying no power. But he did hit 24 home runs in 1987, and has led the league three times in turning double plays.

Wade Boggs Checklist

Year	Company	No.	Price
1983	Donruss	586	25.00
1983	Fleer	179	25.00
1983	Topps	498	35.00
1984	Donruss	26/151	4.00/18.00
1984	Fleer	392/630	12.00/1.00
1984	O-Pee-Chee/Topps	30	9.00/5.00
1984	Topps	131	.50
1984	Topps	786	.40
1985	Donruss	172	5.00
1985	Fleer	151	4.00
1985	Leaf	179	3.00

Wade Boggs Checklist

Year	Company	No.	Price
1985	O-Pee-Chee/Topps	350	3.00/2.00
1986	Donruss	371	3.00
1986	Fleer	341/634/639	2.25/.60/1.00
1986	Leaf	168	1.50
1986	O-Pee-Chee	262	1.50
1986	Topps	510	1.25
1987	Donruss	252	.80
1987	Fleer	29/637	1.50/.35
1987	Leaf	193	.80
1987	O-Pee-Chee/Topps	150	.80/.70
1987	Topps	608	.40
1988	Donruss	153	.60
1988	Fleer	345	.70
1988	Leaf	65	.70
1988	O-Pee-Chee/Topps	200	.70/.30
1988	Score	2	.40
1988	Topps	21/388	.15/.35
1989	Bowman	32	.40
1989	Donruss	68	.90
1989	Fleer	81/633	.50/.40
1989	O-Pee-Chee	184	.60
1989	Score	175/654	.35/.30
1989	Topps	2/399/600	.20/.20/.40
1989	Upper Deck	389/687	.60/.08
1990	Bowman	281	.10
1990	Donruss	68/712	.30/.09
1990	Fleer	268/632	.40/.10
1990	Leaf	51	2.00
1990	O-Pee-Chee/Topps	387	.35/.20
1990	O-Pee-Chee	760	.50/.25
1990	Score	245/683/704	.30/.20/.25
1990	Upper Deck	555	.50
1991	Bowman	129	.15
1991	Donruss	55/178	.10/.20
1991	Donruss Studio	11	.60
1991	Fleer	86	.20
1991	Fleer Ultra	27	.25
1991	Leaf	273	.40
1991	O-Pee-Chee/Topps	450	.35/.15
1991	Score	12/393/889	.20/.20/.20
1991	Topps Stadium Club	170	1.50
1991	Upper Deck	546	.25
1992	Donruss	23/210	.20/.20
1992	Fleer	32/707	.15/.08
1992	Fleer Ultra	311	.50
1992	Leaf	286	.30
1992	Leaf Studio	131	.80
1992	Score	434/660/885	.10/.12/.20
1992	Score Pinnacle	175/282	.40/.15
1992	Topps	10/399	.15/.10
1992	Topps Stadium Club	520	.80
1992	Topps Stadium Club Dome	18	.30
1992	Upper Deck	443/646	.15/.20

 **Gregg Jefferies**

Gregg Jefferies: 1988 Fleer #137, $2; $7 in July 1991.

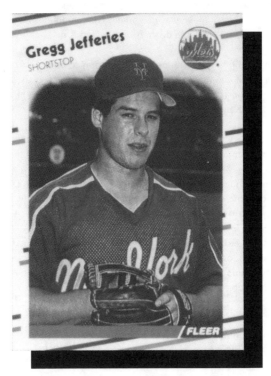

Gregg Jefferies

Aug. 1, 1967; 5-10, 185; throws right, switch-hitter; second base, third base; active; six seasons (New York Mets 1987-91, Kansas City 1992, St. Louis 1993).

G: 617; AB: 2,317; R: 312; H: 644; 2B: 132; 3B: 12; HR: 52;
TB: 956; RBI: 280; Ave.: .278; SB: 82.

Led N.L. in doubles (40) in 1990; led A.L. third basemen in errors in 1992 (26).

As Baseball America's only two-time Minor League Player of the Year ever, Gregg Jefferies had some big expectations to live up to as he started his major league career in New York as the Mets' 1988 season concluded. It didn't help that he hit .321 in 29 games to close out the season, and hit a spectacular .333 in post-season play against the Los Angeles Dodgers.

And it didn't help, as the 1989 season started, that Jefferies was projected as the Rookie of the Year.

Perhaps the best thing to happen for Jefferies, who found it difficult to live up to all those expectations, was his escape from the spotlights of the New York media, where his every move was magnified. His tumultuous days behind him, Jefferies has been able to settle down mentally, and is making great strides as a hitter.

A potential .300 hitter, Jefferies has all the tools to bust out. He's capable of hitting 15 to 20 home runs each season, and throw in 20 steals, too. Don't be surprised if he consistently hits .285, with 75 RBIs, each season, matching his 1992 totals with Kansas City.

As an infielder who can play every position, Jefferies may have found a home in St. Louis, where he'll play first base. He won't generate the power numbers that are generally supplied by first basemen, but he'll be a dependable hitter.

On Memorial Day in 1988, Jefferies told a Sports Collectors Digest reporter during the epitome of rookie card mania that he wouldn't pay $3.50 for his rookie card. "I'm overrated," he said, adding that he'd only proven himself at the minor league level.

His 1988 Fleer card eventually peaked at around $7 late in 1991, and has fallen ever since, down to $2. The time to buy is now, because Jefferies, 25, will be hitting his prime soon. And he'll put up some solid numbers. And his card value will shoot up.

Gregg Jefferies Checklist

Year	Company	No.	Price
1988	Donruss	657	1.25
1988	Fleer	137	2.00
1988	Leaf	259	2.00
1988	Score	645	1.25
1989	Bowman	381	.20
1989	Donruss	35	.40
1989	Fleer	38	.30
1989	O-Pee-Chee/Topps	233	.50/.30
1989	Score	600	.30
1989	Upper Deck	9	1.00
1990	Bowman	140	.25
1990	Donruss	270	.25
1990	Fleer	207	.20
1990	Leaf	171	.50
1990	O-Pee-Chee/Topps	457	.25/.30
1990	Score	468	.60
1990	Upper Deck	166	.30

Gregg Jefferies Checklist

Year	Company	No.	Price
1991	Bowman	481	.08
1991	Donruss	79	.15
1991	Donruss Studio	206	.20
1991	Fleer	151	.15
1991	Fleer Ultra	221/397	.15/.06
1991	Leaf	465	.15
1991	O-Pee-Chee/Topps	30	.20/.15
1991	Score	660	.15
1991	Upper Deck	95/156	.10/.15
1992	Donruss	372	.15
1992	Fleer	508	.12
1992	Fleer Ultra	372	.25
1992	Fleer Update	26	.12
1992	Leaf	215	.25
1992	Leaf Studio	184	.20
1992	Score	192	.12
1992	Score Pinnacle	330	.20
1992	Score Traded	39	.08
1992	Topps	707	.12
1992	Topps Traded	55	.08
1992	Topps Stadium Club	737	.25
1992	Upper Deck	133	.15

 # Mark Grace

Mark Grace: 1988 Score Traded #80, $15; $25 in July 1991.

June 28, 1964; 6-2, 190; bats and throws left; first baseman; active; five seasons (Chicago Cubs 1988-92).

Career statistics entering the 1993 season
G: 751; AB: 2,807; R: 370; H: 840; 2B: 148; 3B: 18; HR: 46; TB: 1,162; RBI: 355; Ave.: .299; SB: 41.

Won Gold Glove Award at first base in 1992; led N.L. first basemen in total chances in 1991 (1,695) and 1992 (1,725); shares major league record for most assists by a first baseman in one inning (3, May 23, 1990); holds N.L. single-season record for most assists by a first baseman (180, in 1990); led N.L. in at bats in 1991 (619); hit a home run in his first championship series at bat (Oct. 4, 1989).

Although he plays in the friendly confines of Wrigley Field and has the opportunity to be seen nationally on the Cubs' cable television network, Mark Grace just doesn't receive the recognition he deserves. Maybe it's because he doesn't have the arrogance of a Will "The Thrill" Clark. Or maybe it's because Grace has only reached double figures in home runs in one of his five seasons. He doesn't hit the tape-measure monster home runs like Fred McGriff does.

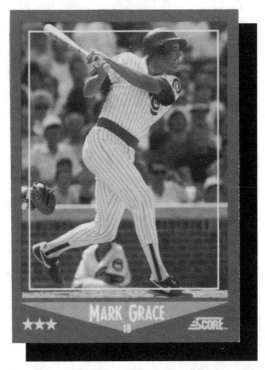

Mark Grace

But, as the old golfer's expression goes, you drive for show and putt for dough. As one of the best young "putters" in the league, sporting a lifetime .299 batting average, Grace would be considered a very wealthy man.

This bright young star is a confident hitter who can handle almost any pitch. An established hitter with a good eye, Grace walks twice as many times as he strikes out. His sweet swing will keep him in the hunt for a batting title, and a top-10 finish every year.

Grace should be the cornerstone of the Cubs infield for many years to come. If he plays 13 more years at his current 168 hits per year, Grace will finish with slightly more than 3,000 hits — and be a virtual lock as a Hall of Famer.

At $15, Grace's 1988 Score Traded may seem a bit steep right now, but the set itself (at $100, including Roberto Alomar at $65) offers above average investment potential due to its scarcity. Since some dealers may be hesitant to break the set down, an individual Grace card might logically in turn be even more difficult to come by.

Mark Grace Checklist

Year	Company	No.	Price
1988	Donruss	40	1.25
1988	Donruss Rookies	1	2.50
1988	Fleer	641	4.00
1988	Fleer Update	U77	2.50
1988	Leaf	40	4.00
1988	Score Traded	80T	15.00
1988	Topps Traded	42T	2.00
1989	Bowman	291	.30
1989	Donruss	17/255	.20/.60
1989	Fleer	426	.40
1989	O-Pee-Chee	297	.50
1989	Score	362	.80
1989	Topps	465	.70
1989	Upper Deck	140	1.25
1990	Bowman	29	.20
1990	Donruss	577	.25
1990	Fleer	32	.25
1990	Leaf	137	.50
1990	O-Pee-Chee/Topps	240	.35/.40
1990	Score	150	.25
1990	Upper Deck	128	.50
1991	Bowman	433	.08
1991	Donruss	199	.10
1991	Donruss Studio	157	.40
1991	Fleer	422	.15
1991	Fleer Ultra	61	.15
1991	Leaf	170	.20
1991	O-Pee-Chee/Topps	520	.25/.15
1991	Score	175	.15
1991	Topps Stadium Club	290	.50
1991	Upper Deck	99/134	.10/.15
1992	Donruss	281	.15
1992	Fleer	381	.08
1992	Fleer Ultra	175	.30
1992	Leaf	26	.20
1992	Leaf Studio	14	.15
1992	Score	445	.08
1992	Score Pinnacle	136	.20
1992	Topps	140	.12
1992	Topps Stadium Club	174	.25
1992	Upper Deck	143	.15

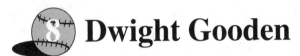 # Dwight Gooden

Dwight Gooden: 1985 Donruss #190, $8; $15 in July 1991.

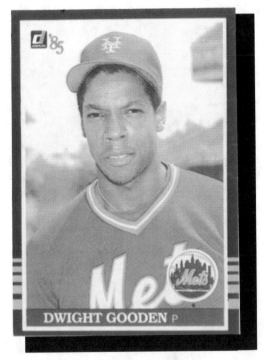

Dwight Gooden

Nov. 16, 1964; 6-3, 210; bats and throws right; pitcher; active; nine seasons (New York Mets 1984-92).

Career statistics entering the 1993 season

W: 142; L: 66; Pct.: .683 (4th); ERA: 2.99; G: 269; GS: 267; CG: 60; ShO: 21; Saves: 1; IP: 1,919 2/3; H: 1,664; R: 702; ER: 638; BB: 575; SO: 1,686 (74th).

Named N.L. Rookie of the Year in 1984; named N.L. Cy Young Award winner in 1985; led N.L. pitchers in wins (24), ERA (1.53), complete games (16), innings pitched (276 2/3) and strikeouts (268) in 1985; led N.L. in strikeouts in 1984 (276); holds major-league rookie single-season record for strikeouts (276, in 1984); shares modern major league record for most strikeouts in two consecutive games (32, Sept. 12 and Sept. 17, 1984), and three consecutive games (43, Sept. 7, Sept. 12, Sept. 17, 1984); holds championship single-series record for most strikeouts (20, in 1988); shares N.L. championship single-game record for most innings pitched (10, Oct. 14, 1986).

Dwight Gooden sprang from the gates quickly with a 17-9 rookie campaign and a Rookie of the Year Award in 1984. So, Fleer included him in its 1984 update set. As a result, Gooden redefined the meaning of update and traded sets when his card, with its perceived scarcity, hit $10 the season immediately after it was issued.

Dr. K didn't experience a sophomore jinx, either; his 24-4 record and 1985 Cy Young Award fanned the fires as his card continued to rise in value. By the end of 1985 it had reached $25.

From that point, the card took off — by June it was $40; by August it was $48; by the end of September it was $60. And then by the first week of November, the card peaked at $120.

But Gooden's off-the-field battles (alleged alcohol and drug abuse) limited his appearances and production in 1987, and by the end of the year his card dropped to $70. It gradually climbed to $100 by mid-1991 (aided by Gooden's 19-7 season in 1990) and has fluctuated around that mark ever since.

Although he had rotator cuff surgery before the 1992 season, Gooden rebounded with a 10-13 record and a 3.67 ERA. He isn't the overpowering pitcher he once was, but if Doc can utilize his savvy and excellent control, he'll be able to battle hitters and finesse them out instead of relying on his fastball.

He's not even halfway to 300 wins, which might be an unreachable number. But he's only 67 wins away from Hall of Famer Don Drysdale, and is on pace to match Drysdale's 2.95 career ERA and surpass his 2,486 strikeouts, numbers which landed Drysdale in the Hall of Fame. Take a chance that Gooden's arm holds out; pick up one of his 1985 Donruss cards for $8, and hope he gets traded to a contender where he can accumulate several more wins.

Dwight Gooden Checklist

Year	Company	No.	Price
1984	Fleer Update	U43	90.00
1984	Topps Traded	42	25.00
1985	Donruss	190	8.00
1985	Fleer	82/634	8.00/1.00
1985	Leaf	234	6.00
1985	O-Pee-Chee	41	10.00
1985	Topps	3/620	1.00/3.00
1986	Donruss	26/75	1.00/2.00

Dwight Gooden Checklist

Year	Company	No.	Price
1986	Fleer	81/626	1.50/.50
1986	Fleer	638/641	.70/.40
1986	Leaf	26	.80
1986	O-Pee-Chee/Topps	250	1.25/1.00
1986	Topps	202/709	.40/.40
1987	Donruss	199	.60
1987	Fleer	9/629	1.00/.60
1987	Leaf	84	.70
1987	O-Pee-Chee/Topps	130	.50/.60
1987	Topps	603	.30
1988	Donruss	69	.60
1988	Fleer	135	.60
1988	Leaf	48	.40
1988	O-Pee-Chee	287	.30
1988	Score	350	.40
1988	Topps	405/480	.15/.40
1989	Bowman	376	.25
1989	Donruss	270	.50
1989	Fleer	36/635	.20/.20
1989	O-Pee-Chee/Topps	30	.25/.20
1989	Score	200	.20
1989	Topps	661	.10
1989	Upper Deck	565	.50
1990	Bowman	126	.20
1990	Donruss	171	.15
1990	Fleer	204	.20
1990	Leaf	139	.80
1990	O-Pee-Chee/Topps	510	.20/.25
1990	Post Cereal	29	.80
1990	Score	313	.25
1990	Upper Deck	62/114	.06/.20
1991	Bowman	472	.08
1991	Donruss	266	.20
1991	Donruss Studio	204	.35
1991	Fleer	148	.20
1991	Fleer Ultra	218	.20
1991	Leaf	165	.25
1991	O-Pee-Chee/Topps	330	.15/.20
1991	Score	540/685/866	.15/.20/.08
1991	Topps Stadium Club	100	.70
1991	Upper Deck	224	.25
1992	Donruss	446	.10
1992	Fleer	505	.12
1992	Fleer Ultra	232	.40
1992	Leaf	112	.25
1992	Leaf Studio	65	.25
1992	Score	10	.12
1992	Score Pinnacle	111	.35
1992	Topps	725	.12
1992	Topps Stadium Club	455/602	.40/.50
1992	Upper Deck	84/135	.10/.15

 # Ryne Sandberg

Ryne Sandberg: 1983 Topps #83, $40; $50 in July 1991.

Ryne Sandberg

Sept. 18, 1959; 6-2, 185; throws and bats right; second baseman; active; 12 seasons (all with the Chicago Cubs).

Career statistics entering the 1993 season
G: 1,705; AB: 6,705; R: 1,076; H: 1,939; 2B: 320; 3B: 67; HR: 231;
TB: 3,086; RBI: 836; Ave.: .289; SB: 314.

Named N.L. MVP in 1984; led N.L. in total bases in 1990 (344); led the N.L. in runs in 1984 (114) and 1990 (116) and tied in 1989 (104); led the N.L. in triples in 1984 (13); led the N.L. in home runs in 1990 (40); is 15-39 in championship series play for a .385 batting average; has been selected for the All-Star game nine times.

Holds major league career records for highest fielding percentage by a second baseman (.990) and most consecutive errorless games by a second baseman (123, in 1989-90); shares major league record for most years with 500 or more assists by a second baseman (6); shares major league record for most assists in a game by a second baseman (12, on June 12, 1983); has won Gold Gloves from 1983-91; has led N.L. second basemen in total chances four times; led N.L. second basemen in fielding percentage (.986), assists (571) and double plays (126) in 1983.

If you were building a team around one player, perennial MVP candidate Ryne Sandberg wouldn't be a bad choice. He's been the dominant offensive second baseman from his 1984 MVP season on, blending power and speed with a .289 lifetime average.

Ryno's 1984 MVP season was pretty good — 19 homers, 84 RBI and a .314 batting average. But he's a second baseman, and second basemen aren't supposed to generate such power, which makes those numbers that much more impressive.

To prove it wasn't a fluke, Sandberg has followed that season with three seasons of 26 homers, one 30-homer season, and a 40-spot in 1990, when he, coupled with his .306 batting average, 100 RBI and 25 stolen bases, became only the third player in history to have a .300 batting average, 40 home runs, 25 stolen bases and 100 RBI in a season (Hank Aaron and Jose Canseco have also done it.)

Sandberg, ever so self-effacing, carries himself with graceful elegance and modesty, shunning the spotlight. He lets his bat do his talking for him, and, although he doesn't, he has bragging rights about his fielding, too. The nine-time Gold Glove winner holds major league records for highest lifetime fielding percentage for his position (.989) and most consecutive games without an error (123).

Sandberg's 1983 Topps card is in a set which has excellent investment potential, considering it has rookie cards for Wade Boggs ($35) and Tony Gwynn ($40). Sandberg is exceptionally popular, which should keep his card in greater demand than the other two players' cards. Ryno's card will eventually become the driving force in that set's value, because Sandberg is a definite first-ballot Hall of Famer. Boggs and Gwynn are Hall of Famers too, but maybe not on the first ballot.

Ryne Sandberg Checklist

Year	Company	No.	Price
1983	Donruss	277	35.00
1983	Fleer	507	30.00
1983	O-Pee-Chee/Topps	83	10.00/40.00
1984	Donruss	311	25.00
1984	Fleer	504	18.00
1984	O-Pee-Chee	64	5.00

Ryne Sandberg Checklist

Year	Company	No.	Price
1984	Topps	596	8.00
1985	Donruss	1/67	4.00/10.00
1985	Fleer	65/630	8.00/.30
1985	Leaf	1	1.00
1985	O-Pee-Chee	296	.30
1985	Topps	460/713	3.00/.60
1986	Donruss	67	4.00
1986	Fleer	378	4.00
1986	Leaf	62	3.00
1986	O-Pee-Chee	19	.25
1986	Topps	690	2.00
1987	Donruss	77	1.00
1987	Fleer	572/639	2.50/.12
1987	Leaf	234	1.00
1987	O-Pee-Chee	143	.20
1987	Topps	680	1.00
1988	Donruss	242	.50
1988	Fleer	431/628	1.00/.12
1988	Leaf	207	.50
1988	O-Pee-Chee/Topps	10	.15/.15
1988	Score	26	.40
1989	Bowman	290	.15
1989	Donruss	105	.40
1989	Fleer	437	.40
1989	Score	35	.40
1989	Topps	360/387	.30/.10
1989	Upper Deck	120/675	.80/.08
1990	Bowman	30	.40
1990	Donruss	105/692	.25/.09
1990	Fleer	40/625/639	.35/.25/.10
1990	Leaf	98/528	4.00/.40
1990	O-Pee-Chee	210	.12/.30
1990	O-Pee-Chee	398	.12/.15
1990	Score	90/561/691	.30/.50/.30
1990	Upper Deck	324	.30
1991	Bowman	377/416	.12/.15
1991	Donruss	14/404	.15/.15
1991	Donruss	433/504	.10/.15
1991	Donruss Studio	158	1.25
1991	Fleer	431/709/713	.20/.25/.15
1991	Fleer Ultra	66	.50
1991	Leaf	207	.80
1991	O-Pee-Chee/Topps	7	.10/.10
1991	O-Pee-Chee/Topps	398	.10/.10
1991	O-Pee-Chee/Topps	740	.10/.20
1991	Score	3/665	.20/.15
1991	Score	815/862	.20/.15
1991	Topps Stadium Club	230	3.00
1991	Upper Deck	132	.20
1991	Upper Deck Extended	725	.25
1991	Upper Deck Final Edition	79/93	1.00/.50
1992	Donruss	429/576	.15/.20
1992	Fleer	389	.20
1992	Fleer Ultra	181	1.50
1992	Leaf	317	.70
1992	Leaf Studio	18	.80
1992	Score	200/442/774	.20/.35/.10
1992	Score Pinnacle	10/617	.60/.40
1992	Topps	110/387	.20/.10
1992	Topps Stadium Club	50/600	1.00/1.00
1992	Topps Stadium Club Dome	162	1.00
1992	Upper Deck	145	.25

37

 # **10 Roberto Clemente**

Roberto Clemente: 1973 Topps #50, $35; $25 in July 1991.

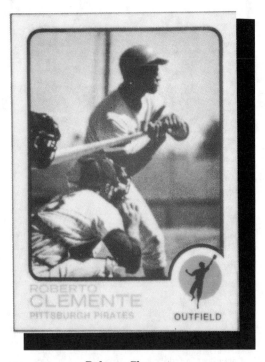

Roberto Clemente

Aug. 18, 1934-Dec. 31, 1972; 5-11, 175; bats and throws right; outfielder; retired; 18 seasons (Pittsburgh 1955-72); Hall of Fame 1973.

G: 2,433 (44th); AB: 9,454 (28th); R: 1,416 (61st); H: 3,000 (17th); 2B: 440 (62nd); 3B: 166 (27th); HR: 240; TB: 4,492 (26th); RBI: 1,305 (66th); Ave.: .317 (52nd); SB: 83.

Led N.L. in hits in 1964 (211) and 1967 (209); led N.L. in triples (12) in 1969; led the N.L. in batting average in 1961 (.351); 1964 (.339); 1965 (.329) and 1967 (.357); 12-time Gold Glove Award winner; 1966 N.L. MVP; 12-time All-Star.

Quite simply, he was one of the game's best, but Roberto Clemente's career doesn't need embellishing...

This pick is a sentimental one, and a tribute to a player who sometimes was accused of not giving 100 percent on the field. But he gave 100 percent off the field...and his 1973 Topps card eerily reminds us of that, as his career tragically ended at exactly 3,000 hits.

The 1973 Topps set contains rookie cards for Mike Schmidt ($425), Bob Boone ($40) and Dwight Evans ($50), but Roberto Clemente, considered by many leading dealers across the country to be one of their, if not the, top sellers, will forever remain one of the most popular players ever. Who doesn't like Roberto Clemente?

Roberto Clemente Checklist

Year	Company	No.	Price
1955	Topps	164	1,800.00
1956	Topps	33	450.00
1957	Topps	76	250.00
1958	Topps	52	225.00
1959	Topps	478/543	125.00/50.00
1960	Topps	326	110.00
1961	Post Cereal (box or company)	132	25.00
1961	Topps	41/388	4.00/110.00
1962	Post Cereal	173	25.00
1962	Topps	10/52	125.00/5.00
1963	Fleer	56	125.00
1963	Jell-O	143	75.00
1963	Post Cereal	143	20.00
1963	Topps	18/540	10.00/225.00
1964	Bazooka	14	50.00
1964	Topps	7/440	7.00/125.00
1965	O-Pee-Chee/Topps	2	5.00/5.00
1965	O-Pee-Chee/Topps	160	70.00/85.00
1966	Topps	215/300	20.00/110.00
1967	Topps	242/400	12.00/85.00
1968	O-Pee-Chee/Topps	1	4.00/15.00
1968	O-Pee-Chee/Topps	3	3.00/4.00
1968	O-Pee-Chee/Topps	150	50.00/70.00
1968	Topps	374/480	15.00/25.00
1969	O-Pee-Chee/Topps	50	50.00/55.00
1970	O-Pee-Chee/Topps	61	2.50/5.00
1970	O-Pee-Chee/Topps	350	40.00/50.00
1971	O-Pee-Chee/Topps	630	50.00/65.00
1972	O-Pee-Chee/Topps	226	1.25/1.50
1972	O-Pee-Chee/Topps	309	30.00/35.00
1972	O-Pee-Chee/Topps	310	15.00/15.00
1973	O-Pee-Chee/Topps	50	12.00/35.00
1975	O-Pee-Chee/Topps	204	4.00/1.50
1975	Topps Mini	204	2.25
1987	Leaf	163	.06
1987	Topps	313	.15

 **Barry Bonds**

Barry Bonds: 1987 Fleer 604, $20; $12 in July 1991.

Barry Bonds

July 24, 1964; 6-1, 190; throws and bats left; outfielder; active; seven seasons (Pittsburgh 1986-92, San Francisco 1993).

Career statistics entering the 1993 season
G: 1,010; AB: 3,582; R: 672; H: 984; 2B: 220; 3B: 36; HR: 176;
TB: 1,804; RBI: 556; Ave.: .275; SB: 251.

Led the N.L. in slugging percentage in 1990 (.565) and 1992 (.624); led the N.L. in intentional walks in 1992 (32); led the N.L. in on base percentage in

1992 (.456); led the N.L. in runs scored in 1992 (109); named N.L. MVP in 1990 and 1992; won N.L. Gold Glove awards in 1990-92; shares the championship series record for most hits in an inning (2) in 1992; has played in two All-Star games.

Over the last three seasons, no one has compiled better statistics than Barry Bonds' 92 home runs, 96 doubles, 134 stolen bases, 333 RBI and .300 batting average. And he's only 29 years old, just in his prime. Those statistics average out to 30 homers, 32 doubles, 44 stolen bases, 111 RBI, and a .300 batting average per season.

The superstar has all the tools to put up some staggering numbers if he continues at that pace. If he chooses to continue playing for 10 more years, and instead has average seasons of 140 hits, 25 home runs, 79 RBI and 35 stolen bases (based on his lifetime statistics), Bonds will have somewhere near 2,500 hits, 400 home runs, 1,300 RBI, 600 stolen bases and a .275 batting average. Those look awfully close to the numbers compiled by Hall of Famer Billy Williams (2,711 hits, 426 home runs, 1,475 RBI, 90 stolen bases and a .290 batting average).

With the speed of a lead-off hitter and the power of a cleanup hitter, Bonds has already become only the fifth player to post multiple 30 home run/30 stolen base seasons (something his father, Bobby would be proud of, since he did it also) and is the first ever to have a 30 home run/50 stolen base/.300 season, which he did in his 1990 MVP season.

Bonds' 1987 Fleer card is more popular than the 1986 Fleer Update, which generates interest among the investors. But are they somewhat readily available because Bonds is perceived as cocky and arrogant?

Maybe, but pick one up at $20 and watch this intensely proud ballplayer let his bat do the talking instead, and, as he compiles Hall-of-Fame-caliber numbers, watch his card value continue to escalate, too. He's a two-time MVP, and with Will Clark and Matt Williams protecting him in the San Francisco Giants' batting order, has the potential to add a few more MVP awards.

Barry Bonds Checklist

Year	Company	No.	Price
1986	Donruss Rookies	11	12.00
1986	Fleer Update	U14	10.00
1986	Topps Traded	11T	6.00
1987	Donruss	361	10.00
1987	Fleer	604	20.00
1987	Leaf	219	2.00
1987	O-Pee-Chee/Topps	320	.60/2.50
1988	Donruss	326	.40
1988	Fleer	322	1.75
1988	Leaf	113	.12
1988	O-Pee-Chee	267	.09
1988	Score	265	.60
1988	Topps	450	.60
1989	Bowman	426	.30

Barry Bonds Checklist

Year	Company	No.	Price
1989	Donruss	92	.30
1989	Fleer	202	.40
1989	O-Pee-Chee	263	.10
1989	Score	127	.25
1989	Topps	620	.20
1989	Upper Deck	440	1.50
1990	Bowman	181	.10
1990	Donruss	126	.25
1990	Fleer	461	.10
1990	Leaf	91	2.00
1990	O-Pee-Chee/Topps	220	.10/.10
1990	Score	4	.12
1990	Upper Deck	227	.10
1991	Bowman	380/513	.10/.12
1991	Donruss	4/495/762	.10/.15/.12
1991	Donruss Studio	222	.60
1991	Fleer	33/710	.20/.30
1991	Fleer Ultra	275/391	.25/.20
1991	Leaf	261/364	.50/.08
1991	O-Pee-Chee/Topps	401	.12/.10
1991	O-Pee-Chee/Topps	570	.15/.15
1991	Score	330/668	.20/.12
1991	Score	868/876	.10/.10
1991	Topps Stadium Club	220	1.00
1991	Upper Deck	94/154	.10/.20
1992	Donruss	243	.20
1992	Fleer	550	.15
1992	Fleer Ultra	251	1.00
1992	Leaf	275	.60
1992	Leaf Studio	82	.50
1992	Score	555/777	.20/.10
1992	Score Pinnacle	500	.40
1992	Topps	380/390	.15/.10
1992	Topps Stadium Club	604/620	1.00/.80
1992	Upper Deck	134	.20

 # Dale Murphy

Dale Murphy: 1977 Topps #476, $30; $25 in July 1991.

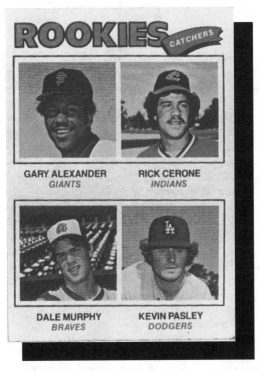

Dale Murphy

March 12, 1956; 6-4, 221; throws and bats right; outfielder; active; 17 seasons (Atlanta 1976-1990, Philadelphia 1990-92).

Career statistics entering the 1993 season
G: 2,154 (100th); AB: 7,918 (97th); R: 1,196; H: 2,105; 2B: 349; 3B: 39; HR: 398 (27th); TB: 3,726 (74th); RBI: 1,529 (78th); Ave.: .266; SB: 161.

Shares the major league record for most years (six) leading the league in games by an outfielder; shares the major league record for most home runs (2) and RBI (6) in one inning, on July 27, 1989; shares the N.L. single-season record for most intentional walks by a right-handed batter (29, in 1987); won Gold Gloves from 1982-86; tied for the N.L. lead in double plays by an outfielder, 4, in 1981 and 1985; named N.L. Most Valuable Player by the Baseball Writers' Association of America in 1982 and 1983; hit three home runs in a game on May 18, 1979; led the N.L. in slugging percentage in 1983 (.540) and 1984 (.547); led the N.L. in total bases (332) in 1984; led the N.L. in intentional walks (29) in 1987; tied or led the N.L. in home runs in 1984 (36) and 1985 (37); tied or led the N.L. in RBI in 1982 (109) and 1983 (121); led the N.L. in runs in 1985 (118); has made seven All-Star appearances and one championship series appearance.

Dale Murphy needs but two home runs to become just the 25th player in major league history to hit 400 home runs in a career, which would virtually guarantee him a spot in Cooperstown. Check out his numbers compared to Hall of Famer Ralph Kiner's (369 home runs, 1,015 RBI, 1,451 hits, .279 batting average).

Although two other players have hit 400 home runs (Darrell Evans and Dave Kingman) and remain on the outside, Murphy has a better batting average than both (.266 to .248 and .236), more hits (2,105 to 2,223 and 1,575) and more RBI (1,529 to 1,354 and 1,210). Those factors alone rank Murphy above Evans and Kingman. It doesn't hurt Murphy's case that he's a two-time MVP winner, either, and a five-time Gold Glove winner.

The quiet, dignified Murphy was baseball's player of the 1980s; no one compiled better power numbers over that decade than Murphy did — 1,037 hits, 218 home runs, 629 RBI, 105 stolen bases, a .289 batting average and a .531 slugging percentage.

Perhaps playing for a Braves team which made only one playoff appearance took its toll on Murphy, who was expected to carry the offensive burden as the primary run producer on a team that, more often than not, finished last. The Phillies released Murphy at the end of spring training in 1993, but Murphy was picked up by the expansion Colorado Rockies.

A class act, Murphy will quietly close out a Hall of Fame career. His 1977 Topps card is the second key rookie card in the set, behind the $75 Andre Dawson card. But Murphy's card, when he is inducted, should fall in between that value and the $35 value placed on the third-year cards for two other future Hall of Famers — Robin Yount and George Brett.

Dale Murphy Checklist

Year	Company	No.	Price
1977	Topps	476	30.00
1978	Topps	708	15.00
1979	O-Pee-Chee	15	7.00
1979	Topps	39	6.00
1980	O-Pee-Chee	143	4.50

Dale Murphy Checklist

Year	Company	No.	Price
1980	Topps	274	4.00
1981	Donruss	437	.90
1981	Fleer	243	.90
1981	O-Pee-Chee	118	2.25
1981	Topps	504	2.00
1982	Donruss	299	.90
1982	Fleer	443	.90
1982	O-Pee-Chee	391	1.75
1982	Topps	668	1.50
1983	Donruss	47	.70
1983	Fleer	142	.90
1983	O-Pee-Chee	21/23	.60/1.25
1983	Topps	401/502	.70/.50
1983	Topps	703/760	.35/1.25
1984	Donruss	66	2.00
1984	Fleer	186	1.00
1984	O-Pee-Chee	150/391	1.25/.60
1984	Topps	126/133	.25/.40
1984	Topps	150/391	.70/.40
1985	Donruss	66	.80
1985	Fleer	335	.60
1985	Leaf	222	.40
1985	O-Pee-Chee/Topps	320	.50/.60
1985	Topps	716	.35
1986	Donruss	66	.60
1986	Fleer	522/635/640	.50/.30/.30
1986	Leaf	60	.40
1986	Topps	456/600/705	.25/.50/.30
1987	Donruss	78	.40
1987	Fleer	522	.40
1987	Leaf	3/141	.30/.30
1987	O-Pee-Chee	359	.35
1987	Topps	490	.40
1988	Donruss	78	.40
1988	Fleer	544/639	.40/.20
1988	Leaf	83	.30
1988	O-Pee-Chee/Topps	90	.25/.30
1988	Score	450	.30
1988	Topps	549	.08
1989	Bowman	276	.08
1989	Donruss	104	.30
1989	Fleer	596	.40
1989	O-Pee-Chee/Topps	210	.20/.30
1989	Score	30	.30
1989	Upper Deck	357/672	.35/.08
1990	Bowman	19	.10
1990	Donruss	168	.09
1990	Fleer	591/623	.15/.25
1990	Fleer Update	U46	.10
1990	Leaf	243	.50
1990	O-Pee-Chee/Topps	750	.20/.10
1990	Score	66	.12
1990	Score Traded	31T	.10
1990	Upper Deck	533	.15
1991	Bowman	486	.08
1991	Donruss	484/744	.12/.25
1991	Donruss Studio	220	.20
1991	Fleer	409	.10
1991	Fleer Ultra	270	.10
1991	Leaf	412	.15
1991	O-Pee-Chee	545	.15
1991	Score	650	.12

Dale Murphy Checklist

Year	Company	No.	Price
1991	Topps	545	.10
1991	Topps Stadium Club	243	.50
1991	Upper Deck	447	.12
1992	Donruss	146	.10
1992	Fleer	541	.12
1992	Fleer Ultra	249	.15
1992	Leaf	527	.12
1992	Leaf Studio	79	.15
1992	Score	80	.12
1992	Score Pinnacle	124	.15
1992	Topps	680	.08
1992	Upper Deck	127	.10

 **Pete Rose**

Pete Rose: 1964 Topps #125, $175; $120 in July 1991.

Pete Rose

46

April 14, 1941; 5-11, 192; switch hits, throws right; outfielder, third base, first base; retired; 24 seasons (Cincinnati 1963-78; Philadelphia 1979-83; Montreal 1984; Cincinnati 1984-86).

G: 3,562 (1st); AB: 14,053 (1st); R: 2,165 (4th); H: 4,256 (1st);
2B: 746 (2nd); 3B: 135 (72nd); HR: 160; TB: 5,752 (6th);
RBI: 1,314 (62nd); Ave.: .303; SB: 198.

Managerial record: six seasons (Cincinnati 1984-89). W: 412; L: 373; .525; led the Reds to three straight second-place finishes (1985-87).

Led the N.L. in hits in 1965 (209), 1968 (210), 1970 (205), 1972 (198), 1973 (230), 1976 (215) and 1981 (140); led the N.L. in runs in 1969 (120), 1974 (110), 1975 (112) and 1976 (130); led the N.L. in doubles in 1974 (45), 1975 (47), 1976 (42), 1978 (51), 1980 (42); led the N.L. in batting average in 1968 (.335), 1969 (.348), 1973 (.338) and 1981 (.325); two-time Gold Glove winner as an outfielder; 1963 Rookie of the Year; 1973 N.L. MVP; 17-time All-Star; compiled a 44-game hitting streak in 1978, the longest in N.L. history and second longest in major league history.

Pete Rose, baseball's all-time hit king, will eventually be inducted into the Hall of Fame. In the meantime, his cards will just keep on going up. His 1963 Topps rookie card is on its way to $1,000, which shouldn't be too surprising, since Rose cards are always in demand.

"Charlie Hustle" won three batting titles, had 14 .300 years and 10 200-hit seasons. An N.L. All-Star 17 times, he made the team at five different positions.

If the fact that he shares his rookie card with three other players, or the $900 price tag, makes the card less appealing, the recommended buy here is the 1964 Topps card, Rose's second-year card, at $175. It's a much more attractive card, and carries the rookie trophy as part of its design.

It's going to jump in price as soon as the Hall of Fame beckons, and might become in greater demand than the rookie card, simply because many can't afford the 1963 card. It might even surpass and stay ahead of the value of Phil Niekro's 1964 rookie card, which is at $225.

Pete Rose Checklist

Year	Company	No.	Price
1963	Topps	537 (Rookies)	900.00
1964	Topps	125	175.00
1965	O-Pee-Chee/Topps	207	125.00/150.00
1966	O-Pee-Chee/Topps	30	50.00/60.00
1967	Topps	430	75.00
1968	Topps	230	40.00
1969	O-Pee-Chee/Topps	2	3.00/4.00
1969	O-Pee-Chee/Topps	120	35.00/35.00
1969	Topps	424	12.00
1970	O-Pee-Chee/Topps	61	2.50/5.00
1970	O-Pee-Chee/Topps	458	8.00/8.00
1970	Topps	580	70.00
1971	O-Pee-Chee/Topps	100	40.00/45.00
1972	Topps	559/560	50.00/25.00

Pete Rose Checklist

Year	Company	No.	Price
1973	O-Pee-Chee/Topps	130	15.00/20.00
1974	O-Pee-Chee/Topps	201	2.50/4.00
1974	O-Pee-Chee/Topps	300	18.00/15.00
1974	O-Pee-Chee/Topps	336	2.00/2.50
1975	O-Pee-Chee/Topps	211	5.00/4.00
1975	O-Pee-Chee/Topps	320	18.00/18.00
1975	Topps Mini	211/320	7.00/40.00
1976	O-Pee-Chee/Topps	240	15.00/12.00
1977	O-Pee-Chee	240	10.00
1977	Topps	450	9.00
1978	O-Pee-Chee	100/240	5.00/1.75
1978	Topps	5/20	2.00/4.00
1979	O-Pee-Chee	343	6.00
1979	Topps	204/650	1.50/5.00
1980	O-Pee-Chee	282	3.50
1980	Topps	4/540	2.00/4.00
1981	Donruss	131/251/371	1.25/1.00/1.50
1981	Fleer	1/645	1.75/2.00
1981	O-Pee-Chee	180	3.00
1981	Topps	180/205	3.00/1.00
1982	Donruss	1/168/585	2.00/1.50/.70
1982	Fleer	256/640	1.00/1.50
1982	O-Pee-Chee	24/361	1.00/2.00
1982	O-Pee-Chee/Topps	337	.75/.80
1982	Topps	4/636	.70/.50
1982	Topps	780/781	2.25/1.00
1983	Donruss	42	1.50
1983	Fleer	171/634	1.50/.40
1983	O-Pee-Chee/Topps	100	1.50/1.75
1983	O-Pee-Chee/Topps	101	.70/.80
1983	O-Pee-Chee	373	.60
1983	Topps	397	.70
1984	Donruss	61	3.00
1984	Fleer	46/636	3.00/.50
1984	O-Pee-Chee/Topps	300	2.50/1.00
1984	Topps	701/702	.35/.35
1984	Topps Traded	103T	8.00
1985	Donruss	254/641	1.75/2.00
1985	Fleer	550/640	2.00/.50
1985	Leaf	144	.80
1985	O-Pee-Chee	116	.75
1985	Topps	6/547/600	.60/.60/1.00
1986	Donruss	62/644/653	1.00/.50/.70
1986	Fleer	191/628/638	.70/.50/1.00
1986	Leaf	53/209/260	.80/.30/.50
1986	O-Pee-Chee/Topps	1	.70/.90
1986	Topps	2/3/4	.30/.30/.30
1986	Topps	5/6/7	.30/.30/.30
1986	Topps	206/741	.50/.40
1987	Donruss	186	.60
1987	Fleer	213	.60
1987	Leaf	129	.50
1987	O-Pee-Chee/Topps	200	.50/.40
1987	Topps	281/393	.10/.40
1988	Topps	475/505	.20/.20

 **Dave Winfield**

Dave Winfield: 1974 Topps #456, $200; $50 in July 1991

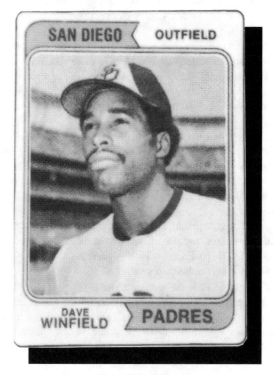

Dave Winfield

Oct. 3, 1951; 6-6, 245; throws and bats right; outfielder; active; 19 seasons (San Diego 1973-80; New York Yankees 1981-90; California 1990-91; Toronto 1992, Minnesota Twins 1993).

Career statistics entering the 1993 season
G: 2,707 (18th); AB: 10,047 (15th); R: 1,551 (38th); H: 2,866 (30th); 2B: 493 (33rd); 3B: 83; HR: 432 (20th); TB: 4,821 (17th); RBI: 1,710 (15th); Ave.: .285; SB: 218.

Won Gold Glove Awards in 1979-80; led N.L. in total bases (333) and intentional walks (24) in 1979; led the N.L. in RBI in 1979 (118); hit three homers in one game on April 13, 1991; shares A.L. single-game championship series record for most at-bats (6, on Oct. 11, 1992, in 11 innings); has been selected for the All-Star game 12 times; holds career record for most doubles (7) in All-Star games; shares record for most consecutive games with one or more hits (7); shares single-game record for most at-bats in a nine-inning game (5, July 17, 1979); selected by the National Basketball Association's Atlanta Hawks in the 1973 draft, fifth round, 58th pick overall; selected by the Minnesota Vikings in the 17th round of the 1973 draft, 429th pick overall;

It's safe to say that if Dave Winfield had decided to play professional football or basketball, his 1974 rookie card wouldn't even be in the triple-figures, even if he'd compiled statistics which would put him in those sports' respective Hall of Fames. He'd be around $50-$75, which is where Hall of Famer Bill Walton's 1974 rookie card is at. That's just the way the card market is; football and basketball will always lag behind baseball. But at $200, Winfield's baseball card is worth a look.

By the time he's finished, Winfield will have compiled statistics which will fit in somewhere between two other Hall of Famers — Al Kaline and Carl Yastrzemski. Yet, his career numbers go unnoticed, basically because he's been so consistent throughout his career. But, he'll call national attention to himself sometime during the 1993 season, when he gets his 3,000th hit. That will help his card's value.

A 12-time All-Star, Winfield, however, played in relative obscurity for eight seasons with the Padres, but does have two World Series appearances to his credit, and one ring. He also benefits from having played for the New York Yankees, which helps influence his card's value.

Winfield's rookie card is the key card in the 1974 set. It will always stay somewhere between the range set by Mike Schmidt's $425 1973 Topps rookie card and Schmidt's $90 1974 second-year card, probably closer to Schmidt's rookie card value. As those two cards appreciate, so should Winfield's, after it makes its initial jump after his 3,000th hit and makes its second jump when he's inducted.

Dave Winfield Checklist

Year	Company	No.	Price
1974	O-Pee-Chee/Topps	456	80.00/200.00
1975	O-Pee-Chee/Topps	61	30.00/60.00
1975	Topps Mini	61	20.00
1976	O-Pee-Chee/Topps	160	6.00/35.00
1977	O-Pee-Chee	156	4.00
1977	Topps	390	25.00
1978	O-Pee-Chee	78	3.00
1978	Topps	530	18.00
1979	O-Pee-Chee	11	3.50

Dave Winfield Checklist

Year	Company	No.	Price
1979	Topps	30	12.00
1980	O-Pee-Chee	122	1.50
1980	Topps	230	9.00
1981	Donruss	364	3.00
1981	Fleer	484	3.00
1981	Topps	370	5.00
1981	Topps Traded	855	15.00
1982	Donruss	18/31/575	1.00/2.50/2.00
1982	Fleer	56/646	2.50/2.00
1982	O-Pee-Chee	76/352	.20/.40
1982	Topps	553/600	2.00/4.00
1983	Donruss	409	2.50
1983	Fleer	398/633	2.50/.25
1983	O-Pee-Chee	258	.40
1983	Topps	770	3.00
1984	Donruss	51	9.00
1984	Fleer	143	5.00
1984	O-Pee-Chee	266/378	.60/.60
1984	Topps	402/460	.30/1.50
1985	Donruss	51/651	3.00/6.00
1985	Fleer	146/629	3.00/.30
1985	Leaf	127/140	.30/2.00
1985	O-Pee-Chee/Topps	180	.30/1.25
1985	Topps	705	.20
1986	Donruss	248	1.25
1986	Fleer	121	1.25
1986	Leaf	125	1.00
1986	O-Pee-Chee/Topps	70	.25/.60
1986	Topps	717	.20
1987	Donruss	20/105	.25/.30
1987	Fleer	120	.30
1987	Leaf	20/70	.80/1.00
1987	O-Pee-Chee	36	.20
1987	Topps	770	.25
1988	Donruss	298	.30
1988	Fleer	226	.30
1988	Leaf	116	.25
1988	Score	55	.20
1988	Topps	392/510	.12/.20
1989	Bowman	179	.20
1989	Donruss	159	.25
1989	Fleer	274	.30
1989	O-Pee-Chee/Topps	260	.15/.25
1989	Score	50	.25
1989	Topps	407	.12
1989	Upper Deck	349	.30
1990	Bowman	432	.12
1990	Donruss	551	.20
1990	Fleer	458	.15
1990	Fleer Update	U81	.12
1990	Leaf	426	.50
1990	O-Pee-Chee/Topps	380	.12/.15
1990	Score	307	.15
1990	Score Traded	1T	.15
1990	Topps Traded	130T	.15
1990	Upper Deck	337	.12
1990	Upper Deck Extended	745	.20
1991	Bowman	210	.10
1991	Donruss	468	.12
1991	Donruss Studio	30	.25
1991	Fleer	329	.12
1991	Fleer Ultra	54	.15

Dave Winfield Checklist

Year	Company	No.	Price
1991	Leaf	499	.25
1991	O-Pee-Chee/Topps	630	.10/.10
1991	Score	83	.12
1991	Topps Stadium Club	263	.50
1991	Upper Deck	337	.15
1992	Donruss	133	.10
1992	Fleer	72/686	.12/.10
1992	Fleer Ultra	454	.50
1992	Fleer Update	67	.10
1992	Leaf	171	.40
1992	Leaf Studio	260	.25
1992	Score	32	.08
1992	Score Pinnacle	375	.25
1992	Score Traded	7	.10
1992	Topps	5/792	.06/.12
1992	Topps Traded	130	.08
1992	Topps Stadium Club	745	.50
1992	Upper Deck	28/222	.10/.15

 # Ted Simmons

Ted Simmons: 1971 Topps #117, $25; $12 in July 1991.

Aug. 8, 1949; 5-11, 193; switch-hitter, throws right; catcher; retired; 21 seasons (St. Louis 1968-80; Milwaukee 1981-85; Atlanta 1986-88).

G: 2,456 (40th); AB: 8,680 (63rd); R: 1,074; H: 2,472 (70th); 2B: 483 (41st); 3B: 47; HR: 248 (96th); TB: 3,793 (65th); RBI: 1,389 (47th); Ave.: .285; SB: 21.

As one of the best hitting catchers in major league history, Ted Simmons had eight seasons with 90 or more RBI, including three 100+ seasons; hit over .300 in seven seasons; and had five seasons with 20 home runs. During his 21-year career, Simmons collected 2,272 hits, 248 home runs, 1,389 RBI and had a .285 career batting average. If he were playing today, there'd be no comparisons; he'd be considered the best.

However, Simmons played in Johnny Bench's shadow. Although he played four more years than Bench, Simmons only added 102 hits, 10 home runs and 67 RBI to his totals during those years. His career numbers still compare favorably to Bench's 2,048 hits, 389 home runs, 1,376 RBI and .267 batting average.

Bench benefited from playing for the "Big Red Machine," which made four World Series appearances. But Simmons shouldn't be denied Hall of Fame induction for only playing in one World Series. And he won't.

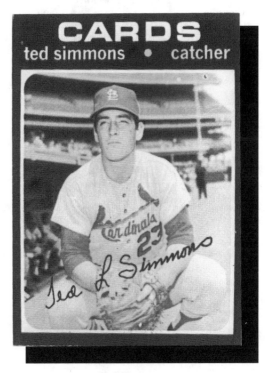

Ted Simmons

Considering 1971 Topps rookie cards for Bert Blyleven ($50), Don Baylor ($60) and Dave Concepcion ($20) are where they are at, Simmons' card at $25 is a real steal. Buy two; for the price of a Baylor, you can get a card of a player who has a better shot at the Hall of Fame. Expect Simmons (eligible in 1994 with, among others, Steve Carlton and Don Sutton) to pass Baylor's value after the catcher finally gets inducted.

Ted Simmons Checklist

Year	Company	No.	Price
1971	O-Pee-Chee/Topps	117	12.00/25.00
1972	O-Pee-Chee/Topps	154	1.25/2.00
1973	O-Pee-Chee/Topps	85	1.00/2.00
1974	O-Pee-Chee/Topps	260	.75/.80
1975	O-Pee-Chee/Topps	75	.60/.70
1975	Topps Mini	75	1.00
1976	O-Pee-Chee/Topps	191	.50/.60
1976	O-Pee-Chee/Topps	290	.60/.60
1976	Topps	290	.90

Ted Simmons Checklist

Year	Company	No.	Price
1977	O-Pee-Chee	196	.50
1977	Topps	470	.60
1978	O-Pee-Chee	150	.40
1978	Topps	380	.40
1979	O-Pee-Chee	267	.30
1979	Topps	510	.40
1980	O-Pee-Chee	47	.30
1980	Topps	85	.40
1981	Donruss	308	.12
1981	Fleer	528	.12
1981	O-Pee-Chee	352	.20
1981	Topps	705	.25
1981	Topps Traded	830	.40
1982	Donruss	106	.12
1982	Fleer	152	.12
1982	O-Pee-Chee/Topps	150	.20/.20
1983	Donruss	332	.12
1983	Fleer	45	.12
1983	O-Pee-Chee	33/284	.12/.15
1983	Topps	450/451	.20/.12
1984	Donruss	473	.20
1984	Fleer	213	.15
1984	O-Pee-Chee	94/122	.30/.30
1984	Topps	404/630	.15/.15
1984	Topps	713/726	.20/.12
1985	Donruss	414	.15
1985	Fleer	596	.12
1985	Leaf	104	.20
1985	O-Pee-Chee	318	.12
1985	Topps	318	.12
1986	Donruss	292	.06
1986	Fleer	503	.12
1986	Fleer Update	U106	.20
1986	Leaf	167	.10
1986	Topps	237	.12
1986	Topps Traded	102T	.20
1987	Donruss	537	.12
1987	Fleer	528	.12
1987	Topps	516	.10
1988	Donruss	560	.10
1988	Fleer	549	.10
1988	Leaf	222	.10
1988	Score	285	.08
1988	Topps	791	.08
1989	Fleer	599	.10
1989	Score	611	.08
1989	Upper Deck	570	.10

Lee Smith

Lee Smith: 1982 Topps #452, $12; $1.25 in July 1991.

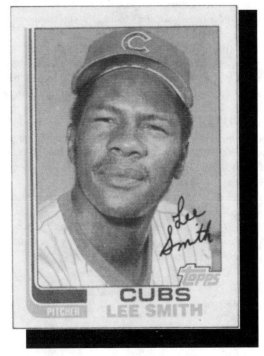

Lee Smith

Dec. 4, 1957; 6-6, 269; throws and bats right; pitcher; active; 13 seasons (Chicago 1980-87; Boston 1988-90; St. Louis 1990-92).

Career statistics entering the 1993 season

W: 65; L: 74; Pct.: .468; ERA: 2.86; G: 787 (18th); GS: 6; CG: 0; ShO: 0; Saves: 355 (2nd); IP: 1,067 1/3; H: 919; R: 375; ER: 339; BB: 402; SO: 1,050.

Holds the major league career record for most consecutive errorless games by a pitcher (546, July 5, 1982, through 1992); holds N.L. single-season record for most saves (47, in 1991); led N.L. in saves in 1983 (29), 1991 (47) and 1992 (43); has one save in two championship series playoffs; has been selected for the All-Star game four times.

When the Boston Red Sox acquired Jeff Reardon, the current all-time saves leader, for the 1990 season, it made Lee Smith, who's right behind him, expendable. "Big Daddy" was traded to St. Louis. But it's the Red Sox who've lost out on the deal...

A rejuvenated Smith continued throwing bullets, on his way to leading the National League in saves two out of the last three years — in 1991 (47) and 1992 (43). During those three years, he's had 121 saves, compared to Reardon's 91.

Smith, in the twilight of his career, has been in Dennis Eckersley's shadow the last five years, considering Eck has had 220 saves during that time, compared to Smith's 175. But Smith has been a consistent closer for the last 10 seasons, averaging 33 saves each season, and he's had a record 10 straight 25+ save seasons, too.

The four-time All-Star has only one save in two championship series playoffs. Since Reardon, also a four-time All-Star, has been in four playoff series and has played on two World Series teams, he has the advantage over Smith in those categories. But Smith's 1982 Topps rookie card is $12, compared to Reardon's $8 1981 Topps rookie card.

Both players' cards, each at about $1.50 at the time, benefited when Rollie Fingers was elected into the Hall and rose to where they are now. Smith had a better 1992 season (43 saves to 30) than Reardon, which is why his card has pulled ahead. You can't go wrong with either card, but we're banking that Smith finishes as the all-time saves leader.

Lee Smith Checklist

Year	Company	No.	Price
1982	Donruss	252	12.00
1982	Fleer	603	9.00
1982	Topps	452	12.00
1983	Donruss	403	2.00
1983	Fleer	508	2.00
1983	Topps	699	2.50
1984	Donruss	289	3.00
1984	Fleer	505	.15
1984	O-Pee-Chee/Topps	176	.20/.15
1985	Donruss	311	.12
1985	Fleer	67	.10
1985	Leaf	128	.07
1985	O-Pee-Chee	43	.10
1985	Topps	511	.10
1986	Donruss	144	.10
1986	Fleer	380	.10
1986	Leaf	64	.07

Lee Smith Checklist

Year	Company	No.	Price
1986	O-Pee-Chee/Topps	355	.07/.10
1986	Topps	636	.07
1987	Donruss	292	.10
1987	Fleer	574	.10
1987	Leaf	80	.08
1987	O-Pee-Chee/Topps	23	.07/.10
1988	Donruss	292	.10
1988	Fleer	433	.10
1988	Fleer Update	U8	.10
1988	O-Pee-Chee/Topps	240	.05/.08
1988	Score	31	.08
1988	Score Traded	20T	.25
1988	Topps Traded	110T	.10
1989	Bowman	19	.03
1989	Donruss	66	.08
1989	Fleer	99	.10
1989	O-Pee-Chee	149	.05
1989	Score	150	.08
1989	Topps	760	.08
1989	Upper Deck	521	.10
1990	Bowman	263	.06
1990	Donruss	110	.05
1990	Fleer	287	.05
1990	Fleer Update	U53	.08
1990	Leaf	524	.40
1990	O-Pee-Chee/Topps	495	.05/.06
1990	Score	37	.06
1990	Score Traded	48T	.08
1990	Topps Traded	118T	.08
1990	Upper Deck	393	.08
1991	Bowman	387	.06
1991	Donruss	169/403	.08/.05
1991	Donruss Studio	237	.15
1991	Fleer	645	.08
1991	Fleer Ultra	295	.08
1991	Leaf	44	.10
1991	O-Pee-Chee/Topps	660	.05/.06
1991	Score	81	.08
1991	Upper Deck	348	.08
1992	Donruss	112	.08
1992	Fleer	591/697	.06/.05
1992	Fleer Ultra	270	.12
1992	Leaf	254	.15
1992	Leaf Studio	97	.15
1992	Score	630/781	.06/.06
1992	Score Pinnacle	195	.12
1992	Topps	565	.05
1992	Topps Stadium Club	180	.15
1992	Topps Stadium Club Dome	174	.30
1992	Upper Deck	376	.08

 # Kirby Puckett

Kirby Puckett: 1985 Donruss #438, $50; $25 in July 1991.

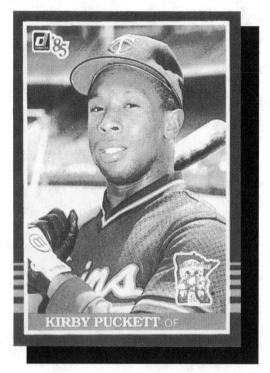

Kirby Puckett

March 16, 1961; 5-9, 220; bats and throws right; outfielder; active; nine seasons (all with Minnesota).

Career statistics entering the 1993 season
G: 1,382; AB: 5,645; R: 820; H: 1,812; 2B: 304; 3B: 51; HR: 142;
TB: 2,644; RBI: 785; Ave.: .321; SB: 117.

Shares the major league record for most consecutive years leading the league in hits, three, from 1987-89 (with 207, 234 and 215 hits); shares major league single-game records for most doubles (4, May 13, 1989) and most doubles in two consecutive games (6, May 13-14, 1989); shares modern major league record for most hits in a first game in the majors (4, May 8, 1984); holds A.L. record for most hits in two consecutive nine-inning games (10, Aug. 29-30, 1987); hit for the cycle Aug. 1, 1986; had six-hit games on Aug. 30, 1987, and May 23, 1991; led the A.L. in total bases in 1988 (358) and 1992 (313); led the A.L. in hits in 1992 (210) and in batting average in 1989 (.339); shares A.L. single-game championship series record for most at bats (6, Oct. 12, 1987); has hit .311 in two championship series (14 for 45); shares World Series record for most runs scored in a game (4, Oct. 24, 1987); has hit .308 in World Series play, including two home runs in the 1991 Series; has been selected to the All-Star game seven straight seasons; shares A.L. record for most seasons with 400 or more putouts by an outfielder (5); won A.L. Gold Gloves from 1986-89 and 1991-92; has led the A.L. outfielders in total chances three times.

Before the 1993 season Kirby Puckett signed what he says might be his last contract — a five-year deal with the Minnesota Twins, worth $30 million. It would be a shame if Puckett, 32, plays just five more years, for he could make a serious run at 3,000 hits, instead of finishing with a projected 2,800 or so.

But the seven-time All-Star, who's been the most popular player ever in Twins history, isn't concerned about personal stats; he just wants to play baseball, win, and have fun doing it. His power numbers have been on the decline, but his batting average has been over the .300 mark in six of his nine seasons.

If a prototype mold of a baseball player was being made, it might not necessarily have the body of Kirby Puckett, although he's been quite reliable and durable; he's never been on the disabled list in his entire career. But the player created would surely have the work ethic and devotion that Puckett displays toward the game. He's a spark plug, an impact player, a franchise player, which is why he was given a club-record contract amount by the Twins.

Even if you're a fan of any other American League West team, it's impossible not to like Kirby Puckett. Which is one of the reasons, in addition to scarcity, why his 1984 Fleer Update card is $400. The set, which also contains a $450 first card of Roger Clemens, is at $1,000, and is driven by those two cards and the fact that it's a low production run.

If $400 is too steep, Puckett's 1985 Donruss, at $50, has to be considered a bargain, and one of the key cards in the set. That $200 set, which had a record low print run, also contains a card for Clemens ($60) and has above average investment potential. Because the cards are black-bordered, it will be difficult to find a set in Mint condition.

Buy one of these cards now, while it's still low. Puckett isn't going to get any less popular, and his cards aren't going to decrease in value. They're going to keep going up, just as Puckett's career hits will keep on doing.

Kirby Puckett Checklist

Year	Company	No.	Price
1984	Fleer Update	U93	400.00
1985	Donruss	438	50.00
1985	Fleer	286	50.00
1985	Leaf	107	20.00
1985	O-Pee-Chee	10	15.00
1985	Topps	536	21.00
1986	Donruss	72	10.00
1986	Fleer	401	10.00
1986	Leaf	69	6.00
1986	O-Pee-Chee/Topps	329	3.00/4.00
1987	Donruss	149	2.00
1987	Fleer	549/633	4.00/.70
1987	Leaf	19/56	.80/1.00
1987	O-Pee-Chee	82	.25
1987	Topps	450/611	1.00/.15
1988	Donruss	368	.50
1988	Fleer	19/638	.60/.20
1988	Leaf	144	.60
1988	O-Pee-Chee	120	.20
1988	Score	24/653	.25/.12
1988	Topps	120/391	.40/.12
1989	Bowman	162	.35
1989	Donruss	182	.30
1989	Fleer	124/639	.35/.15
1989	O-Pee-Chee	132	.15
1989	Score	20	.35
1989	Topps	403/650	.12/.25
1989	Upper Deck	376	.30
1990	Bowman	424	.20
1990	Donruss	269/683	.30/.09
1990	Fleer	383/635	.40/.10
1990	Leaf	123	1.50
1990	O-Pee-Chee/Topps	391	.10/.20
1990	O-Pee-Chee/Topps	700	.10/.25
1990	Score	400/690	.40/.30
1990	Upper Deck	48/236	.06/.35
1991	Bowman	320	.15
1991	Donruss	490	.15
1991	Donruss Studio	90	.70
1991	Fleer	623	.15
1991	Fleer Ultra	195	.25
1991	Leaf	208	.50
1991	O-Pee-Chee/Topps	300	.07/.15
1991	Score	200/855/891	.15/.08/.20
1991	Topps Stadium Club	110	3.00
1991	Upper Deck	544	.20
1992	Donruss	617	.15
1992	Fleer	217/704	.15/.10
1992	Fleer Ultra	97	1.50
1992	Leaf	98	.80
1992	Leaf Studio	209	.80
1992	Score	600/796/886	.15/.08/.20
1992	Score Pinnacle	20/289	.50/.40
1992	Topps	575	.15
1992	Topps Stadium Club	500	1.25
1992	Topps Stadium Club Dome	144/145	.80/.80
1992	Upper Deck	254	.20

 # Nolan Ryan

Nolan Ryan: 1971 Topps #513, $250; $150 in July 1991.

Nolan Ryan

Jan. 31, 1947; 6-2, 212; bats and throws right; pitcher; active; 26 seasons (New York Mets 1966-71; California 1972-79; Houston 1980-88; Texas 1989-92).

Career statistics entering the 1993 season
W: 319 (13th); L: 287 (3rd); Pct.: .526; ERA: 3.17; G: 794 (17th);
GS: 760 (2nd); CG: 222; ShO: 61 (8th); IP: 5,320 2/3 (6th);
H: 3,869; R: 2,131; ER: 1,875; BB: 2,755; SO: 5,668 (1st).

Holds the major league career record for most strikeouts (5,668), most seasons with 300 or more strikeouts (6), most seasons with 200 or more strikeouts (15), and most consecutive seasons with 100 or more strikeouts (23); holds major league records for most games with 15 or more strikeouts (26), most games with 10 or more strikeouts (213), most no-hit games (7); holds major league record for most strikeouts in three consecutive games (47, in 1974); holds modern major league record for most consecutive starting assignments (582, July 30, 174, through 1992); shares major league career records for most seasons played (26); shares major league record for no-hitters in a season (2, in 1973); has struck out the side on nine pitches twice, a major league record; tied for the N.L. lead in sacrifice hits in 1985 (14); led the N.L. in ERA in 1981 (1.69) and 1987 (2.76); tied for A.L. lead in complete games in 1977 (22); led A.L. in shutouts in 1972 (9) and 1976 (7) and tied in 1979 (5); led the A.L. in innings pitched in 1974 (333); led the A.L. in strikeouts in 1972 (329), 1973 (383), 1974 (367), 1976 (327), 1977 (341), 1978 (260), 1979 (223), 1989 (301) and 1990 (232); led the N.L. in strikeouts in 1987 (270) and (228); shares career record for most strikeouts in championship series play (46); is 1-1 in championship play, and has one save in World Series play; has been selected to the All-Star team eight times.

Until four seasons ago, people could debate whether Nolan Ryan deserves to be in the Hall of Fame. He's given up too many walks, is third in lifetime losses, and has the second lowest winning percentage among pitchers who have 250 or more wins. And despite his 319 victories, he's only won 20 games in a season twice.

But in 1989, at age 42, Ryan, with 301 strikeouts, shattered the age barrier for a 300+ strikeout season by 11 years. Mickey Lolich, at a youthful 31, had held the honor previously; he struck out 308 hitters in 1971.

In 1990, baseball's all-time leading strikeout pitcher collected his 300th win and sixth no-hitter. For an encore in 1991, Ryan threw an unprecedented seventh no-hitter.

Finally, in 1992 Ryan had a sub-par year, with a 5-9 record and a 3.72 ERA. His 157 strikeouts in 157 innings pitched, however, kept his career strikeout ratio above one K per every inning he's pitched.

The Ryan Express, which has six 300+ strikeout seasons, is slowly coming to a halt. As he grew older, Ryan, who relied on an overpowering fastball, developed an effective curveball and changeup to complement his outstanding heater. As a result, he's held his career ERA to 3.17, which is pretty impressive. His name is going to dot the record books; he won't be denied his place in the Hall of Fame.

Not too many people are going to be able to afford a $1,600 1968 Nolan Ryan rookie card. The recommendation here is to go after a fourth-year card from 1971 — Topps #513. At $250 it's a lot more affordable and has more potential to grow. It's also difficult to find Mint cards from this set, due to the cards' black borders, which "chip" easier.

If you can find a 1971 Ryan in Mint shape, buy it and hang on to it for another six years. When Ryan is inducted on the first ballot as a representative of the class of 1999, someone's going to want a Mint Ryan fourth-year card. You'll have one, and it will surely be worth more than the $250 you paid for it.

Nolan Ryan Checklist

Year	Company	No.	Price
1968	O-Pee-Chee/Topps	177	1,500.00/1,600.00
1969	Topps	533	550.00
1970	O-Pee-Chee/Topps	197	15.00/20.00
1970	Topps	712	550.00
1971	O-Pee-Chee/Topps	513	200.00/250.00
1972	Topps	595	275.00
1973	O-Pee-Chee/Topps	67	12.00/15.00
1973	O-Pee-Chee/Topps	220	3.00/5.00
1974	O-Pee-Chee/Topps	20	50.00/70.00
1974	O-Pee-Chee/Topps	207	7.00/7.00
1975	O-Pee-Chee/Topps	5	15.00/20.00
1975	O-Pee-Chee/Toops	7	.75/1.00
1975	O-Pee-Chee/Topps	312	2.50/4.00
1975	O-Pee-Chee/Topps	500	50.00/65.00
1975	Topps Mini	5/7	3.25/1.50
1975	Topps Mini	312/500	2.50/60.00
1976	O-Pee-Chee/Topps	330	50.00/60.00
1977	O-Pee-Chee/Topps	6	4.50/6.00
1977	O-Pee-Chee	65/264	4.00/1.25
1977	Topps	234/650	10.00/35.00
1978	O-Pee-Chee/Topps	6	.35/.70
1978	O-Pee-Chee	105/241	3.00/.75
1978	Topps	206/400	.35/30.00
1979	O-Pee-Chee	51	10.00
1979	Topps	6/115/417	3.00/20.00/.40
1980	O-Pee-Chee	303	12.00
1980	Topps	206/580	2.00/25.00
1981	Donruss	260	8.00
1981	Fleer	57	8.00
1981	O-Pee-Chee/Topps	240	9.00/12.00
1982	Donruss	13/419	4.00/9.00
1982	Fleer	229	9.00
1982	O-Pee-Chee/Topps	90	7.50/10.00
1982	Topps	5/66/167	2.00/.25/.20
1983	Donruss	118	7.00
1983	Fleer	463	8.00
1983	O-Pee-Chee/Topps	360	7.50/10.00
1983	O-Pee-Chee/Topps	361	3.00/4.00
1984	Donruss	60	25.00
1984	Fleer	239	20.00
1984	O-Pee-Chee/Topps	66	.25/.50
1984	Topps	4/470/707	.30/6.00/.35
1985	Donruss	60	10.00
1985	Fleer	359	10.00
1985	Leaf	216	.30
1985	O-Pee-Chee	63	.30
1985	Topps	7/760	1.00/5.00
1986	Donruss	258	6.00
1986	Fleer	310	6.00
1986	Leaf	132	3.00
1986	O-Pee-Chee/Topps	100	2.50/3.00

Nolan Ryan Checklist

Year	Company	No.	Price
1987	Donruss	138	2.00
1987	Fleer	67	4.00
1987	Leaf	257	1.50
1987	O-Pee-Chee	155	.75
1987	Topps	757	1.25
1988	Donruss	61	.50
1988	Fleer	455	1.25
1988	Leaf	77	.50
1988	O-Pee-Chee/Topps	250	.35/.70
1988	Score	575	.60
1988	Topps	6/661	.10/.08
1989	Bowman	225	.70
1989	Donruss	154	.60
1989	Donruss Traded	19	1.50
1989	Fleer	368	.50
1989	Fleer Update	67	1.75
1989	O-Pee-Chee	366	.35
1989	Score	300	.50
1989	Score Traded	2	1.50
1989	Topps	530	.50
1989	Topps Traded	106T	1.50
1989	Upper Deck	145/669	4.00/.60
1989	Upper Deck Extended	774	4.00
1990	Bowman	486	.40
1990	Donruss	166/659/665	.40/1.00/1.00
1990	Fleer	313/636	.50/.10
1990	Fleer Update	131	.70
1990	Leaf	21/264	7.00/.50
1990	O-Pee-Chee/Topps	1	.25/.35
1990	O-Pee-Chee/Topps	2	.15/.20
1990	O-Pee-Chee/Topps	3	.15/.20
1990	O-Pee-Chee/Topps	4	.15/.20
1990	O-Pee-Chee/Topps	5	.15/.20
1990	Score	250/696	.50/.50
1990	Upper Deck	34/544	1.25/1.25
1990	Upper Deck Extended	734	2.00
1991	Bowman	280	.25
1991	Donruss	89	.35
1991	Donruss Studio	128	2.50
1991	Fleer	302	.25
1991	Fleer Ultra	355/395/400	1.00/.40/.06
1991	Leaf	423	3.00
1991	O-Pee-Chee/Topps	1	.20/.30
1991	O-Pee-Chee/Topps	6	.15/.20
1991	Score	4/417	.30/.30
1991	Score	686/701	.20/.20
1991	Topps Stadium Club	200	15.00
1991	Upper Deck	345	.30
1992	Donruss	154/555/707	.40/.20/.30
1992	Fleer	320/682/710	.25/.20/.80
1992	Fleer Ultra	141	3.00
1992	Leaf	41	1.00
1992	Leaf Studio	248	1.50
1992	Score	2/425	.25/.30
1992	Score Pinnacle	50/294/618	1.50/1.00/.40
1992	Topps	1/4	.30/.10
1992	Topps Stadium Club	605/770	3.00/3.00
1992	Upper Deck	92/655	.05/.40

 # Cal Ripken Jr.

Cal Ripken Jr.: 1982 Topps #21, $70; $35 in July 1991.

Cal Ripken Jr.

Aug. 24, 1960; 6-4, 220; throws and bats right; shortstop; active; 12 seasons (all with Baltimore).

Career statistics entering the 1993 season
G: 1,800; AB: 6,942; R: 1,043; H: 1,922; 2B: 369; 3B: 34;
HR: 273 (77th); TB: 3,178; RBI: 1,014; Ave.: .277; SB: 32.

Named A.L. Rookie of the Year in 1982; named A.L. Most Valuable Player in 1983 and 1991; hit for the cycle on May 6, 1984; tied for the A.L. lead with

15 game-winning RBI in 1986; tied for the A.L. lead with 10 sacrifice flies in 1988; led the A.L. in total bases in 1991 (368); led the A.L. in runs (121), hits (211) and doubles (47) in 1983; has made one playoff and World Series appearance, in 1983; has been selected to the All-Star team 10 times; holds A.L. career record for most home runs by a shortstop (265); holds major league record for most years leading the league in games by a shortstop, eight, and most consecutive games, 1,708; holds major league records for highest fielding percentage by a shortstop for a season (.996 in 1990) and fewest errors in 150 or more games (3, in 1990); holds record for most consecutive errorless games at shortstop (95, April 14-July 27, 1990) and most consecutive chances accepted without an error (431, April 14-July 28, 1990); shares major league career record for most years as a shortstop leading the league in double plays (6); won Gold Gloves in 1991 and 1992; led A.L. shortstops in total chances four times; led A.L. shortstops in double plays six times.

At 32, Ripken has already accomplished virtually everything he can — he's been a Rookie of the Year, is a two-time MVP winner, a 10-time All-Star, and owns a World Series ring. All that's left for this future Hall of Famer, aside from duplicating his previous efforts, is to keep on adding to his statistics.

During his 12-year career, Ripken has had nine straight 20-home run seasons as a shortstop, a streak broken in 1992, before he could set his sights on Eddie Mathews' record of 14 seasons. His 1991 MVP season (34 home runs, 210 hits, 114 RBI and a .323 batting average) ranks as one of the better seasons ever compiled by a shortstop.

Nevertheless, Ripken has averaged each season 86 runs, 160 hits, 22 home runs, 84 RBI and a .277 batting average, putting him on pace with Hall of Famer Ernie Banks' career numbers (2,583 hits, 1,305 runs, 1,636 RBI, 512 home runs and a .274 batting average) if he plays another six or so seasons.

Of course, one would be remiss if he didn't mention "The Streak;" the reliable, durable shortstop, currently at 1,735 consecutive games played, is closing in on the June 1995 date when he will break Lou Gehrig's record of 2,130 consecutive games played. Some say the streak has taken its toll; but like Gary Carter, Ripken is a gamer; he isn't going to stay out of the lineup.

Ripken's card, at $260, is the gem in the 1982 Topps Traded set. But that might be too steep for most collectors, so the recommendation is to buy his 1982 Topps card; it has more room to increase in value, so will yield a higher percentage on your return.

There are no other cards in this set which are even above $20; Ripken's is the key. Pick it up now, while it's still a value. If Ripken breaks Gehrig's streak, his card will probably reach $100. From then on, it won't be too difficult to reach the $140 mark, which will be double your initial investment.

Cal Ripken Jr. Checklist

Year	Company	No.	Price
1982	Donruss	405	50.00
1982	Fleer	176	50.00
1982	Topps	21 (Rookies)	70.00
1982	Topps Traded	98T	260.00
1983	Donruss	279	18.00
1983	Fleer	70	18.00
1983	O-Pee-Chee/Topps	163	17.50/25.00
1984	Donruss	106	25.00
1984	Fleer	17	18.00
1984	O-Pee-Chee	2/363	.80/.60
1984	Topps	400/426/490	1.75/.25/8.00
1985	Donruss	169	10.00
1985	Fleer	187/626	10.00/2.50
1985	Leaf	14	1.50
1985	O-Pee-Chee/Topps	30	3.00/4.00
1985	Topps	704	.30
1986	Donruss	210	5.00
1986	Fleer	284/633	5.00/.30
1986	Leaf	142	4.00
1986	O-Pee-Chee/Topps	340	1.50/2.00
1986	Topps	715	.80
1987	Donruss	89	2.00
1987	Fleer	478	3.00
1987	Leaf	98	2.00
1987	O-Pee-Chee	312	.25
1987	Topps	609/784	.20/1.25
1988	Donruss	26/171/625	.35/.35/.15
1988	Fleer	570/635/640	.60/.15/.12
1988	O-Pee-Chee	74	.20
1988	Score	550/651	.40/.20
1988	Topps	650	.40
1989	Bowman	9/260	.20/.15
1989	Donruss	51	.50
1989	Fleer	617	.40
1989	O-Pee-Chee/Topps	250	.20/.40
1989	Score	15	.40
1989	Upper Deck	467/682	3.00/.08
1990	Bowman	255	.20
1990	Donruss	96/676	.15/.09
1990	Fleer	187/624	.30/3.00
1990	O-Pee-Chee/Topps	8	.15/.15
1990	O-Pee-Chee/Topps	388	.20/.15
1990	O-Pee-Chee/Topps	570	.20/.35
1990	Score	2	.40
1990	Upper Deck	266	.30
1991	Bowman	104	.12
1991	Donruss	52/223	.05/.10
1991	Donruss Studio	9	1.00
1991	Fleer	490	.20
1991	Fleer Ultra	24	.50
1991	Leaf	430	1.50
1991	O-Pee-Chee/Topps	5	.12/.08
1991	O-Pee-Chee/Topps	150	.15/.12
1991	Score	95/849	.30/.12
1991	Topps Stadium Club	430	2.50
1991	Upper Deck	347	.15
1991	Upper Deck Final Edition	85	.50
1992	Donruss	22/35	.20/.30
1992	Fleer	26/703/711	.20/.15/.70
1992	Fleer Ultra	11	2.00

Cal Ripken Jr. Checklist

Year	Company	No.	Price
1992	Leaf	52	.80
1992	Leaf Studio	129	.80
1992	Score	433/540/788	.15/.20/.10
1992	Score	794/884	.08/.30
1992	Score Pinnacle	200/605	1.00/.15
1992	Topps	40/400	.20/.15
1992	Topps Stadium Club	1/595	2.00/1.50
1992	Topps Stadium Club Dome	154	1.00
1992	Upper Deck	82/165/645	.15/.30/.25

 # Carlton Fisk

Carlton Fisk: 1972 Topps #79, $135; $150 in July 1991.

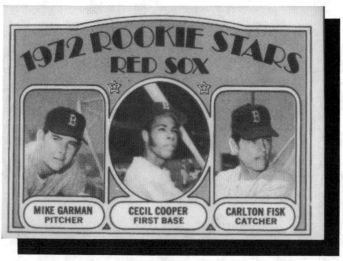

Carlton Fisk

Dec. 26, 1947; 6-2, 225; bats and throws right; catcher; active; 23 seasons (Boston 1971-80, Chicago White Sox 1981-92).

Career statistics entering the 1993 season

G: 2,474 (37th); AB: 8,703 (61st); R: 1,274 (92nd); H: 2,346 (86th); 2B: 421 (78th); 3B: 47; HR: 375 (36th); TB: 3,986 (53rd); RBI: 1,326 (59th); Ave.: .270; SB: 128.

Named A.L. Rookie of the Year in 1972; won a Gold Glove Award in 1972; holds major league career record for most home runs by a catcher (350); shares major league record for most at bats in a game (11) and plate appearances (12, May 8-9, 1984, in 25 innings); holds A.L. record for most home runs in a season by a catcher (33, in 1985); hit for the cycle May 16, 1984; shares World Series single-game record for most at bats in an inning (2, Oct. 15, 1975); has been selected for 11 All-Star games; holds A.L. career records for years catching (23), games (2,201), putouts (11,294) and chances accepted (12,337); shares A.L. season record for fewest passed balls in 150 or more games (4, in 1977); holds major league record for longest game with no passed balls, and most innings played by a catcher in a game (25, May 8-9, 1984); led A.L. catchers in total chances four times; led A.L. catchers in double plays in 1981 (10) and 1987 (15).

Set his statistics aside for a while. We'll get back to them in a minute. If but for no other reason, Carlton Fisk has to be admired for the Ryan-like condition he's kept himself in for 23 seasons while playing a position which delivers the most wear and tear.

Although he's slowed a bit, this veteran could be considered the game's best catcher up until about 1990 or so, when he was but 42 years old, and 10-15 years older than most. He's winding down an illustrious career and should, during the 1993 season, break Bob Boone's record (2,225) for most games caught by a catcher.

"Pudge" is the prototypical catcher. A fierce competitor, he's also been a calming influence for the pitching staffs he's worked with. During his career, he's caught six 20-game winners (Luis Tiant three times, and LaMarr Hoyt, Dennis Eckersley and Jack McDowell once each) and one Cy Young Award winner (Hoyt in 1983).

Now, to the offensive highlights. Who can forget the dramatic home run he hit in the thrilling Game 6 of the 1975 World Series? That is but one glorious moment in a career which has seen him hit more home runs than any catcher except Johnny Bench (389) and collect more hits than any catcher except Ted Simmons (2,472).

Fisk shares a 1972 Topps rookie card with Cecil Cooper, who, in his own right, compiled some pretty impressive statistics during his career (2,192 hits, 415 doubles, 241 home runs, 1,125 RBI and a .298 batting average), yet surprisingly didn't garner any votes in 1993 during the Hall of Fame balloting. Nevertheless, Fisk's card is the key rookie in the set, and trails only Nolan Ryan's fifth-year card ($275) in value.

Carlton Fisk Checklist

Year	Company	No.	Price
1972	O-Pee-Chee/Topps	79	125.00/135.00
1973	O-Pee-Chee/Topps	193	25.00/45.00
1974	O-Pee-Chee/Topps	105	20.00/25.00
1974	O-Pee-Chee/Topps	331	1.50/2.00
1975	O-Pee-Chee/Topps	80	18.00/25.00
1976	O-Pee-Chee/Topps	365	10.00/12.00
1977	O-Pee-Chee	137	6.00
1977	Topps	640	8.00
1978	O-Pee-Chee	210	5.50
1978	Topps	270	7.00
1979	O-Pee-Chee	360	4.00
1979	Topps	680	5.00
1980	Topps	40	5.00
1980	O-Pee-Chee	20	3.50
1981	Donruss	335	1.75
1981	Fleer	224	.50
1981	O-Pee-Chee	116	2.50
1981	Topps	480	3.00
1981	Topps Traded	762	7.00
1982	Donruss	20/495	.50/1.50
1982	Fleer	343	1.50
1982	O-Pee-Chee	58	.12
1982	O-Pee-Chee/Topps	110	1.50/2.00
1982	O-Pee-Chee/Topps	111	1.00/1.25
1982	Topps	554	.20
1983	Donruss	104	1.25
1983	Fleer	235/638	1.00/.20
1983	O-Pee-Chee/Topps	20	1.50/2.00
1983	O-Pee-Chee/Topps	393	.12/.15
1984	Donruss	302	4.00
1984	Fleer	58	2.50
1984	O-Pee-Chee	127	.40
1984	Topps	216/560	.15/1.25
1985	Donruss	208	.40
1985	Fleer	513	.40
1985	Leaf	155	.15
1985	O-Pee-Chee	49	.15
1985	Topps	1/770	.15/.40
1986	Donruss	366	.60
1986	Fleer	204/643	.50/.10
1986	Leaf	163	1.00
1986	O-Pee-Chee/Topps	290	.35/.50
1986	Topps	719	.12
1987	Donruss	247	.20
1987	Fleer	496	.30
1987	Leaf	199	.60
1987	O-Pee-Chee	164	.20
1987	Topps	756	.25
1988	Donruss	260	.20
1988	Fleer	397	.20
1988	Leaf	208	.12
1988	O-Pee-Chee/Topps	385	.20/.30
1988	Score	592	.20
1989	Bowman	62	.10
1989	Donruss	7/101	.12/.20
1989	Fleer	495	.20
1989	O-Pee-Chee	46	.15

Carlton Fisk Checklist

Year	Company	No.	Price
1989	Score	449	.12
1989	Topps	695	.20
1989	Upper Deck	609	.60
1990	Bowman	314	.08
1990	Donruss	58	.12
1990	Fleer	530	.10
1990	Leaf	10/174	1.00/.30
1990	O-Pee-Chee/Topps	392	.08/.08
1990	O-Pee-Chee/Topps	420	.08/.08
1990	Score	290	.09
1990	Upper Deck	367	.10
1991	Bowman	345	.10
1991	Donruss	108	.10
1991	Donruss Studio	32	.35
1991	Fleer	118	.10
1991	Fleer Ultra	72	.20
1991	Leaf	384	.30
1991	O-Pee-Chee/Topps	3	.05/.08
1991	O-Pee-Chee/Topps	170	.07/.10
1991	O-Pee-Chee/Topps	393	.05/.08
1991	Score	265/421	.10/.10
1991	Topps Stadium Club	180	.80
1991	Upper Deck	29/643/677	.08/.12/.25
1992	Donruss	543	.10
1992	Fleer	79	.10
1992	Fleer Ultra	33	.30
1992	Leaf	303	.20
1992	Score	72	.25
1992	Score Pinnacle	361	.20
1992	Topps	630	.12
1992	Topps Stadium Club	480	.50
1992	Topps Stadium Club Dome	49	.20
1992	Upper Deck	571	.15

 # Paul Molitor

Paul Molitor: 1978 Topps #707, $60; $50 in July 1991.

Aug. 22, 1956; 6-0, 185; bats and throws right; infielder; active; 15 seasons (Milwaukee 1978-92, Toronto 1993).

Career statistics entering the 1993 season
G: 1,856; AB: 7,520; R: 1,275 (91st); H: 2,281 (100th); 2B: 405 (91st);
3B: 86; HR: 160; TB: 3,338; RBI: 790; Ave.: .303; SB: 412 (53rd).

Shares the major league record for most stolen bases in an inning, 3, on July 26, 1987; hit three home runs in a game on May 12, 1982; hit for the cycle May 15, 1991; led the A.L. in runs in 1982 (136), 1987 (114) and 1991 (133); led the A.L. in hits in 1991 (216); led the A.L. in doubles in 1987 (41); tied for the A.L. lead in triples in 1991 (13); has made one World Series appearance, setting single-game records for most hits, five, and singles, five, on Oct. 12, 1982; shares World Series record for most at bats in a nine-inning game (6, Oct. 12, 1982); has been selected for five All-Star games.

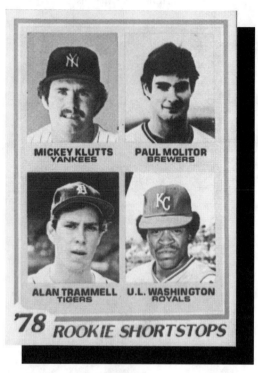

MICKEY KLUTTS
YANKEES

PAUL MOLITOR
BREWERS

ALAN TRAMMELL
TIGERS

U.L. WASHINGTON
ROYALS

'78 ROOKIE SHORTSTOPS

Paul Molitor

During his days in Milwaukee, Paul Molitor was nicknamed "The Ignitor," a rally starter for the big bats behind him — Cecil Cooper, Ben Oglivie, Gorman Thomas, Larry Hisle, Ted Simmons and Robin Yount, among others.

He doesn't have the power or speed of a Rickey Henderson, but "Molly" will be regarded as one of the game's best leadoff hitters. A lifetime .300 hitter, he kept Brewer fans on the edge of their seats with a thrilling 39-game hitting streak in 1987.

The versatile Molitor can be considered a nomad; he's played every infield position and in the outfield, too. The five-time All-Star's always had a strong work ethic, and is a club leader.

Unfortunately, injuries have sidetracked Molitor, an aggressive, hard-nosed ballplayer. He's been on the disabled list 12 times in his 15-year career. As a result, he's only played in about 80 percent of his team's games during his career. But Molitor, who's getting better with age, has stayed healthy the last two seasons. He shows no signs of slowing down; his 89 RBI in 1992 were a career high.

Molitor signed a three-year contract with Toronto before the 1993 season; if he plays another five seasons, he has a shot at 3,000 career hits. That accomplishment will guarantee him a spot in the Hall of Fame.

Can you imagine what his 1978 Topps card would be worth if he and Alan Trammell, who's also on the card, were not so injury prone? If they can both finish their careers strongly, they will get serious Cooperstown consideration. If one or the other is inducted, and we're banking on both, the card will increase, probably hitting the $100 mark.

Molitor's second-year card is a great buy at $15, too. The extra attention he'll get playing for the World Champion Blue Jays will help his cards' values, too.

Paul Molitor Checklist

Year	Company	No.	Price
1978	Topps	707	60.00
1979	O-Pee-Chee	8	12.00
1979	Topps	24	15.00
1980	O-Pee-Chee	211	5.00
1980	Topps	406	7.00
1981	Donruss	203	1.50
1981	Fleer	515	2.00
1981	O-Pee-Chee	300	1.00
1981	Topps	300	2.00
1982	Donruss	78	.20
1982	Fleer	148	.20
1982	O-Pee-Chee	195	.20
1982	Topps	195	.35
1983	Donruss	484	.20
1983	Fleer	40	.20
1983	O-Pee-Chee	371	.20
1983	Topps	630	.30
1984	Donruss	107	1.25
1984	Fleer	207	.20
1984	O-Pee-Chee/Topps	60	.40/.20
1985	Donruss	359	.20
1985	Fleer	588	.15
1985	O-Pee-Chee	395	.15
1985	Topps	522	.15
1986	Donruss	124	.15
1986	Fleer	495	.15
1986	O-Pee-Chee/Topps	267	.12/.15
1987	Donruss	117	.15
1987	Fleer	350	.15
1987	O-Pee-Chee	184	.10
1987	Topps	56/741	.07/.12
1988	Donruss	249	.12
1988	Fleer	169	.12
1988	Leaf	7/168	.10/.12
1988	O-Pee-Chee	231	.09
1988	Score	340/660	.10/.08
1988	Topps	465	.10
1989	Bowman	140	.08
1989	Donruss	291	.12
1989	Fleer	193	.15
1989	O-Pee-Chee	110	.07
1989	Score	565	.08

Paul Molitor Checklist

Year	Company	No.	Price
1989	Topps	110	.12
1989	Upper Deck	525/673	.15/.08
1990	Bowman	399	.08
1990	Donruss	103	.10
1990	Fleer	330	.08
1990	Leaf	242	.35
1990	O-Pee-Chee	360	.07
1990	Score	460	.10
1990	Topps	360	.09
1990	Upper Deck	254	.12
1991	Bowman	32	.08
1991	Donruss	85	.08
1991	Donruss Studio	73	.20
1991	Fleer	591	.10
1991	Fleer Ultra	178	.15
1991	Leaf	302	.15
1991	O-Pee-Chee/Topps	95	.05/.10
1991	Score	49	.12
1991	Topps Stadium Club	245	.30
1991	Upper Deck	324	.12
1992	Donruss	51	.10
1992	Fleer	182/702	.10/.06
1992	Fleer Ultra	81	.15
1992	Leaf	238	.15
1992	Leaf Studio	194	.20
1992	Score	61	.08
1992	Score Pinnacle	8	.12
1992	Topps	600	.10
1992	Topps Stadium Club	230	.20
1992	Topps Stadium Club Dome	122	.25
1992	Upper Deck	423	.10

Alan Trammell

Alan Trammell: 1978 Topps #707, $60; $50 in July 1991.

Feb. 21, 1958; 6-0, 185; throws and bats right; shortstop; active; 16 seasons (all with Detroit).

Career statistics entering the 1993 season

G: 1,965; AB: 7,179; R: 1,077; H: 2,050; 2B: 356; 3B: 51;
HR: 162; TB: 2,994; RBI: 876; Ave.: .286; SB: 212.

Won Gold Gloves in 1980-81 and 1983-84; led the A.L. in sacrifice hits in 1981 (16) and 1983 (15); led A.L. shortstops in double plays in 1990 (102); has played in one World Series (1984 against San Diego), and shares a single-game record for knocking in all his team's runs (4); hit .450 in the World Series, with two homers and six RBI; has been selected for the All-Star game six times.

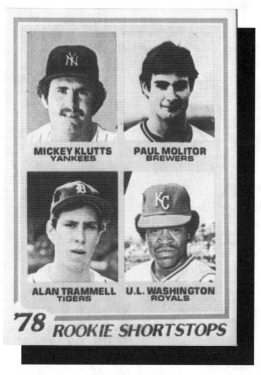

MICKEY KLUTTS
YANKEES

PAUL MOLITOR
BREWERS

ALAN TRAMMELL
TIGERS

U.L. WASHINGTON
ROYALS

78 ROOKIE SHORTSTOPS

Alan Trammell

Recurring back problems and the emergence of Travis Fryman have shifted shortstop Alan Trammell to the outfield in Detroit. He'll always be considered a shortstop, part of the longtime double play combination in Motown with second baseman Lou Whitaker. But he's capable of putting up some outfielder-type numbers, as he did in 1987, when he had 205 hits, 28 home runs, a .343 batting average and 105 RBI.

Trammell and Whitaker broke into the league together in the same game late in the 1977 season. Their career numbers are quite similar. Trammell was the sixth Tiger to get 2,000 hits, behind Ty Cobb, Al Kaline, Charlie Gehringer, Harry Heilmann and Sam Crawford. Whitaker appropriately was the seventh.

Trammell's career numbers are quite similar to Hall of Famer Pee Wee Reese's — 2,166 games, 2,170 hits, 330 doubles, 80 triples, 126 home runs, 1,338 runs, 232 stolen bases and a .269 batting average. Reese had more playoff exposure; as a Brooklyn Dodger he played in seven World Series, compared to Trammell's one. But that shouldn't preclude Trammell from getting the support he needs for induction.

The six-time All-Star has been everything the Tigers needed — a leader, an excellent fielder, a run scorer, a good base runner, a clean up hitter, and one who could hit for average. If he can keep his batting average above .280, he has a legitimate shot at Cooperstown.

The 1978 Trammell/Molitor card is the only rookie card around that has two potential Hall of Famers on it. At $60, it might seem a bit steep, but the potential to double is tremendous if they are both inducted.

Alan Trammell Checklist

Year	Company	No.	Price
1978	Topps	707	60.00
1979	O-Pee-Chee	184	5.00
1979	Topps	358	8.00
1980	O-Pee-Chee	123	1.25
1980	Topps	232	4.00
1981	Donruss	5	.40
1981	Fleer	461	.40
1981	O-Pee-Chee	133	.25
1981	Topps	709	.70
1982	Donruss	5/76	.40/.60
1982	Fleer	283	.40
1982	O-Pee-Chee	381	.40
1982	Topps	475	.50
1983	Donruss	207	.40
1983	Fleer	344	.40
1983	O-Pee-Chee/Topps	95	.40/.50
1984	Donruss	293	.60
1984	Fleer	91	.40
1984	O-Pee-Chee	88	.60
1984	Topps	510	.40
1985	Donruss	171	.40
1985	Fleer	23	.35
1985	Leaf	158	.25
1985	O-Pee-Chee	181	.30
1985	Topps	690	.35
1986	Donruss	171	.35
1986	Fleer	241/633	.30/.30
1986	Leaf	101	.25
1986	O-Pee-Chee	130	.25
1986	Topps	130	.30
1987	Donruss	127	.25
1987	Fleer	167	.25
1987	Leaf	126	.20
1987	O-Pee-Chee	209	.20
1987	Topps	687	.25
1988	Donruss	4/230	.25/.25
1988	Fleer	74	.25
1988	Leaf	4/167	.20/.15
1988	O-Pee-Chee	320	.12
1988	Score	37/651	.15/.20
1988	Topps	320/389	.15/.08
1989	Bowman	105	.05
1989	Donruss	180	.15
1989	Fleer	148	.20
1989	O-Pee-Chee	49	.10
1989	Score	110	.15
1989	Topps	400/609/770	.08/.06/.15
1989	Upper Deck	290/690	.20/.08

Alan Trammell Checklist

Year	Company	No.	Price
1990	Bowman	353	.08
1990	Donruss	90	.10
1990	Fleer	617	.09
1990	Leaf	218	.40
1990	O-Pee-Chee	440	.10
1990	Score	9	.09
1990	Topps	440	.09
1990	Upper Deck	554	.10
1991	Bowman	154/370	.08/.08
1991	Donruss	118	.08
1991	Donruss Studio	59	.25
1991	Fleer	355	.08
1991	Fleer Ultra	129	.15
1991	Leaf	351	.30
1991	O-Pee-Chee/Topps	275	.07/.10
1991	O-Pee-Chee/Topps	389	.07/.06
1991	Score	40/852	.12/.08
1991	Topps Stadium Club	63	.40
1991	Upper Deck	223	.12
1992	Donruss	164	.10
1992	Fleer	148	.10
1992	Fleer Ultra	64	.15
1992	Leaf	172	.25
1992	Leaf Studio	179	.30
1992	Score	515	.08
1992	Score Pinnacle	113	.20
1992	Topps	120	.10
1992	Topps Stadium Club	850	.15
1992	Upper Deck	273	.10

 **Tony Gwynn**

Tony Gwynn: 1983 Topps #482, $40; $20 in July 1991.

May 9, 1960; 5-11, 215; bats and throws left; outfielder; active; 11 seasons (San Diego 1982-92).

Career statistics entering the 1993 season
G: 1,463; AB: 5,701; R: 842; H: 1,864; 2B: 275; 3B: 75;
HR: 59; TB: 2,466; RBI: 591; Ave.: .327 (31st); SB: 249

Holds N.L. season record for lowest batting average by leader (.313, in 1988); shares N.L. record for most years leading the league in singles (4); led the N.L. in on base percentage in 1984 (.410); led N.L. in hits in 1984 (213), 1986 (211), 1987 (218) and 1989 (203); led the N.L. in at bats in 1986 (642) and tied in runs (107); led the N.L. in batting average in 1984 (.351), 1987 (.370), 1988 (.313) and 1989 (.336); has been named to the All-Star team eight times; won Gold Glove Awards in 1986, 1987, 1989-91; led N.L. outfielders in total chances in 1986 (360).

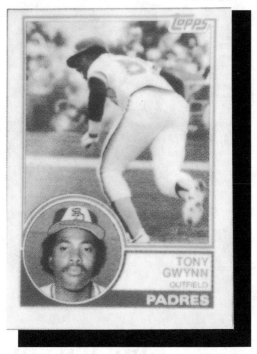

Tony Gwynn

Tony Gwynn never seems satisfied with his performance; he's constantly reviewing tapes of his swing. The eight-time All-Star is meticulous in his preparation in the batting cage before each game, practicing his game situation execution.

It's paid off, too. A lifetime .327 hitter (31st overall), Gwynn, always a threat for a batting title, has strung together 10 straight .300 seasons, with four batting titles to his credit. His league-leading .370 average in 1990 was the highest the National League has seen since 1948, when Stan Musial hit .376.

Gwynn has also shown some speed, too, averaging 22 steals each season, and has flashed some leather, too. He's won five Gold Gloves.

Gwynn's 1983 Topps card is a best-kept secret, considering Ryne Sandberg is the marquee player featured in the set. But Gwynn's rookie card is keeping pace with Sandberg's rookie card, and is a step ahead of another possible Hall of Famer, Wade Boggs, whose rookie card ($35) is in the set, also.

Tony Gwynn Checklist

Year	Company	No.	Price
1983	Donruss	598	25.00
1983	Fleer	360	25.00
1983	O-Pee-Chee	143	30.00
1983	Topps	482	40.00
1984	Donruss	324	20.00
1984	Fleer	301	12.00
1984	Topps	251	4.00
1985	Donruss	25/63	1.75/5.00
1985	Fleer	34	5.00
1985	O-Pee-Chee	383	1.00
1985	Topps	660/717	2.00/.35
1986	Donruss	112	2.00
1986	Fleer	323	2.00
1986	Leaf	41	1.00
1986	O-Pee-Chee/Topps	10.	.75/1.00
1987	Donruss	64	.35
1987	Fleer	416	1.00
1987	Leaf	235	.25
1987	O-Pee-Chee	198	.30
1987	Topps	530/599	.50/.20
1988	Donruss	164	.35
1988	Fleer	585/631/634	.35/.15/.12
1988	Leaf	90	.50
1988	Score	385	.25
1988	Topps	360/402/699	.25/.15/.12
1989	Bowman	461	.20
1989	Donruss	6/128	.35/.30
1989	Fleer	305	.35
1989	O-Pee-Chee	51	.25
1989	Score	90	.20
1989	Topps	570	.30
1989	Upper Deck	384/683	.30/.08
1990	Bowman	217	.08
1990	Donruss	86/705	.15/.09
1990	Fleer	157	.25
1990	Leaf	154	1.00
1990	O-Pee-Chee/Topps	403	.20/.15
1990	O-Pee-Chee/Topps	730	.20/.20
1990	Score	255/685	.35/.20
1990	Upper Deck	344	.20
1991	Bowman	647	.10
1991	Donruss	243	.10
1991	Donruss Studio	245	.50
1991	Fleer	529	.15
1991	Fleer Ultra	303	.20
1991	Leaf	290	.40
1991	O-Pee-Chee/Topps	180	.15/.12
1991	Score	500	.15
1991	Topps	180	.12
1991	Upper Deck	255	.15
1991	Upper Deck Final Edition	97	.30
1992	Donruss	425/441	.10/.15
1992	Fleer	605	.12
1992	Fleer Ultra	277/371	.70/.12
1992	Leaf	206	.60
1992	Leaf Studio	104	.50
1992	Score	625/779/886	.15/.10/.20
1992	Score Pinnacle	400/591	.40/.25
1992	Topps	270	.12
1992	Topps Stadium Club	825	.80
1992	Topps Stadium Club Dome	73	.30
1992	Upper Deck	83/274	.10/.15

 # Will Clark

Will Clark: 1987 Fleer #269, $20; $25 in July 1991.

Will Clark

March 13, 1964; 6-0, 196; throws and bats left; first baseman; active; seven seasons (San Francisco 1986-92).

Career statistics entering the 1993 season
G: 1,028; AB: 3,778; R: 605; H: 1,139; 2B: 222; 3B: 35;
HR: 162; TB: 1,917; RBI: 636; Ave.: .301; SB: 50.

Member of the 1984 United States Olympic Team; led the N.L. in slugging percentage (.536) and tied for the league lead in total bases (303) in 1991; led the N.L. in walks (100), RBI (109) and games (162) in 1988; tied for the N.L. lead in runs in 1989 (104); led N.L. first basemen in double plays in 1987 (130), 1988 (126), 1990 (118), 1991 (115) and 1992 (130); led N.L. first basemen in total chances in 1988 (1,608), 1989 (1,566) and 1990 (1,587); won a Gold Glove Award in 1991; has been named to the All-Star team five times; holds championship single-series records for most hits (13) and total bases (24, in 1989); holds championship series single-game record for RBI (6, Oct. 4, 1989); shares single-series record for most runs (8) and consecutive hits (5, in 1989); shares single-game record for most runs (4) and grand slams (1) and RBI in an inning (4, Oct. 4, 1989); shares N.L. single-game record for most hits (4, Oct. 4, 1989).

Will "The Thrill" Clark has a picture-perfect swing, the classic left-handed swing, á la Ted Williams. He's obviously never going to touch the statistics Williams compiled, but the confident, somewhat arrogant Clark has the potential to put up some very good numbers by the end of his career.

At age 27, he's entering his prime and should have his most productive years ahead of him. Having Matt Williams and the newly-acquired superstar Barry Bonds protecting him in the Giants' powerful lineup will also help.

If he keeps on his current pace of 162 hits, 31 doubles, 23 home runs and 90 RBI per season, Clark could hit the coveted 3,000 hit mark in 10 more seasons, with close to 400 home runs. If he maintains his lifetime .301 batting average, he'll be a shoo-in come election time.

The highly-touted 1984 Olympian hit a career high .333 in 1989, but lost the batting title by .003 to Tony Gwynn. Clark will always be a threat to win a title.

In his two playoff appearances Clark is hitting a robust .489, with 22 hits in 45 at bats, including a 13-20 (.650 average) in 1989 against Chicago, which gives him the record for most hits in a championship series.

Every card in the 1987 Fleer set has always been more valuable than its counterpart in the 1986 Fleer Update set, due in part to the perceived scarcity of the 1987 set and the apparent overproduction of the 1986 set. The 1987 set has also always been in great demand because it's one of Fleer's better-looking designs. If you're going to spend $20 on a card that's only six years old, this is the one to spend it on.

Will Clark Checklist

Year	Company	No.	Price
1986	Donruss Rookies	32	12.00
1986	Fleer Update	U25	10.00
1986	Topps Traded	24T	6.00
1987	Donruss	66	8.00
1987	Fleer	269	20.00
1987	Leaf	144	5.00
1987	O-Pee-Chee	361	1.50
1987	Topps	420	2.50
1988	Donruss	21/204	.35/.60
1988	Fleer	78	1.25
1988	Leaf	21	.40

Will Clark Checklist

Year	Company	No.	Price
1988	Leaf	170	.80
1988	O-Pee-Chee/Topps	350	.45/.80
1988	Score	78	.80
1988	Topps	261	.10
1989	Bowman	476	.40
1989	Donruss	249	.40
1989	Fleer	325/631/632	.50/.40/.30
1989	O-Pee-Chee	321	.25
1989	Score	450	.50
1989	Topps	660	.50
1989	Upper Deck	155/678	2.00/.08
1990	Bowman	231	.35
1990	Donruss	230/707	.40/.15
1990	Fleer	54/630/637	.40/1.50/.10
1990	O-Pee-Chee/Topps	100	.25/.50
1990	O-Pee-Chee/Topps	397	.20/.25
1990	Score	300/684/699	.60/.20/.25
1990	Upper Deck	50/556	.40/.60
1991	Bowman	616	.20
1991	Donruss	86/441	.25/.15
1991	Donruss Studio	254	1.00
1991	Fleer	259	.25
1991	Fleer Ultra	318	.50
1991	Leaf	238	1.00
1991	O-Pee-Chee/Topps	500	.15/.30
1991	Score	7/664	.20/.15
1991	Score	871/886	.20/.30
1991	Topps Stadium Club	5	2.00
1991	Upper Deck	445	.40
1991	Upper Deck Final Edition	92	.50
1992	Donruss	214/428	.30/.15
1992	Fleer	631/699	.25/.10
1992	Fleer Ultra	287	1.00
1992	Leaf Studio	114	.80
1992	Score	3/773/883	.25/.10/.20
1992	Score Pinnacle	122	.80
1992	Topps	330/386	.20/.10
1992	Topps Stadium Club	460/598	1.00/1.00
1992	Topps Stadium Club Dome	28	.80
1992	Upper Deck	175	.25

 # Ozzie Smith

Ozzie Smith: 1979 Topps #116, $75; $45 in July 1991

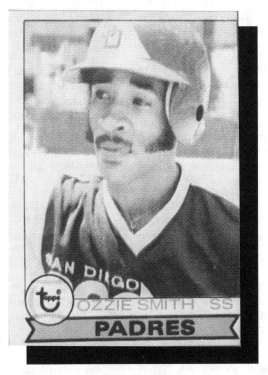

Ozzie Smith

Dec. 26, 1954; 5-10, 168; throws right, switch-hitter; shortstop; active; 15 seasons (San Diego 1978-1981; St. Louis 1982-92).

Career statistics entering the 1993 season
G: 2,208 (87th); AB: 8,087 (86th); R: 1,079; H: 2,108; 2B: 347;
3B: 57; HR: 22; TB: 2,635; RBI: 681; Ave.: .261; SB: 542 (24th).

Holds major league records for most years with 500 or more assists by a shortstop (8), and most years leading the league in assists and chances (8); holds major league single-season record for most assists by a shortstop (621, in 1980); shares major league record for most double plays by a shortstop in an extra-inning game (6, on Aug. 25, 1979, in 19 innings); holds N.L. career record for most double plays by a shortstop (1,361); holds N.L. single-season record for fewest errors by a shortstop in 150 or more games (8, in 1991); holds N.L. record for most years leading the league in fielding percentage (7) and double plays (5); holds N.L. record for highest fielding percentage in a season in 150 or more games (.987, in 1987 and 1991); has won Gold Gloves from 1980-92; has led the N.L. in total chances seven times and in double plays five times; led N.L. in sacrifice hits in 1978 (28) and 1980 (23); has hit .351 in championship series play; has played in three World Series; has been named to the All-Star team 12 times.

At first glance, you'll say a .261 lifetime hitter doesn't belong in the Hall of Fame; but that's not what's going to land baseball's best fielding shortstop ever, Ozzie Smith, there. It's his glovework, which is also why such defensive standouts as Rabbit Maranville and Luis Aparicio are in the Hall.

The 12-time All-Star owns 13 Gold Gloves, more than any other shortstop, and trails only Jim Kaat (14) and Brooks Robinson (16) for the most in a career. His fielding is magical; he's an acrobatic "Wizard" who owns several major league fielding records.

But Smith has been a consistent, steady threat at the plate, too. He's a switch-hitter who's coming off consecutive .285 and .295 batting average seasons. When his career is finished, he should have about 2,500 hits and 700 stolen bases — first-rate offensive numbers for a shortstop known more for his fielding.

During the 1976 free-agent draft, Detroit selected Alan Trammell in the second round. Later, in the seventh round, the team picked Ozzie Smith. Smith waited a year and was drafted by the San Diego Padres in 1977. His decision to play in San Diego instead of competing with Trammell in Detroit paved the way for two shortstops to compile Hall-of-Fame-calibre statistics.

Although it's a year newer, Smith's 1979 Topps rookie card, at $75, is $15 more than Trammell's 1978 card. That's due mainly to the Wizard's overall popularity; Smith has been the top vote-getter in All-Star balloting twice, in 1987 and 1988, and his 10th straight election as a starter in 1992 broke Johnny Bench's record.

It's difficult to find a perfectly-centered Smith rookie card; most are 60-40 centered. The closer it is to a perfect 50-50 centering, the better it is. Nevertheless, don't be surprised if Smith's card makes a serious run at Luis Aparicio's 1956 Topps rookie card, which is undervalued at $135.

Ozzie Smith Checklist

Year	Company	No.	Price
1979	O-Pee-Chee	52	60.00
1979	Topps	116	75.00
1980	O-Pee-Chee	205	15.00
1980	Topps	393	20.00
1981	Donruss	1	3.00
1981	Fleer	488	2.00
1981	O-Pee-Chee	254	2.00
1981	Topps	207/254	.20/4.00
1982	Donruss	21/94	.20/2.00
1982	Fleer	582	1.00
1982	O-Pee-Chee/Topps	95	1.50/2.50
1982	Topps Traded	109T	20.00
1983	Donruss	120	1.50
1983	Fleer	22/636	1.50/.10
1983	O-Pee-Chee	14	1.50
1983	Topps	540	2.00
1984	Donruss	59/625	5.00/.30
1984	Fleer	336	1.50
1984	O-Pee-Chee/Topps	130	.45/.70
1984	O-Pee-Chee/Topps	389 (All-Star)	.20/.15
1985	Donruss	59	1.50
1985	Fleer	240/631	.15/.06
1985	Leaf	60	.08
1985	O-Pee-Chee	191	.12
1985	Topps	605/715	.15/.12
1986	Donruss	59	1.00
1986	Fleer	46	1.00
1986	Leaf	47	.15
1986	O-Pee-Chee	297	.12
1986	Topps	704/730	.10/.15
1987	Donruss	5/60	.12/.15
1987	Fleer	308	.80
1987	Leaf	5/108	.30/.15
1987	O-Pee-Chee	107	.12
1987	Topps	598/749	.07/.35
1988	Donruss	263	.15
1988	Fleer	47/628	.15/.12
1988	Leaf	115	.12
1988	O-Pee-Chee	38	.09
1988	Score	12	.12
1988	Topps	400/460	.08/.12
1989	Bowman	436	.08
1989	Donruss	63	.12
1989	Fleer	463	.15
1989	O-Pee-Chee	230	.08
1989	Score	80	.10
1989	Topps	230/389	.12/.08
1989	Upper Deck	265/674	.15/.08
1990	Bowman	195	.10
1990	Donruss	201/710	.10/.08
1990	Fleer	260	.09
1990	Leaf	142/364	.80/.30
1990	O-Pee-Chee	400/590	.07/.07
1990	Score	285	.10
1990	Topps	400/590	.10/.10
1990	Upper Deck	225	.20
1991	Bowman	398	.10
1991	Donruss	240/437	.10/.10
1991	Donruss Studio	238	.40
1991	Fleer	646	.10

Ozzie Smith Checklist

Year	Company	No.	Price
1991	Fleer Ultra	296	.20
1991	Leaf	80	.40
1991	O-Pee-Chee	130	.07
1991	Score	825	.10
1991	Topps	130	.08
1991	Topps Stadium Club	154	.70
1991	Upper Deck	162	.10
1992	Upper Deck Final Edition	95F	.25
1992	Donruss	423/432	.08/.08
1992	Fleer	592	.12
1992	Fleer Ultra	271	.50
1992	Leaf	400	.20
1992	Leaf Studio	98	.25
1992	Score	590	.08
1992	Score Pinnacle	6	.30/
1992	Topps	396/760	.08/.10
1992	Topps Stadium Club	680	.40
1992	Topps Stadium Club Dome	175	.30
1992	Upper Deck	177	.15

 # George Brett

George Brett: 1975 Topps #228, $250; $200 in July 1991.

May 15, 1953; 6-0, 205; bats left, throws right; third baseman/first baseman; active; 20 seasons; (Kansas City 1973-92).

Career statistics entering the 1993 season
G: 2,562 (26th); AB: 9,789 (19th); R: 1,514 (45th); H: 3,005 (16th);
2B: 634 (8th); 3B: 134 (73rd); HR: 298 (64th); TB: 4,801 (18th);
RBI: 1,520 (33rd); Ave.: .307 (97th); SB: 194.

Named A.L. Most Valuable Player in 1980; won A.L. Gold Glove Award in 1985 for third basemen; led A.L. in total bases in 1976 (286); led the A.L. in hits in 1975 (195), 1976 (215) and 1979 (212); led the A.L. in batting average in 1976 (.333), 1980 (.390) and 1990 (.329); led the A.L. in doubles in 1978 (45) and 1990 (45); led the A.L. in triples in 1975 (13), 1976 (14) and 1979 (20); holds the major league single-season record for most consecutive games with three or more hits (6, May 8-13, 1976); shares the major league record for most home runs in October (4, in 1985); holds A.L. career record for most intentional walks (220); holds A.L. record for most seasons with 10 or more intentional walks received (11); hit three home runs in a game twice, on July 22, 1979, and April 20, 1983; led the A.L. in on base percentage in 1980 (.461); hit for the cycle twice, on May 28, 1979, and July 25, 1990; led the A.L. in intentional walks in 1985 (31) and 1986 (18); led the A.L. in slugging percentage in 1980

(.664), 1983 (.563) and 1985 (.585); led A.L. third basemen in double plays in 1985 (33); holds the career highest slugging average (50 at bats or more) in championship series (.728); holds career championship series record for runs (22), triples (4), home runs (9), total bases (75); shares single-game records for most runs (4, Oct. 11, 1985) and home runs (3, Oct. 6, 1978); holds single-game record for total bases (12, Oct. 6, 1978); named to the All-Star team 13 times.

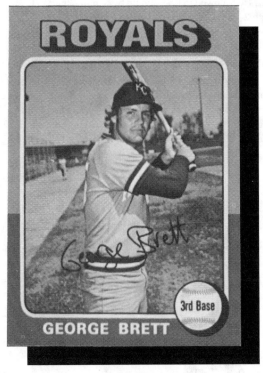

George Brett

His .390 batting average in 1980 is the closest to hitting .400 that anyone has come since Ted Williams hit .406 in 1941.

But people probably still remember George Brett more for the famous pine-tar incident in 1983, when Brett came storming out of the dugout at Yankee Stadium after a game-winning two-run home run was disallowed because he had too much pine tar on his bat.

American League President Lee MacPhail later overruled the umpires, letting the home run stand, giving the Kansas City Royals a win. That's what George Brett is all about — winning. The fierce competitor has won three batting titles, one MVP Award and one World Series ring during his Hall-of-Fame-calibre career.

The lifetime .307 hitter is the only player to win batting titles in three decades — 1976 (.333), 1980 (.390) and 1990 (.329). A 13-time All-Star, Brett became only the fifth player in history to have 20 doubles, 20 triples and 20 home runs in a season, doing so in 1979 when he had 42 doubles, 20 triples and 20 home runs. He followed that season up by winning the MVP Award, after hitting .390, with 24 home runs and 114 RBI.

Had Brett not missed nearly two full seasons to injuries throughout his career, his statistics would be even more impressive. But he's accomplished his own personal goal — 3,000 hits — and has definite Hall of Fame numbers.

Since it's already at $250, a 1975 George Brett rookie card shouldn't be considered a short-term investment. It won't increase as dramatically as cards do for active players, so you'll have to wait longer to get the higher percentage return on your initial investment. Consider it a long-term investment, but a safe bet. It won't decline; Brett's on his way to the Hall of Fame.

George Brett Checklist

Year	Company	No.	Price
1975	O-Pee-Chee/Topps	228	210.00/250.00
1975	Topps Mini	228	200.00
1976	O-Pee-Chee/Topps	19	45.00/60.00
1977	O-Pee-Chee/Topps	1	3.00/4.00
1977	O-Pee-Chee	170/261	15.00/3.00
1977	Topps	231/580/631	6.00/35.00/3.00
1978	O-Pee-Chee	215	20.00
1978	Topps	100	25.00
1979	O-Pee-Chee	167	8.00
1979	Topps	330	15.00
1980	O-Pee-Chee	235	7.00
1980	Topps	450	12.00
1981	Donruss	100/491	4.00/1.75
1981	Fleer	28/655	2.00/2.00
1981	O-Pee-Chee	113	3.00
1981	Topps	1/700	2.00/6.00
1982	Donruss	15/34	1.50/3.00
1982	Fleer	405	3.00
1982	O-Pee-Chee/Topps	200	2.00/4.00
1982	O-Pee-Chee/Topps	201	.75/1.50
1982	O-Pee-Chee	261	.60
1982	Topps	96/549	.35/2.00
1983	Donruss	338	3.00
1983	Fleer	108	3.00
1983	O-Pee-Chee	3	2.00
1983	O-Pee-Chee/Topps	388	.40/1.25
1983	Topps	600	4.00
1984	Donruss	53	10.00
1984	Fleer	344/638	6.00/.30
1984	O-Pee-Chee	212/223	.40/1.00
1984	Topps	399/500/710	.50/2.00/.30
1985	Donruss	53	4.00
1985	Fleer	199	4.00
1985	Leaf	176	.40
1985	O-Pee-Chee	100	.40

George Brett Checklist

Year	Company	No.	Price
1985	Topps	100/703	1.00/.35
1986	Donruss	53	2.00
1986	Fleer	5/634	2.00/.60
1986	Leaf	42	1.00
1986	O-Pee-Chee/Topps	300	.35/.50
1986	Topps	714	.30
1987	Donruss	15/54	.40/.40
1987	Fleer	366	.50
1987	Leaf	15/96	.30/1.00
1987	O-Pee-Chee	126	.30
1987	Topps	400	.35
1988	Donruss	102	.40
1988	Fleer	254	.40
1988	Leaf	93	.50
1988	O-Pee-Chee	312	.25
1988	Score	11	.30
1988	Topps	700	.30
1989	Bowman	121	.15
1989	Donruss	204	.30
1989	Fleer	277	.35
1989	O-Pee-Chee/Topps	200	.20/.30
1989	Score	75	.50
1989	Upper Deck	215/689	.35/.08
1990	Bowman	382	.12
1990	Donruss	144	.10
1990	Fleer	103/621	.15/.50
1990	Leaf	178	.80
1990	O-Pee-Chee/Topps	60	.20/.15
1990	Score	140	.15
1990	Upper Deck	124	.15
1991	Bowman	300	.12
1991	Donruss	201/396	.10/.10
1991	Donruss Studio	62	.30
1991	Fleer	552	.12
1991	Fleer Ultra	144	.25
1991	Leaf	335	.25
1991	O-Pee-Chee/Topps	2	.10/.10
1991	O-Pee-Chee/Topps	540	.15/.12
1991	Score	120/769/853	.15/.08/.08
1991	Topps Stadium Club	159	.80
1991	Upper Deck	525	.15
1992	Donruss	143	.15
1992	Fleer	154	.15
1992	Fleer Ultra	68	.40
1992	Leaf	255	.25
1992	Leaf Studio	181	.20
1992	Score	650	.10
1992	Score Pinnacle	60	.40
1992	Topps	620	.12
1992	Topps Stadium Club	150/609	.40/.60
1992	Upper Deck	444	.15

 Robin Yount

Robin Yount: 1975 Topps 223, $250; $200 in July 1991.

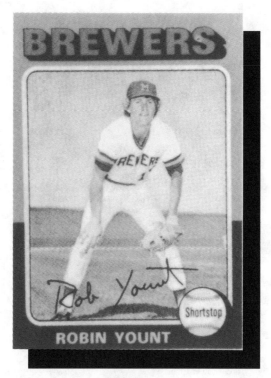

Robin Yount

Sept. 16, 1955; 6-0, 180; throws and bats right; shortstop/outfielder; active; 19 seasons (all with Milwaukee).

Career statistics entering the 1993 season

G: 2,729 (17th); AB: 10,554 (8th); R: 1,570 (35th); H: 3,025 (13th);
2B: 558 (12th); 3B: 123; HR: 243; TB: 4,558 (23rd);
RBI: 1,355 (52nd); Ave.: .287; SB: 262.

Named A.L. MVP in 1982 and 1989; led the A.L. in total bases (367) and slugging percentage (.578) in 1982; won Gold Glove as a shortstop in 1982; led A.L. shortstops in total chances (831) and double plays (104) and tied for the lead in putouts (290) in 1976; led A.L. outfielders in fielding percentage in 1986 (.997); hit for the cycle on June 12, 1988; led the A.L. in doubles in 1980 (49) and tied in 1982 (46); led the A.L. in hits (210) in 1982; led the A.L. in triples in 1983 (10) and tied in 1988 (11); has made one championship series appearance and one World Series appearance; shares World Series single-game record for most at bats in a nine-inning game (6, Oct. 12, 1982); hit .414 in the World Series, including 6 RBI; has been selected for the All-Star game three times, all as a shortstop.

Although he's a 19-year veteran, Robin Yount still plays with the enthusiasm of a rookie. A throwback to the early days of baseball, Yount, during a take-the-money-and-run era, turned down a higher offer from the California Angels in 1989 to stay in Milwaukee. He's driven by his love for the game and his desire to win — not the monetary rewards or personal statistics.

As an 18-year-old rookie, "The Kid" was named the Brewers' starting short-stop in 1974. He reigned as the American League's best overall shortstop until 1985, when he was converted to the outfield because of shoulder problems.

In 1982 Yount compiled one of the best offensive seasons ever by a shortstop — 210 hits, 46 doubles, 12 triples, 29 home runs, 114 RBI, a .331 batting average, and a Gold Glove Award. He capped that MVP season with his personal highlight of his career — his only World Series appearance, when he hit .414 against the victorious St. Louis Cardinals.

The three-time All-Star shortstop captured his second MVP Award in 1989, when, as an outfielder, he had 195 hits, 38 doubles, nine triples, 21 home runs, 103 RBI and a .318 batting average. Yount joined Stan Musial and Hank Greenberg as the only players to win MVP Awards while playing two different positions.

In 1992, Yount became the 18th player in baseball history to collect 3,000 hits, just three weeks before Kansas City's George Brett did it. It's quite fitting that the two, who will follow each other into the Hall of Fame, have rookie cards in the 1975 Topps set.

Although Brett has had more playoff and World Series exposure, Yount's card has kept pace in value and should stay even with Brett's as they both rise in value. The 1975 set, at $900, has average investment potential, but does contain rookie cards for three Hall of Famers — Yount, Brett and Gary Carter.

Robin Yount Checklist

Year	Company	No.	Price
1975	O-Pee-Chee/Topps	223	210.00/250.00
1975	Topps Mini	223	200.00
1976	O-Pee-Chee/Topps	316	45.00/60.00

Robin Yount Checklist

Year	Company	No.	Price
1977	O-Pee-Chee	204	25.00
1977	Topps	635	35.00
1978	O-Pee-Chee	29	17.50
1978	Topps	173	25.00
1979	O-Pee-Chee	41	12.00
1979	Topps	95	15.00
1980	O-Pee-Chee	139	9.00
1980	Topps	265	12.00
1981	Donruss	323	4.00
1981	Fleer	511	4.00
1981	O-Pee-Chee	4	3.00
1981	Topps	515	6.00
1982	Donruss	510	3.00
1982	Fleer	155	3.00
1982	O-Pee-Chee	237	2.00
1982	Topps	435	4.00
1983	Donruss	258	3.00
1983	Fleer	51/632	3.00/.15
1983	O-Pee-Chee/Topps	350	2.00/4.00
1983	O-Pee-Chee/Topps	389	.75/1.25
1983	Topps	321	.20
1984	Donruss	1/48	4.00/10.00
1984	Fleer	219	6.00
1984	O-Pee-Chee/Topps	10	1.00/2.00
1985	Donruss	48	4.00
1985	Fleer	601	4.00
1985	Leaf	44	.80
1985	O-Pee-Chee/Topps	340	.50/1.00
1986	Donruss	48	2.00
1986	Fleer	506	2.00
1986	Leaf	31	.25
1986	O-Pee-Chee	144	.25
1986	Topps	780	.50
1987	Donruss	126	.50
1987	Fleer	361	.50
1987	Leaf	67	1.00
1987	O-Pee-Chee	76	.20
1987	Topps	773	.35
1988	Donruss	295	.30
1988	Fleer	178	.30
1988	Leaf	106	.20
1988	O-Pee-Chee/Topps	165	.15/.20
1988	Score	160	.30
1989	Bowman	144	.25
1989	Donruss	5/55	.25/.25
1989	Fleer	200	.25
1989	O-Pee-Chee	253	.15
1989	Score	151	.25
1989	Topps	615	.25
1989	Upper Deck	285	.35
1990	Bowman	404	.15
1990	Donruss	146	.20
1990	Fleer	340	.20
1990	Leaf	71	1.00
1990	O-Pee-Chee/Topps	290	.12/.20
1990	O-Pee-Chee/Topps	389	.12/.20
1990	Score	320	.20
1990	Upper Deck	91/567	.06/.40
1991	Bowman	55	.10
1991	Donruss	272	.10
1991	Donruss Studio	80	.35
1991	Fleer	601	.15

Robin Yount Checklist

Year	Company	No.	Price
1991	Fleer Ultra	184	.20
1991	Leaf	116	.40
1991	O-Pee-Chee	575	.10
1991	Score	525/854	.15/.08
1991	Topps	575	.15
1991	Topps Stadium Club	509	1.00
1991	Upper Deck	344	.15
1992	Donruss	173	.20
1992	Fleer	194/708	.15/.40
1992	Fleer Ultra	87	.40
1992	Leaf	64	.25
1992	Leaf Studio	200	.20
1992	Score	525	.12
1992	Score Pinnacle	38/287	.50/.30
1992	Topps	90	.12
1992	Topps Stadium Club	450/607	.50/.60
1992	Upper Deck	456	.20

Ken Griffey Jr.

Ken Griffey Jr.: 1989 Upper Deck #1, $50; $40 in July 1991.

Nov. 21, 1969; 6-3, 205; bats and throws left; outfielder; active; four seasons (Seattle 1989-92).

Career statistics entering the 1993 season

G: 578; AB: 2,165; R: 311; H: 652; 2B: 132; 3B: 12; HR: 87; TB: 1,069; RBI: 344; Ave.: .301; SB: 60.

Won Gold Glove Awards in 1990-92; led A.L. outfielders in double plays (6) in 1989; named to three All-Star teams.

It doesn't hurt that his father, Ken Sr., was a five-time All-Star during his 18-year career, but Ken Griffey Jr. has enough natural talent to be as good, if not better, than his father.

After all, Griffey, the first Seattle Mariner to ever start in an All-Star game, has already made three appearances in the mid-summer classic, and he's only been in the league four years. And, he's still only 23 years old!

"The Kid" is baseball's most exciting player, effortlessly making miraculous catches and cannon-like throws. He's emerged as the game's brightest young star, one to build a franchise around. He's a potential Triple Crown winner, and a good bet to win an MVP Award, too, especially if the Mariners can make a play-off run.

Ken Griffey Jr.

It's hard to even imagine what kind of numbers he'll post by the time his career is over. But he's annually averaged 163 hits, 33 doubles, 21 home runs, 86 RBI and a .301 batting average. And he hasn't even reached his prime. Let's say he keeps up that pace for another 10 years — he'd finish with 300 home runs, 2,200 hits and 1,200 RBI, quite comparable to those of Hall of Famer Ralph Kiner, who played only 10 seasons but hit 369 home runs, had 1,451 hits and 1,105 RBI. But Griffey would still only be 33!

Griffey has fun on the field; it's one of the reasons he's such a popular player. So popular, in fact, that a Ken Griffey Jr. candy bar came out just shortly after he made the team during his 1989 rookie season. He's even been on Kellogg's Frosted Flakes boxes, too.

There's no telling how high Griffey's 1989 Upper Deck card could go, but if you want one, get it now while it's still only $50. Or, buy 10 1989 Donruss cards at $5 each, and let them sit.

If you don't have one already, it'll cost you around $6 a pop to try to find an '89 Upper Deck Griffey in a wax pack, or about $175 for a 36-count box. Since the investment potential is above average for the entire 1989 Upper Deck set, which is currently at $125, setting aside a few unopened packs or boxes might be a wise idea, too, with a high-yield return quite likely.

Ken Griffey Jr. Checklist

Year	Company	No.	Price
1989	Bowman	220/259	3.00/1.00
1989	Donruss	33	5.00
1989	Donruss Rookies	3	7.00
1989	Fleer	548	7.00
1989	Score Traded	100	5.00
1989	Topps Traded	41T	4.00
1989	Upper Deck	1	50.00
1990	Bowman	481	1.50
1990	Donruss	4/365	.80/1.00
1990	Fleer	513	1.00
1990	Leaf	245	20.00
1990	O-Pee-Chee/Topps	336	1.50/1.00
1990	Score	560	2.00
1990	Upper Deck	24/156	.06/4.00
1991	Bowman	246	1.00
1991	Donruss	49/77/392	.40/.80/.40
1991	Donruss Studio	112	3.00
1991	Fleer	450/710	1.00/.30
1991	Fleer Ultra	336	2.00
1991	Leaf	372	3.00
1991	O-Pee-Chee/Topps	392	1.00/.30
1991	O-Pee-Chee/Topps	790	1.00/1.00
1991	Score	2/396/697	.80/.40/.30
1991	Score	841/858/892	1.25/1.00/1.50
1991	Topps Stadium Club	270	18.00
1991	Upper Deck	555	1.50
1992	Donruss	24/165	.60/.50
1992	Fleer	279/709	.70/.80
1992	Fleer Ultra	123	4.00
1992	Leaf	392	1.50
1992	Leaf Studio	232	1.75
1992	Score	1/436	.50/.40
1992	Score Pinnacle	283/549	2.50/2.00
1992	Topps	50	.50
1992	Topps Stadium Club	400/603	3.00/3.00
1992	Topps Stadium Club Dome	70	2.00
1992	Upper Deck	85/424/650	.80/.80/.50

 **Bret Saberhagen**

Bret Saberhagen: 1985 Donruss #222, $6; $9 in July 1991.

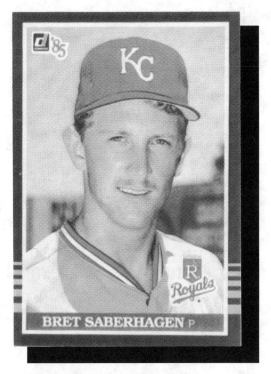

Bret Saberhagen

April 11, 1964; 6-1, 190; throws and bats right; pitcher; active; nine seasons
(Kansas City 1984-91; New York Mets 1992).

Career statistics entering 1993 season

W: 113; L: 83; Pct.: .577; ERA: 3.23; G: 269; GS: 241;
CG: 65; ShO: 15; IP: 1,758; H: 1,635; R: 689;
ER: 631; BB: 358; SO: 1,174.

Named A.L. Cy Young Award Winner in 1985 and 1989; won a Gold Glove Award in 1989; pitched a 7-0 no-hitter against Chicago Aug. 26, 1991; has been used as a pinch runner; is 3-3 in championship series play and was 2-0 in his only World Series performance in 1985; has been selected for the All-Star game two times, and was the winning pitcher for the A.L. in 1990.

Perhaps it's quite fitting that Bret Saberhagen was a World Series hero in 1985, picking up two wins as the Kansas City Royals topped the St. Louis Cardinals for the title. After all, it was an odd-numbered year.

Throughout Saberhagen's roller-coaster career, he's 39-53 during even-numbered years and 74-30 in odd-numbered years, including Cy Young Award seasons in 1985 (20-6, 2.87 ERA) and 1989 (23-6, 2.16 ERA).

Baseball's answer to Dr. Jeckyll and Mr. Hyde maintains exceptional control and has an excellent walks-per-nine-innings ratio (358 walks in 1,758 innings). Although he was limited to 17 games in 1992 due to an injured finger, when Saberhagen is healthy he's as good as the best.

Pitchers' cards don't offer the best investment potential, compared to hitters' cards. Saberhagen's 1985 Donruss card value has dropped since 1991, but now's the time to buy. At $5, it has plenty of room to grow; it could easily double in value.

Saberhagen is only 29; he's in his prime, and, although he's only collected 21 wins since his 1989 Cy Young season, he has the potential to win another Cy Young Award. If that happens, you'll surely get $10 for your $5 investment.

Bret Saberhagen Checklist

Year	Company	No.	Price
1984	Fleer Update	U103	38.00
1984	Topps Traded	104T	10.00
1985	Donruss	222	6.00
1985	Fleer	212	5.00
1985	O-Pee-Chee/Topps	23	2.75/2.50
1986	Donruss	11/100	.25/.60
1986	Fleer	19	1.00
1986	Leaf	11	.20
1986	O-Pee-Chee	249	.25
1986	Topps	487/720	.70/.15
1987	Donruss	132	.25
1987	Fleer	379	.30
1987	Leaf	261	.15
1987	O-Pee-Chee/Topps	140	.15/.15
1988	Donruss	96	.15
1988	Fleer	268/626	.15/.10
1988	O-Pee-Chee	5	.12
1988	Score	89	.20
1988	Topps	540	.25
1989	Bowman	111	.10
1989	Donruss	144	.12
1989	Fleer	291	.15
1989	O-Pee-Chee	157	.10
1989	Score	251	.10
1989	Topps	750	.12
1989	Upper Deck	37	.15

Bret Saberhagen Checklist

Year	Company	No.	Price
1990	Bowman	364	.10
1990	Donruss	89	.15
1990	Fleer	116	.10
1990	O-Pee-Chee/Topps	35	.10/10
1990	Score	195	.25
1990	Topps	393	.10
1990	Upper Deck	326	.15
1991	Bowman	291	.08
1991	Donruss	88	.10
1991	Donruss Studio	69	.15
1991	Fleer	567	.10
1991	Fleer Ultra	154	.10
1991	Leaf	118	.15
1991	O-Pee-Chee/Topps	280	.08/.08
1991	Score	6	.12
1991	Topps Stadium Club	38	.30
1991	Upper Deck	33/435	.10/.12
1992	Donruss	128/434	.10/.08
1992	Fleer	167	.08
1992	Fleer Ultra	537	.06
1992	Leaf	376	.15
1992	Leaf Studio	69	.15
1992	Score	6/786	.08/.06
1992	Score Pinnacle	442	.20
1992	Score Traded	20	.08
1992	Topps	75	.08
1992	Topps Traded	97	.08
1992	Topps Stadium Club	755	.20
1992	Upper Deck	233	.10

 # Dennis Eckersley

Dennis Eckersley: 1976 Topps #98, $70; $30 in July 1991.

Oct. 3, 1954; 6-2, 195; throws and bats right; pitcher, relief pitcher; active; 18 seasons (Cleveland 1975-77; Boston 1978-84; Chicago Cubs 1984-86; Oakland 1987-92).

Career statistics entering the 1993 season
W: 181; L: 145; Pct.: .555; ERA: 3.43; G: 740 (30th);GS: 361; CG: 100; ShO: 20; Saves: 239 (8th);IP: 2,971 1/3; H: 2,747; R: 1,224; ER: 1,133; BB: 679; SO: 2,118 (38th).

Named A.L. Cy Young Award winner and MVP in 1992; pitched a 1-0 no-hitter victory against the California Angels May 30, 1977; led the A.L. in saves (51) in 1992; holds career record for most saves in championship series play (10); holds single-series save record (4, in 1988); shares major-league career record for most games pitched in championship series play (15), and most games pitched in the A.L. championship series (14, all as a relief pitcher, also a record); named to the All-Star team six times.

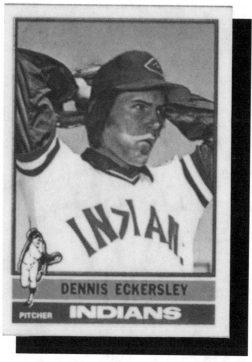

Dennis Eckersley

When Dennis Eckersley went 6-11 in 1986 as a starter for the Chicago Cubs, some thought it was the beginning of the end. It was; his career as a starter was over. But his career as the premiere relief pitcher was just beginning.

"Eck" has successfully converted from a starter to the bullpen. He's the only pitcher in history to have 100 complete games and 100 saves, featuring one 20-win season in 1978 (20-8) and one 51-save season 14 seasons later (1992).

In 1990, Eckersley set the standard for future relievers. As the Oakland A's closer, he had 48 saves, with an amazing 0.61 ERA in 73 1/3 innings pitched. That's the lowest ERA in history for a season, even if 25 innings is the minimum requirement.

During his six seasons as a relief pitcher, Eckersley has amassed 239 saves (eighth all-time), averaging nearly 40 saves per season. In 1992, he set a career high of 51, which led the American League. As a result, Eckersley was named the A.L. MVP and Cy Young Award winner, becoming just the fourth player in league history to win both awards in the same season.

Eckersley has an above-average fastball and nasty slider. He's most efficient with his repertoire, too. He has such great control he has hitters swinging at anything that looks decent, and is often able to retire the side with but a few pitches. His walks-per-innings-pitched ratio of 19.2 in 1989, when he walked but three batters in 57 2/3 innings, is an all-time best, followed by his 1990 ratio of 18.3, when he walked four in 73 1/3 innings.

Before being converted to a specialist, Eckersley had a 151-128 record, primarily as a starter. He'll need to hang on for a few more seasons, and catch a few breaks, by uncharacteristically blowing some saves, but he could hit 200 wins.

Eckersley's cards should follow the route of current Hall of Famer Rollie Fingers, whose 1969 Topps rookie cards, prior to his election, were $80. Now they're $150. Don't be surprised to see the same pattern occur with Eckersley when he's inducted.

Dennis Eckersley Checklist

Year	Company	No.	Price
1976	O-Pee-Chee/Topps	98	55.00/70.00
1976	O-Pee-Chee/Topps	202	.75/.90
1977	O-Pee-Chee	15	15.00
1977	Topps	525	20.00
1978	O-Pee-Chee	138	8.00
1978	Topps	122	12.00
1979	O-Pee-Chee	16	6.00
1979	Topps	40	8.00
1980	O-Pee-Chee	169	3.00
1980	Topps	320	4.00
1981	Donruss	96	2.00
1981	Fleer	226	1.50
1981	O-Pee-Chee	109	2.00
1981	Topps	620	3.00
1982	Donruss	30	1.25
1982	Fleer	292	1.50
1982	O-Pee-Chee	287	.12
1982	Topps	490	.20
1983	Donruss	487	1.00
1983	Fleer	182/629	.12/.25
1983	O-Pee-Chee/Topps	270	1.50/2.00
1984	Donruss	639	5.00
1984	Fleer	396	.20
1984	Fleer Update	U34	20.00
1984	O-Pee-Chee	218	.25
1984	Topps	745	.15
1984	Topps Traded	34	8.00
1985	Donruss	442	1.50
1985	Fleer	57	1.25
1985	O-Pee-Chee/Topps	163	.10/.12
1986	Donruss	239	.12
1986	Fleer	368	.12
1986	Leaf	113	.10
1986	O-Pee-Chee	199	.10
1986	Topps	538	.40
1987	Donruss	365	.12
1987	Fleer	563	.12
1987	Fleer Update	U30	.30
1987	O-Pee-Chee	381	.10
1987	Topps	459	.10

Dennis Eckersley Checklist

Year	Company	No.	Price
1987	Topps Traded	31T	.30
1988	Donruss	349	.20
1988	Fleer	279	.12
1988	O-Pee-Chee/Topps	72	.07/.10
1988	Score	104	.10
1989	Bowman	190	.08
1989	Donruss	67	.10
1989	Fleer	7	.12
1989	O-Pee-Chee/Topps	370	.07/.10
1989	Score	276	.10
1989	Upper Deck	289	.12
1990	Bowman	451	.08
1990	Donruss	210	.09
1990	Fleer	6	.12
1990	Leaf	29	.50
1990	O-Pee-Chee/Topps	670	.05/.09
1990	Score	315	.10
1990	Upper Deck	513	.08
1991	Bowman	237	.10
1991	Donruss	270	.10
1991	Donruss Studio	102	.25
1991	Fleer	6	.10
1991	Fleer Ultra	245	.10
1991	Leaf	285	.20
1991	O-Pee-Chee/Topps	250	.05/.10
1991	Score	485	.12
1991	Topps Stadium Club	332	.35
1991	Upper Deck	172	.15
1992	Donruss	147	.10
1992	Fleer	255	.08
1992	Fleer Ultra	421	.35
1992	Leaf	100	.25
1992	Leaf Studio	223	.20
1992	Score	190	.08
1992	Score Pinnacle	25	.15
1992	Topps	738	.08
1992	Topps Stadium Club	190	.25
1992	Topps Stadium Club Dome	42	.30
1992	Upper Deck	331	.10

Robin Ventura

Robin Ventura: 1988 Topps Traded #124, $10; $2 in July 1991.

July 14, 1967; 6-1, 198; bats right, throws left; third base; active; four seasons (all with Chicago White Sox).

Career statistics entering the 1993 season

**G: 480; AB: 1,736; R: 230; H: 470; 2B: 83; 3B: 3;
HR: 44; TB: 691; RBI: 254; Ave.: .271; SB: 5.**

Robin Ventura

Won a Gold Glove Award at third base in 1991 and 1992; led A.L. third basemen in putouts in 1991 (134); led A.L. third basemen in putouts (141), assists (372) total chances (563) and tied for the lead in double plays (29) in 1992; was a member of the 1988 United States Olympic baseball team; played in the 1992 All-Star game and was 2-2.

A two-time NCAA player of the year, Robin Ventura was a hitting machine, hitting .430 over three years, with 66 home runs, 319 RBI and an incredible 58-game hitting streak at Oklahoma State.

Drafted by the Chicago White Sox as the team's third baseman of the future, he started out shakily in the field in 1990, committing 25 errors. But he's quickly settled down as a fielder, and has won Gold Gloves the last two seasons.

As a hitter, Ventura is quite poised, and has a good eye for the strike zone; in each of his three seasons, Ventura's walked more times than he's struck out. He has the potential to consistently hit 20 home runs, with 100 RBI, solid numbers for a third basemen.

At 24, he made his first All-Star appearance in 1992. He's stepped forward among the younger third basemen in the league (Dean Palmer and Edgar Martinez) and is the odds-on-favorite to be a perennial All-Star favorite at third base. He should keep getting better as he heads into his prime.

Topps included Ventura in its 1988 Traded set. At $10, the card sets the pace among the special subset of United States Olympians, which is loaded with several potential Cy Young Award winners, including Jim Abbott, Jack McDowell, Andy Benes and Charles Nagy. Since hitters' cards command higher prices than pitchers' cards, Ventura is a better investment.

Robin Ventura Checklist

Year	Company	No.	Price
1988	Topps Traded	124	10.00
1989	Bowman	65	1.25
1989	Fleer Update	23	3.00
1989	Topps	764	2.50
1990	Bowman	311	.50
1990	Donruss	28	.80
1990	Donruss Rookies	15	.80
1990	Fleer	550	.60
1990	Leaf	167	12.00
1990	O-Pee-Chee/Topps	121	.50/.60
1990	Score	595	1.00
1990	Upper Deck	21	3.00
1991	Bowman	358	.15
1991	Donruss	315	.10
1991	Fleer	139	.25
1991	Fleer Ultra	86	1.00
1991	Leaf	271	1.00
1991	O-Pee-Chee/Topps	461	.08/.08
1991	Score	320	.25
1991	Topps Stadium Club	274	5.00
1991	Upper Deck	263/677	.30/.25
1992	Donruss	145	.25
1992	Fleer	101	.20
1992	Fleer Ultra	343	1.00
1992	Leaf	17	.80
1992	Leaf Studio	160	.60
1992	Score	122	.15
1992	Score Pinnacle	121/286	.60/.50
1992	Topps	255	.15
1992	Topps Stadium Club	591	5.00
1992	Upper Deck	263	.15

THE REST OF THE BEST

31) Eddie Murray 1978 Topps #36, $75/was $50 in July 1991: The stats speak for themselves — he's 23rd all-time in home runs, 26th in RBI and 52nd in hits.

32) Andre Dawson 1977 Topps #473, $75/$50: When he finishes his career with more than 400 home runs and 2,500 hits, "Hawk's" flight pattern will take him straight to the Hall of Fame.

33) Rickey Henderson 1980 Topps #482, $80/$175: Baseball's all-time stolen base king, and one of the game's best leadoff hitters ever.

34) Juan Gonzalez 1991 Fleer Ultra Update #U55, $10/not available: At 28, he's got a home run title under his belt, and is just hitting his prime.

35) Fred McGriff 1986 Donruss #28, $30/$18: He hits 30 home runs each year and his Donruss card is scarcer than its competitors.

36) Cecil Fielder 1986 Donruss #512, $25/$18: If you don't buy this one, at least buy Fielder's 1986 Topps (#386) card for $8.

37) Travis Fryman 1991 Topps Stadium Club #355, $10/not available: He's being groomed to fill Alan Trammell's spot at shortstop. If he keeps hitting 20+ home runs each season, he'll stay there for a long, long while.

38) Carlos Baerga 1993 Score Pinnacle #6, 25 cents: The potential is unlimited. His 1992 season of 20 home runs, 105 RBI and a .312 batting averge compares with what Ryne Sandberg consistently does.

39) Roger Clemens 1985 Donruss #273, $60/$25: The "Rocket" has three Cy Young Awards and he's gunning for more.

40) Ruben Sierra 1987 Fleer #138, $12/$12: He was sent to Oakland as part of a three-for-one deal for Jose Canseco, but Sierra is almost good enough to be traded straight up for Canseco.

41) Frank Thomas 1990 Leaf #300, $50/$12: He's going to be putting a hurt on the ball for quite some time, probably 30 home runs, 100 RBI and a .300 average each year.

42) Mark McGwire 1985 Topps #401, $30/$30: After a 22 home run, 75 RBI, .201 average season in 1991, some thought McGwire had peaked. But he came back with 42 homers, 104 RBI and a .268 average, his second highest ever, in 1992.

43) Joe Carter 1984 Donruss #41, $50/$15: He's had four 30+ home run seasons during his 10-year career. If he stays in Toronto and has the SkyDome fences to shoot for, he should have another 5-10 similar seasons.

44) Don Sutton 1966 Topps #288, $150/$125: Hall of Fame Class of 1994, along with Steve Carlton.

45) Roberto Alomar 1988 Score Traded #105, $65/$8: If this is too steep, try a 1988 Donruss (#34) for $4. He's so young, and has put up more hits at his age than Pete Rose did at the same age.

46) Rafael Palmeiro 1987 Donruss #43, $6/$3.50: He's a threat to win a batting title, has a shot at 3,000 career hits and can end up as a lifetime .300 hitter.

47) John Olerud 1990 Leaf #237, $6/$2.75: OK, we confess. This was written at the end of July when Olerud was still hitting above .400. His card had hit $15, with $25 looming if he wins a batting title and $75-$100 if he hits .400.

48) Matt Williams 1988 Fleer #101, $4/$6: He's only played in one-third as many games as Cal Ripken has, but his career statistics are on pace with what Cal Ripken has done.

49) Mike Schmidt 1973 Topps #615, $425/$450: This Hall of Famer's card is the key one in this set.

50) Mickey Mantle 1961 Topps #578, $400/$300: A good-looking card among the scarce third-series high numbers (523-589) in the set. Commons in that series go for $25.

51) Ernie Banks 1955 Topps #28, $225/$175: Although it won't offer a high percentage yield, for a second-year card at this price, let's buy two!

52) Yogi Berra 1952 Topps #191, $350/$350: He's a Hall of Famer, and a New York Yankee. Who doesn't like Yogi Berra?

53) Sandy Koufax 1956 Topps #79, $400/$275: It's a long-term investment, but this second-year Koufax card will keep on rising.

54) Willie Mays 1954 Topps #90, $500/$350: The "Say Hey Kid" remains among the top 10 best sellers among major card dealers across the country.

55) Ted Williams 1954 Topps #1, $650/$600: It's usually difficult to find a Near Mint first-numbered card in any set from the pre-binder era of collecting.

The 52 cards (not including Juan Gonzalez, Travis Fyrman and Carlos Baerga cards) which had a collective value of $4,474.50 in July 1991 have jumped to $5,743. Ten have decreased; three have stayed the same in value. The 15 football cards selected for this book have collectively increased from $213.70 in July 1991 to $264. Four cards have decreased in value, while one has stayed the same. The 14 basketball (not including Alonzo Mourning) cards have increased from $227 to $415; only one has decreased and one has stayed the same. The 15 hockey cards have jumped from $732.50 to $1,292. Only one card has dropped in value.

Editor's note: The hockey cards shown for 1) Mario Lemieux, 9) Jari Kurri and 12) Bryan Trottier are their Topps cards. The cards for 3) Steve Yzerman and 6) Larry Robinson are from the 1992-93 O-Pee-Chee Hockey set's 25th Anniversary Series of 26 cards. They are replicas of the players' rookie cards.

 Eddie Murray
1978 Topps #36
$75

 Andre Dawson
1977 Topps #473
$75

 Rickey Henderson
1980 Topps #482
$80

 Juan Gonzalez

1991 Fleer Ultra Update #U55
$10

 Fred McGriff

1986 Donruss #28
$30

Cecil Fielder

1986 Donruss #512
$25

 Travis Fryman

1991 Topps Stadium Club #355
$10

 Carlos Baerga

1993 Score Pinnacle #6
$00.25

 Roger Clemens

1985 Donruss #273
$60

Ruben Sierra
1987 Fleer #138
$12

Frank Thomas
1990 Leaf #300
$50

Mark McGwire
1985 Topps #401
$30

 Don Sutton
1966 Topps #288
$150

 Joe Carter
1984 Donruss #41
$50

 Roberto Alomar
1988 Score Traded #105
$65

 Rafael Palmeiro

1987 Donruss #43
$6

 John Olerud

1990 Leaf #237
$6

 Matt Williams

1988 Fleer #101
$4

 Mike Schmidt

1973 Topps #615
$425

 Mickey Mantle

1961 Topps #578
$400

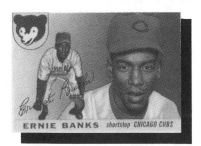

 **Ernie
Banks**

1955 Topps #28
$225

 **Yogi
Berra**

1952 Topps #191
$350

 **Sandy
Koufax**

1956 Topps #79
$400

 **Willie
Mays**

1954 Topps #90
$500

 **Ted
Williams**

1954 Topps #1
$650

FOOTBALL

 **Tony Dorsett**

Tony Dorsett: 1978 Topps #315, $30; $50 in July 1991.

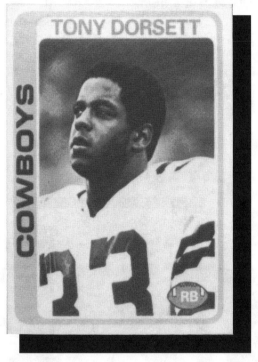

Tony Dorsett

April 7, 1954; 5-11, 190; University of Pittsburgh; Dallas Cowboys' first-round pick in 1977, second overall; running back; retired; 12 seasons (all with Dallas).

Att.: 2,936; Yds.: 12,739 (3rd); Ave.: 4.3; TDs: 77; Rec.: 398; Yds.: 3,554; Ave.: 8.9; TDs: 13; Total TDs: 91 (12th); Pts.: 546; All-Purpose Yds.: 16,326 (2nd).

During the early 1970s, the Dallas Cowboys had Roger Staubach, Billy Joe DuPree, Bob Hayes, Drew Pearson and Tony Hill leading the passing attack. Although Duane Thomas, Calvin Hill, Walt Garrison and Robert Newhouse were contributing from the backfield, the organization decided it needed a premiere back. So the Cowboys, after trading four high draft choices to Seattle for the second pick in the 1977 draft, went big time, taking the most prolific runner in collegiate history, Tony Dorsett.

Appropriately nicknamed T.D., Dorsett would conclude his 12-year career as the 12th-leading touchdown scorer in National Football League history, and is the team's all-time leading touchdown scorer. His 12,739 rushing yards ranks third in NFL history.

But the collegiate statistics which made Dorsett the first pick in the 1977 draft are impressive, too. The 1976 Heisman Trophy winner finished his collegiate career with 202 yards against Georgia in the Sugar Bowl on New Year's Day 1977, leading his team to a National Championship.

In all, Dorsett set 18 collegiate records, becoming the first back to have four 1,000-yard rushing seasons, and the first to gain 6,000 yards in a career. He finished with 6,082 yards on 1,133 attempts, and scored 58 times.

Although he was small, the swift Dorsett, who ran a 9.6-second 100-yard-dash, would prove he was tough enough and strong enough to play in the pros. He did so quickly, earning the NFC Rookie of the Year Award in 1977, and became just the second back to gain 1,000 yards in each of his first three seasons. He added two more 1,000+ seasons to that streak, making him the first back to gain 1,000 yards in each of his first five seasons. In all, Dorsett had eight 1,000-yard rushing seasons.

The Cowboy's team captain relied on his speed, strength and lateral mobility to find and hit the holes. He could stop and start, and change directions, better than most. His NFL record for longest run from scrimmage (99 yards) against the Minnesota Vikings in a Jan. 3, 1983, playoff game, is evidence of his great open field speed.

The four-time Pro Bowl selection played in two Super Bowls, contributing a touchdown in the Cowboys' win over Denver in 1978. He could catch passes out of the backfield, too, and ranks second all-time in all-purpose yardage with 16,326 yards.

Dorsett's rookie card, the key card in the 1978 Topps set, dropped in value due to the out-of-sight, out-of-mind principle. It's a sure bet he'll reach the $50 mark again, since he's a sure Hall of Famer.

Tony Dorsett Checklist

Year	Company	No.	Price
1978	Topps	315	30.00
1978	Topps	507 (Leaders)	2.00
1979	Topps	160	7.00
1979	Topps	469 (Leaders)	1.00
1980	Topps	113 (Leaders)	.75
1980	Topps	330	4.00

Tony Dorsett Checklist

Year	Company	No.	Price
1981	Topps	138 (In Action)	1.00
1981	Topps	376 (Leaders)	.60
1981	Topps	500	2.00
1982	Topps	307 (Leaders)	.50
1982	Topps	311	1.25
1982	Topps	312 (In Action)	.60
1983	Topps	2 (Record Breakers)	.40
1983	Topps	42 (Leaders)	.30
1983	Topps	46	.75
1983	Topps	204 (Leaders)	.50
1984	Topps	235 (Leaders)	.30
1984	Topps	238	.75
1984	Topps	239 (Instant Reply)	.35
1985	Topps	37 (Leaders)	.30
1985	Topps	40	.50
1986	Topps	126	.50
1987	Topps	263	.40
1988	Topps	262	.25
1989	Pro Set	453	.15
1989	Score	326 (Record Breakers)	.25
1989	Topps	240	.15
1992	Pro Line	420	.25

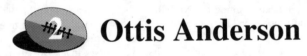 # Ottis Anderson

Ottis Anderson: 1980 Topps #170, $10; $10 in July 1991.

Jan. 19, 1957; 6-2, 225; University of Miami; St. Louis Cardinals' first-round pick in 1979, eighth pick overall running back; active; 14 seasons (St. Louis 1979-86; New York Giants 1986-92).

Career statistics entering the 1993 season

Att..: 2,562; Yds.: 10,273 (8th); Ave.: 4.0; TDs: 81; Rec: 376; Yds.: 3,062; Ave.: 8.1; TDs: 5; Total TDs: 86 (18th); Pts.: 516; All-Purpose Yds.: 13,364 (12th).

Ottis Anderson is football's equivalent of the Energizer rabbit so familiar from television commercials — he keeps on going and going and going, despite nagging injuries throughout his career. He's also signed a one-year contract with the New York Giants for the 1993 season.

Anderson is the prototypical short-yardage back, and one who would be perfect for any time-consuming, ball-control offensive team. He's strong and fast, able to go inside or outside. Just when many thought his career was over — he'd gained just 451 yards in the three previous seasons — a rejuvenated Anderson gained 1,023 yards and scored 14 touchdowns in 1989, becoming the NFL's Comeback Player of the Year. He's also added a Super Bowl MVP award to his resume, gaining 102 yards and scoring a touchdown in Super Bowl XXV against Buffalo in 1991.

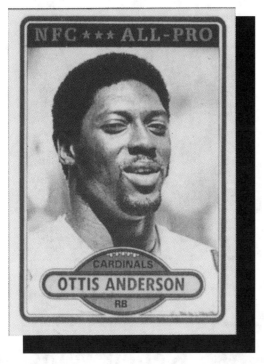

Ottis Anderson

In 1990 Anderson, who appeared as an extra in the movie "Black Sunday," became the eighth back in NFL history to amass 10,000 career yards rushing. The one-time All-Pro currently ranks eighth, and is in the top 20 in total touchdowns.

This card has tremendous potential to double in value, since it's so low to start with. Anderson hasn't retired yet, so his card will have at least six years to appreciate in value before he's inducted into the Hall of Fame.

Ottis Anderson Checklist

Year	Company	No.	Price
1980	Topps	1 (Record Breakers)	1.50
1980	Topps	170	10.00
1980	Topps	359 (Leaders)	.50
1981	Topps	12 (In Action)	1.00
1981	Topps	365	2.00
1981	Topps	468 (Leaders)	.35
1982	Topps	462 (Leaders)	.35
1982	Topps	463	1.00

Year	Company	No.	Price
1982	Topps	464 (In Action)	.50
1983	Topps	152 (Leaders)	.20
1983	Topps	153	.50
1984	Topps	337 (Leaders)	.15
1984	Topps	338	.40
1985	Topps	138	.35
1986	Topps	329	.20
1989	Action Packed	12	2.00
1989	Pro Set	554	.10
1989	Score Supplement	348	.15
1990	Action Packed	181	.20
1990	Fleer	62	.20
1990	Pro Set	591	.10
1990	Score	531	.10
1990	Score	562 (Ground Force)	.10
1990	Topps	59	.10
1991	Action Packed	181	.20
1991	Fleer	305	.08
1991	Fleer Ultra	214	.10
1991	Pro Line Portraits	116	.10
1991	Pro Set	20 (Milestones)	.10
1991	Pro Set	51 (Super Bowl)	.10
1991	Score	433	.10
1991	Score Pinnacle	216	.15
1991	Topps	5 (Highlight)	.10
1991	Topps	20	.10
1991	Upper Deck	161	.10
1991	Upper Deck	469 (Most Valuable)	.10
1992	Pacific	541	.10

Kellen Winslow

Kellen Winslow: 1981 Topps #150, $10; $3.50 in July 1991.

Nov. 5, 1957; 6-5, 245; University of Minnesota; San Diego's first-round pick in 1979, 13th overall; tight end; retired; 10 seasons (all with San Diego).
Rec.: 541 (22nd); Yds..: 6,741; Ave.: 12.5; TDs: 45; Rush: 0; Yds.: 0; Ave.: 0; TDs: 0; Total TDs: 45; Pts.: 270.

There are only two tight ends in the Pro Football Hall of Fame — Mike Ditka and John Mackey, both essentially third tackles on the offensive line. But the player who changed the tight end's duties from blocker to receiver during the 1980s will be the third or fourth inducted, depending on when Ozzie Newsome goes in.

Tight end Kellen Winslow, San Diego's first-round pick in 1979, was one of quarterback Dan Fouts' favorite targets in San Diego's Don "Air" Coryell passing game, featuring wide receivers John Jefferson and Charlie Joiner. Winslow ranks 22nd all-time in receptions, trailing only Newsome's 662 at the tight end position. His speed made him a deep threat, and he often drew double coverage.

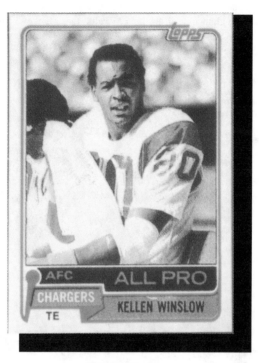

Kellen Winslow

A four-time Pro Bowler, Winslow utilized his size, speed and power to become the first tight end to lead the American Football Conference in receptions two consecutive seasons, in 1980 (89) and 1981 (84). He also led during the strike-shortened 1982 season, and was named All-Pro in each of those three seasons.

In November 1981 he tied a league record when he caught five touchdown passes in a game against the Oakland Raiders. During the 1982 AFC Championship Game against Miami, Winslow caught 13 passes for 166 yards and a touchdown in a 41-38 loss.

Despite a severe knee injury which prematurely ended Winslow's career after 10 years, the Pro Football Hall of Fame named him as a receiver on the AFL-NFL 1960-84 All-Star Team. His numbers after better than Ditka's (12 seasons, 427 receptions, 5,913 yards, 43 touchdowns) and Mackey's (10 seasons, 331 catches, 5,238 yards, 39 touchdowns), so the Hall of Fame should be recognizing him again.

In just two years, Winslow's card has nearly tripled in value, but there's still room for it to double, since it's only $10 right now. He might peak at $20, but there's an outside chance he'll hit the $23 value that Mackey's 1964 Philadelphia rookie card is at, and could possibly settle in somewhere between that value and the $125 value Mike Ditka's 1962 Topps rookie card is at.

Kellen Winslow Checklist

Year	Company	No.	Price
1981	Topps	2 (Leaders)	.50
1981	Topps	150	10.00
1981	Topps	524 (In Action)	3.50
1982	Topps	241	2.50
1982	Topps	242 (In Action)	1.25
1982	Topps	258 (Leaders)	.50
1983	Topps	203 (Leaders)	.35
1983	Topps	382	.60
1984	Topps	186	.35
1984	Topps	187 (Instant Reply)	.20
1985	Topps	379	.30
1986	Topps	237	.25
1987	Topps	343	.20
1988	Topps	203	.15
1988	Topps	209	.15
1992	Pro Line	447	.25

 # Charlie Joiner

Charlie Joiner: 1972 Topps #244, $24; $15 in July 1991.

Oct. 14, 1947; 5-11, 180; Grambling State University; Houston Oilers' fourth-round draft pick in 1969, 69th overall, as a defensive back; wide receiver; retired; 18 seasons (Houston 1969-72; Cincinnati 1972-75; San Diego 1976-86).

Rec.: 750 (tied for third); Yds..: 12,146; Ave.: 16.2; TDs: 65; Rush: 8; Yds.: 22; Ave.: 2.8; TDs: 0; Total TDs: 65; Pts.: 390; All-Purpose Yds..: 12,362.

After concluding a collegiate career at Grambling University as a favorite target for future NFL quarterback James Harris, Charlie Joiner was drafted by the Houston Oilers as a cornerback, a position he also played in college.

But, after he showed his 4.5 speed in the 40-yard dash, and displayed his moves, quick feet and good hands in training camp, the Oilers thought otherwise, and made him strictly a wide receiver, based on his impressive pass-catching skills. His first two seasons started out shakily; he broke his arm each season.

Charlie Joiner

But the team still had enough confidence in Joiner to trade its number two draft pick in 1968, wide receiver Jerry LeVias, to San Diego to make room for Joiner in 1971. Shortly through the 1972 season, however, Joiner was sent to the Cincinnati Bengals, where he and Isaac Curtis formed a potent twosome.

Joiner was an unassuming, consistent, hard worker who mastered his patterns and basic moves. He was an intelligent, perceptive and inspirational technician who quietly put up the numbers in relative obscurity — he was an All-Pro only once (in 1980) and never made a Super Bowl appearance. But he did make three Pro Bowl appearances (in 1976, 1979 and 1980) and from 1979-85 he averaged more than 62 catches per season.

The natural athlete set an Oilers' single-season game record of 200 yards on seven catches against the Browns in 1971. During his career he had 30 100-yard reception games.

Just like his statistics, Joiner's card value quietly keeps on going up. He's missed on a few attempts at induction, but there's no way he'll be kept out. Considering Joiner's rookie card is older and less expensive than the man he's tied with on the all-time receptions list — James Lofton, at $35 — Joiner's card is a steal. Lofton's will always stay ahead, because he was active when the football card boom occurred during the late 1980s-early 1990s, but Joiner will fall right in line.

Charlie Joiner Checklist

Year	Company	No.	Price
1972	Topps	244	24.00
1973	Topps	467	5.00
1976	Topps	89	2.00
1977	Topps	167	1.50
1978	Topps	338	1.00
1978	Topps	524 (Leaders)	.65
1979	Topps	419	.75
1980	Topps	28	.75
1981	Topps	312 (In Action)	.35
1981	Topps	496	.75
1982	Topps	223 (Leaders)	.35
1982	Topps	233	.50
1982	Topps	234 (In Action)	.25
1983	Topps	377	.30
1984	Topps	181	.30
1985	Topps	3 (Record Breakers)	.15
1985	Topps	377	.30
1986	Topps	236	.25
1987	Topps	4 (Record Breakers)	.15

 # Marcus Allen

Marcus Allen: 1983 Topps #294, $8; $9 in July 1991.

March 26, 1960; 6-2, 210; University of Southern California; Los Angeles Raiders' first-round pick in 1982, 10th overall; running back; active; 11 seasons (all with the Los Angeles Raiders).

Career statistics entering the 1993 season

Att..: 2,090; Yds..: 8,545 (11th); Ave.: 4.1; TDs: 79; Rec.: 446; Yds.: 4,258; Ave.: 9.5; TDs: 18; Total TDs: 98 (9th); Pts.: 588; All-Purpose Yds.: 12,532 (18th).

Following in the footsteps of three Heisman Trophy winners at the University of Southern California would be a difficult task for most high school recruits, especially if you're being recruited as a defensive back who also played quarterback.

Marcus Allen

But Marcus Allen not only filled the shoes of his predecessors (Mike Garrett, O.J. Simpson, Charles White), he set a then-collegiate single-season rushing record with 2,342 yards in 1981, taking home a Heisman Trophy for his efforts, too. Allen's 212.9 yards per game average and eight games with 200+ yards rushing were also records, as are his 11 career 200+ yard games.

In his 1982 rookie season in the NFL, Allen, playing with the Raiders, was named the Rookie of the Year, gaining 697 yards rushing. Throughout his career he's been quite durable and an excellent blocker. The classy back runs with a dramatic flair, and is tough enough to take a shot and bounce back up, a la Walter Payton.

Allen tied the NFL record for consecutive games with 100 or more yards rushing (9) in 1985. He's been over the 1,000-yard season mark three times, peaking at 1,759 in 1985, when he was named the NFL's MVP. He's been a Pro Bowler five times and an All-Pro twice.

A four-time winner of the Raiders' "Commitment to Excellence" award, given by teammates who pick the player "who best exemplifies the pride, poise and spirit of the Raiders," Allen has shined in postseason play too, rushing for 100+ yards in five of his 10 games played. He capped his then record-setting 191-yard rushing performance in Super Bowl XVIII in 1984 against Washington with two touchdowns and an MVP award.

The game-breaker, purely a running threat in college, is also a dangerous receiver; his 51 catches in 1986 made him the first back to lead the Raiders in receptions since 1967. He's one of a select few running backs to have rushed for more than 7,000 yards and catch for 3,000. His 12,532 all-purpose yards ranks 18th all-time.

Allen enters the 1993 season with the Kansas City Chiefs, who, with the addition of future Hall of Famer Joe Montana, have a legitimate shot at the Super Bowl; that would just be icing on the cake for the future Hall-of-Famer's career. Allen's card, although it's one of several double prints from the 1983 set, should benefit from the extra attention he'll receive this season, and could double in value if Allen plays a key role if the Chiefs do indeed make a Super Bowl appearance. A repeat performance from Super Bowl XVIII wouldn't hurt, either...

Marcus Allen Checklist

Year	Company	No.	Price
1983	Topps	205 (Leaders)	.60
1983	Topps	293 (Leaders)	.75
1983	Topps	294	8.00
1984	Topps	98	2.00
1984	Topps	99 (Instant Reply)	1.00
1985	Topps	281 (Leaders)	.30
1985	Topps	282	1.00
1986	Topps	1 (Record Breakers)	.35
1986	Topps	62	.75
1986	Topps	227 (Leaders)	.25
1987	Topps	215	.40
1988	Topps	328	.25
1989	Pro Set	182	.10
1989	Score	234	.25
1989	Score	284 (Combos)	.60
1989	Topps	267	.10
1990	Action Packed	121	.25
1990	Fleer	249	.07
1990	Pro Set	538	.15
1990	Score	230	.10
1990	Topps	289	.10
1991	Action Packed	121	.20
1991	Bowman	238	.10
1991	Fleer	102	.10
1991	Fleer Ultra	75	.10
1991	Pacific	Plus 225	.10
1991	Pro Set	45 (Heisman Hero)	.10
1991	Pro Set	541	.15
1991	Score Pinnacle	398	.15
1991	Score	420	.10
1991	Score Pinnacle	232	.15
1991	Topps	87	.10

Marcus Allen Checklist

Year	Company	No.	Price
1991	Topps	640 (Action Card)	.10
1991	Topps Stadium Club	8	.25
1991	Upper Deck	446	.10
1992	Action Packed	122	.20
1992	Fleer Ultra	185	.10
1992	Pacific	153	.10
1992	Pro Set	27	.10
1992	Pro Set	208	.10
1992	Pro Set Power	32	.15
1992	Score Pinnacle	120	.15
1992	Topps	25	.10
1992	Topps Stadium Club	129	.15
1992	Upper Deck	94	.10
1992	Upper Deck	211	.10

Roger Craig

Roger Craig: 1984 Topps #353, $4.50; $7.50 in July 1991.

July 10, 1960; 6-0, 225; University of Nebraska; San Francisco's second-round pick in 1983, 49th overall; running back; active; 17 seasons (San Francisco 1983-90; Los Angeles Raiders 1991; Minnesota 1992).

Att.: 1,953; Yds.: 8,070 (16th); Ave.: 4.1; TDs: 55; Rec.: 547 (19th); Yds..: 4,742; Ave.: 8.6; TDs: 16; Total TDs: 71; Pts.: 426; All-Purpose Yds.: 12,844 (16th).

One of the best all-around backs ever, Roger Craig is the only player in NFL history to rush for more than 1,000 yards (1,050) and catch passes for more than 1,000 yards (1,016) in the same season, which he did in 1985. He's had three 1,000-yard rushing seasons, all with the San Francisco 49ers.

The dedicated all-purpose back ranks 16th all-time in rushing, 19th in receptions, and 16th in all-purpose yardage. He's the NFL's all-time leading pass-catching back and his receiving skills have made him the leading receiver in Super Bowl history, with 20 catches in three appearances. He's also rushed for 198 yards in Super Bowl play.

An explosive big-play man in the 49er offense, he's played halfback and full-back. After eight seasons in San Francisco, he played for the Raiders in 1991, leading the team in rushing. After the Minnesota Vikings made him a Plan B acquisition in 1992, he added another 416 yards rushing to his career total.

A four-time Pro Bowler, Craig appeared in the 1990 movie "Dark Obsession." He has also modeled for Macy's; his ads have appeared in San Francisco newspapers. His name hasn't been in the headlines quite as often as his career winds down, and his cards have actually dropped.

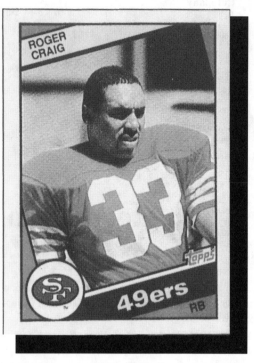

Roger Craig

But when the decade of the 1980s is discussed, inevitably the four-time Super Bowl Champion 49ers will be mentioned. Craig, a vital part on three of those teams, will get his recognition and find his niche in the Hall of Fame beside teammates Joe Montana and Jerry Rice. His cards will rebound.

Roger Craig Checklist

Year	Company	No.	Price
1984	Topps	353	4.50
1985	Topps	151	1.00
1986	Topps	155 (Leaders)	.25
1986	Topps	157	.75
1986	Topps	226 (Leaders)	.25
1987	Topps	113	.35
1988	Topps	37	.20
1988	Topps	40	.25
1989	Pro Set	372	.10
1989	Score	4	.20
1989	Score	297 (All-Pro)	.15
1989	Topps	8	.10
1990	Action Packed	242	.40

Roger Craig Checklist

Year	Company	No.	Price
1990	Fleer	5	.10
1990	Pro Set	287	.10
1990	Pro Set	385 (Pro Bowl)	.04
1990	Score	100	.10
1990	Score	329 (Ground Force)	.04
1990	Topps	12	.10
1991	Action Packed Rookies	78	.20
1991	Action Packed	250	.20
1991	Fleer Ultra Update	41	.10
1991	Pacific Plus	601	.10
1991	Pro Line Portraits	197	.10
1991	Pro Set	21(Milestone)	.10
1991	Score Traded	7	.10
1991	Score Pinnacle	25	.15
1991	Topps	2 (Highlight)	.10
1991	Topps	90	.10
1991	Topps Stadium Club	146	.25
1991	Upper Deck	143	.10
1991	Wild Card NFL	35	.10
1992	Pacific	147	.10
1992	SkyBox Impact	21	.10
1992	SkyBox PrimeTime	171	.15
1992	Topps	511	.10
1992	Wild Card NFL	254	.10

 # Carl Eller

Carl Eller: 1965 Philadelphia #105, $17; $8.50 in July 1991.

Jan. 25, 1942; 6-6, 245; University of Minnesota; drafted by the Minnesota Vikings in the first round in 1964; defensive end; retired; 16 seasons (Minnesota 1964-78; Seattle 1979).

Had one interception for one yard; recovered 23 opponents' fumbles, one for a touchdown; scored two safeties; total points scored: 10.

As a charter member of the Minnesota Vikings' "Purple People Eaters" defensive line, the intimidating Carl Eller was a five-time All-Pro who made six Pro Bowl appearances during his career and played in four Super Bowls.

In college, Eller teamed with future Hall of Famer Bobby Bell at the University of Minnesota. That defensive unit in 1962 compiled the nation's best record against rushing, allowing only 52.2 yards per game. With the Vikings, he helped anchor the "Purple People Eaters" line with Gary Larsen, Jim Marshall and Hall of Famer Alan Page.

Eller used his speed, strength and mobility to become one of the best pass rushers in the league. He could also defend against the run, and had the quickness to cover on pass plays. Despite being one of the NFL's most respected defensive ends, Eller sometimes played on the offensive line, too, where he was a standout blocker on short-yardage plays.

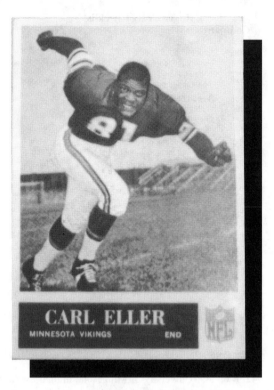

Carl Eller

After becoming the then-highest paid lineman in the history of the NFL in 1970, earning $250,000 for a three-year contract, Eller won the George Halas Trophy in 1971 as the top defensive player of the year.

It's a mystery why one of the premiere defensive lineman has yet to be selected for the Hall of Fame. But his rookie card is from one of the more rarer Philadelphia issues — the 1965 set, which at $750 has above average investment potential. Rookie cards for Paul Warfield ($80), Charley Taylor ($50) and Eller are all underrated.

Carl Eller Checklist

Year	Company	No.	Price
1965	Philadelphia	105	17.00
1970	Topps	175	3.00
1972	Topps	20	1.50
1972	Topps	277 (All-Pro)	24.00
1973	Topps	211	1.50
1974	Topps	5	1.25

Walter Payton

Walter Payton: 1977 Topps #360, $35; $55 in July 1991.

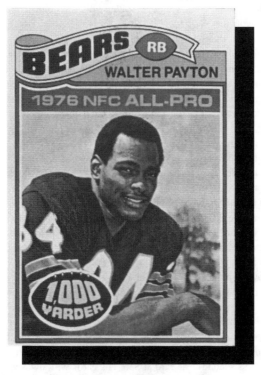

Walter Payton

July 25, 1954; 5-11, 205; Jackson State University; Chicago Bears' first-round pick in 1975, third overall; running back; retired; 13 seasons (all with Chicago); Hall of Fame 1993.

Att.: 3,838; Yds.: 16,726 (1st); Ave.: 4.4; TDs: 110; Rec.: 492; Yds..: 4,538; Ave.: 9.2 TDs: 15; Total TDs: 125 (2nd); Pts.: 750; All-Purpose Yds.: 21,803 (1st).

His resume is the most impressive of all running backs ever to play in the NFL — it's dotted with references to several records he holds, including most yards rushing, most combined yards, most 100-yard games and most rushing yards in one game (275).

He once held the record for nine straight 100-yard games in 1985, but still holds the record for career 100-yard games, with 77. He won an unprecedented fifth consecutive rushing title in 1980, finished his career with 10 1,000-yard seasons, and in 1985 became the first player to accumulate 2,000 yards from scrimmage in three straight seasons and the only player to do it four times in a career. He's also scored an NFL record 110 rushing touchdowns.

And he was a prolific scorer in college too, finding the end zone 66 times, becoming the all-time NCAA scoring leader with 464 points (66 TDs, 54 PATs and five field goals).

Walter Payton, the man nicknamed "Sweetness" due to his quiet, religious nature, quite simply was the busiest, and the best, running back ever in the NFL.

Defenses often chased Payton, even when he didn't have the ball. When tacklers swarmed around him, Payton, an expert at using his arm to brush them away, continued to drive forward, battling for extra yards, which quite often happened. He always seemed to get better as the game wore on.

Payton, a high school record holder in the long jump, had tremendous leg strength — he could press 600+ pounds with his legs — yet remained quite flexible enough to make cuts at full speed. The instinctive, explosive back was also tough and durable, despite his small frame, and possessed superb blocking skills. As a reward to those who blocked for him, Sweetness would hand the football to a lineman to let him spike the ball after he scored.

In 1977, at age 23, Payton became NFL's youngest player to be named the MVP after he rushed for 1,852 yards. In perhaps his most satisfying season, 1985, he was again named the NFL's MVP, gaining 1,551 yards and scoring nine touchdowns in the Bears' 15-1 season. The Bears capped that season with a 46-10 Super Bowl win over the New England Patriots.

A seven-time All-Pro, Payton made nine appearances in the Pro Bowl. The Pro Football Hall of Fame named him to its AFL-NFL 1960-84 All-Star Second Team and recognized him with its highest honor with a 1993 induction.

If you want to spring for a Payton rookie, that's fine, but consider it a long-term investment. If you're looking for a somewhat quicker return on your dollar, pick up Payton's second-year card at $35. His cards will always be in demand, and his 1977 card has more room to grow.

Walter Payton Checklist

Year	Company	No.	Price
1976	Topps	148	190.00
1977	Topps	3 (Leaders)	6.50
1977	Topps	360	35.00
1978	Topps	3 (Highlight)	4.00
1978	Topps	200	16.00
1978	Topps	333 (Leaders)	2.25
1978	Topps	334 (Leaders)	2.25
1978	Topps	504 (Leaders)	1.75
1979	Topps	3 (Leaders)	6.50
1979	Topps	132 (Leaders)	1.25
1979	Topps	335 (Record Breakers)	2.25
1979	Topps	480	9.00
1980	Topps	160	7.50
1980	Topps	226 (Leaders)	1.00
1981	Topps	202 (In Action)	2.50
1981	Topps	264 (Leaders)	1.50
1981	Topps	400	4.00
1982	Topps	269 (Football Brothers)	1.00
1982	Topps	292 (Leaders)	.75
1982	Topps	302	3.00
1982	Topps	303 (In Action)	1.50
1983	Topps	28 (Leaders)	.75
1983	Topps	36 2.50	2.50
1984	Topps	221 (Leaders)	.75
1984	Topps	228	2.00
1984	Topps	229 (Instant Replay)	1.00
1985	Topps	6 (Record Breaker)	.90
1985	Topps	33	1.75
1986	Topps	7 (Record Breaker)	.75
1986	Topps	11	1.50
1987	Topps	46	1.25
1988	Topps	5 (Record Breaker)	.30
1991	Pro Line	215	.15

 # James Lofton

James Lofton: 1979 Topps #310, $40; $12.50 in July 1991.

July 5, 1956; 6-3, 190; University of Stanford; Green Bay's first-round draft choice in 1978, sixth overall; wide receiver; active; 15 seasons (Green Bay 1978-86; Los Angeles Raiders 1987-88; Buffalo 1989-92).

Career statistics entering the 1993 season

Rec.: 750 (tied for 3rd); Yds..: 13,821 (1st); Ave.: 18.4; TDs: 75; Rush: 32; Yds.: 246; Ave.: 7.7; TDs: 1; Total TDs: 76; Pts.: 456; All-Purpose Yds.: 14,094 (8th).

James Lofton

As a world-class sprinter who could run the 200-meter dash in 20.7 seconds and a Stanford University long jumper who won the NCAA long jump title in 1978, James Lofton, a collegiate All-American receiver, has also always had the tools to be one of the most dangerous receivers in the NFL.

But just when you think you may have figured out how to deal with his speed and skills, and possibly contain him, Lofton will pull a trick or two out of his bag — he might throw the ball, as the former high school quarterback did when he, as a Green Bay Packer, once teamed with John Jefferson on a 43-yard pass play in 1982. Or, he might take off on a reverse, as he did when he compiled the third-longest run in Packer history, an 83-yard run against the New York Giants in 1983.

In addition to displaying his skills on the football field, he has shown his exceptional talents as a standout performer in ABC's Superstars competition. The versatile flanker has been quite durable throughout his NFL career, too; he barely misses a game.

Lofton has always been a deep threat, but he's most dangerous after he catches the ball, as evidenced by the yards he's averaged per reception. He's led the NFL in that category twice — in 1983 (22.4), in 1984 (22.0) — and led the National Football Conference in 1991, at 18.8. His career average is 18.4, and in 1991, he became just the second player in NFL history to break the 13,000-yard mark in receiving, finally passing Steve Largent in 1992.

An All-Pro and the NFC's Rookie of the Year in 1978 (46 catches for 818 yards and six touchdowns), Lofton was selected for the Pro Bowl for the eighth time in 1992, making his first appearance since 1985. The NFL's third leading receiver all-time has had two seasons when he's caught 71 passes, and has averaged 50 annually. He's been an All-Pro four times.

Lofton's rookie card might seem a bit steep, but if you can find one for under $40, pick it up. It may not yield the highest return, but will eventually get you $50.

James Lofton Checklist

Year	Company	No.	Price
1979	Topps	310	40.00
1979	Topps	407 (Leaders)	3.00
1980	Topps	78	10.00
1980	Topps	303 (Leaders)	1.25
1981	Topps	151 (Leaders)	1.00
1981	Topps	361 (In Action)	2.50
1981	Topps	430	5.00
1982	Topps	354 (Leaders)	1.00
1982	Topps	364	2.50
1982	Topps	365 (In Action)	1.25
1983	Topps	83	1.50
1984	Topps	263 (Leaders)	.75
1984	Topps	272	1.50
1984	Topps	273 (Instant Reply)	.75
1985	Topps	75	1.00
1986	Topps	218	.60
1987	Topps	354	.50
1988	Topps	329	.50
1989	Score	213	.50
1989	Topps Traded	109	.25
1990	Pro Set	753	.10
1991	Action Packed	15	.20
1991	Bowman	42	.10
1991	Fleer	4	.10
1991	Fleer Ultra Update	10	.20
1991	Pro Set	46 (Super Bowl)	.10
1991	Pro Set	444	.10
1991	Score	180	.10
1991	Score Pinnacle	136	.15
1991	Topps	43	.10
1991	Topps Stadium Club	89	.25
1991	Upper Deck	358	.10
1992	Collectors Edge	8	.50
1992	Fleer Ultra	24	.50
1992	GameDay	232	.15
1992	Pacific	18	.10
1992	Pro Set	21	.10
1992	Pro Set	387	.10

Harold Carmichael

Harold Carmichael: 1974 Topps #121, $16; $9 in July 1991.

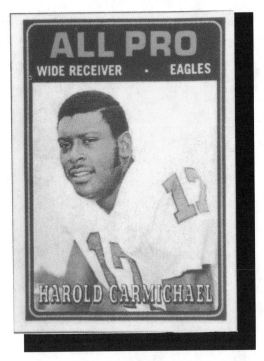

Harold Carmichael

Sept. 22, 1949; 6-8, 225; Southern University; the Philadelphia Eagles' seventh-round pick in 1971, 161st overall; wide receiver; retired; 14 seasons (Philadelphia 1971-84; Dallas 1984).

Rec.: 590 (11th); Yds..: 8,985; Ave.: 15.2; TDs: 79; Rush: 9; Yds.: 64; Ave.: 7.1; TDs: 0; Total TDs: 79; Pts.: 474; All-Purpose Yds.: 9,049.

At 6-8, 225 pounds, Harold Carmichael thought he'd be drafted out of college as a basketball player in 1971. But the Philadelphia Eagles, realizing he played football as well as basketball at Southern University, were willing to take a chance that Carmichael could follow in the footsteps of another professional wide receiver born in Jacksonville, Fla. — Bob Hayes.

The Eagles were right, and this Eagle will land in the Hall of Fame. Using his height and 36-inch vertical leap to his advantage against smaller defensive backs, Carmichael strung together a then-record 127 straight games in which he caught a pass. He ranks 11th in total catches and his statistics are better than another Hall of Famer's, Fred Biletnikoff (589 catches, 8,974 yards, 76 touchdowns), whose 1965 Topps rookie card is $160.

The one-time Pro Bowler also used his size as an extra lineman, becoming one of the league's best pass-blocking ends. He wasn't a fancy shake-and-bake receiver; instead, he concentrated on getting into his pattern as quickly as possible and could make the quick turns necessary to elude defenders.

The NFL's Man of the Year in 1980 for numerous community activities and charitable efforts, Carmichael was consistent throughout his career and could be counted on for 50-60 catches, 800 yards, and 10 touchdowns each year. An All-Pro in 1973, Carmichael played in one Super Bowl, in 1980 against Oakland.

It's a mystery why Carmichael keeps getting passed up for election into the Hall of Fame; his numbers speak for themselves. Considering the 1974 rookie card of Hall of Fame lineman John Hannah is at $15, if the principle that cards for players at the skilled position command higher premiums, then Carmichael's, if he is elected, will fall into the $25-$30 range. That'll put him past Ahmad Rashad, whose $18 1974 rookie card is based on his on-screen personality more than his career accomplishments.

Harold Carmichael Checklist

Year	Company	No.	Price
1974	Topps	121	16.00
1974	Topps	330 (Leaders)	1.25
1975	Topps	80	2.50
1976	Topps	425	1.50
1977	Topps	144	1.00
1978	Topps	379	1.00
1978	Topps	521 (Leaders)	.75
1979	Topps	151 (Leaders)	.60
1979	Topps	250	.75
1980	Topps	2 (Record Breakers)	.35
1980	Topps	132 (Leaders)	.30
1980	Topps	420	.60
1981	Topps	35	.50

Harold Carmichael Checklist

Year	Company	No.	Price
1982	Topps	437 (Leaders)	.25
1982	Topps	440	.30
1982	Topps	441 (In Action)	.25
1983	Topps	137	.30
1984	Topps	326	.20

 # Ozzie Newsome

Ozzie Newsome: 1979 Topps #308, $25; $17.50 in July 1991.

Ozzie Newsome

March 15, 1956; 6-2, 232; University of Alabama; Cleveland Browns' first-round draft choice in 1978, 23rd overall; wide receiver; retired; 13 seasons (all with Cleveland).

Rec.: 662 (5th); Yds..: 7,980; Ave.: 12.1; TDs: 47; Pts.: 282.

Although the Alabama Crimson Tide ran the wishbone offense, which didn't fully utilize Ozzie Newsome's pass-catching skills, Coach Paul "Bear" Bryant has called Ozzie Newsome the finest wide receiver he ever had at the university.

The two-time collegiate All-American is going to be designated as one of the finest ever in the NFL, too, as soon as he's enshrined in the Pro Football Hall of Fame. He's the all-time leading receiver among tight ends, and fifth overall.

An above-average blocker who was converted to tight end by the Cleveland Browns, Newsome, the team captain, often paved the way when Cleveland backs Earnest Byner and Kevin Mack each gained 1,000 yards rushing in 1985. As a receiver, he'd go after the ball, and was also a deep threat.

A two-time All-Pro, the "Wizard of Oz" led the AFC in receptions in 1984 with 89, which equaled his career high from the previous season. Although he only made three Pro Bowl appearances, Newsome, often double-teamed, averaged 50 catches per season during his 13-year career, becoming only the 10th player to catch at least 50 passes in six seasons. His string of 98-straight games catching a pass ranks sixth all-time, and he holds the Browns' single-game record of 14 catches for 191 yards against the Jets in 1984.

Only two tight ends have been elected to the Hall of Fame — Mike Ditka and John Mackey; Ozzie Newsome's statistics are better than both. His card value won't catch Ditka at $125, but he'll stay ahead of Mackey ($23) and Winslow ($10). As the value of the 1979 set rises, Newsome's card will set the pace behind James Lofton's $40 rookie card and Earl Campbell's $35 rookie card.

Ozzie Newsome Checklist

Year	Company	No.	Price
1979	Topps	308	25.00
1980	Topps	110	6.50
1981	Topps	435	3.00
1982	Topps	55 (Leaders)	.15
1982	Topps	67	1.50
1982	Topps	68 (In Action)	.75
1983	Topps	254	.50
1984	Topps	58	.50
1984	Topps	59 (Instant Reply)	.30
1985	Topps	193 (Leaders)	.25
1985	Topps	232	.35
1986	Topps	191	.30
1987	Topps	85	.25
1988	Topps	92	.25
1989	Pro Set	451	.20
1989	Score	124	.25
1989	Topps	151	.15
1990	Action Packed	48	.50
1990	Pro Set	75	.10
1990	Score	443	.10
1990	Topps	168	.10
1991	Action Packed	50	.25

Tom Jackson

Tom Jackson: 1978 Topps #240, 2.50; 90 cents in July 1991.

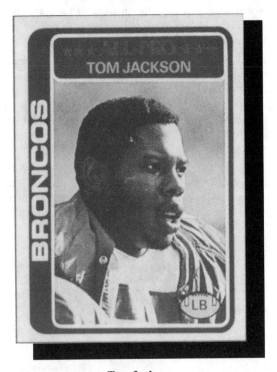

Tom Jackson

5-11, 220; University of Louisville; Denver's fourth-round draft pick in 1973, 88th overall; linebacker; retired; 14 seasons (all with Denver).

20 interceptions for 340 yards, three touchdowns; eight fumble recoveries; 18 points scored; 13 recorded sacks.

During the 1976 NFL season, only three teams scored more than 17 points in a game against the Denver Broncos defense. In 1977, however, only one team scored more than 14 points against that unit, which became known as the Orange Crush.

Lyle Alzado and Paul Smith anchored the line at the ends, while nose tackle Rubin Carter stuffed up the middle. The linebacking corps, one of the best of its time, was led by Randy Gradishar. The secondary included Billy Thompson and Louis Wright. Together, they played an aggressive, swarming defense.

But the inspirational, emotional leader of the bunch was a 5-11 weakside linebacker capable of delivering a big-time play — All-Pro Tom Jackson. It was Jackson who, despite his size, forced opponents to change their offensive philosophies against the Broncos.

In the Bronco offense Jackson was able to play loose and follow the flow. In 1976, he led the team and all other AFC linebackers with seven interceptions. But he could also put pressure on the quarterback, wreaking havoc in the backfield, disrupting plays.

A Tom Jackson rookie card at $2.50 is the safest investment one could make, simply based on the fact that he'll eventually double based on appreciation alone. Some might think he's a longshot to make the Hall of Fame, but at $2.50, what have you got to lose? Buy two of Jackson's cards; if he does get elected, he'll slide in a few paces behind Jack Lambert's $25 1976 rookie card, and you'll have made a substantial return on your initial investment.

Tom Jackson Checklist

Year	Company	No.	Price
1978	Topps	240	$2.50
1979	Topps	83	.50
1980	Topps	323	.40
1982	Topps	80	.35
1984	Topps	65	.25
1985	Topps	241	.20
1989	Pro Set	6 (Announcer insert)	.15

 John Elway

John Elway: 1984 Topps #63, $23; $12.50 in July 1991.

June 28, 1960; 6-3, 215; University of Stanford; first player chosen in the 1983 draft by the Baltimore Colts, refused to report and was traded to the Denver Broncos; quarterback; active; 10 seasons (all with Denver).

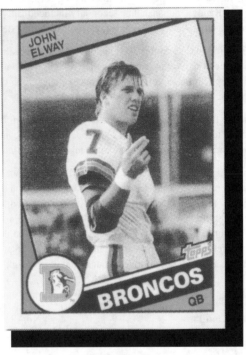

John Elway

Career statistics entering the 1993 season
Att..: 4,339; Comp.: 2,375; Pct.: 54.7; Yds.: 30,316 (14th); TDs: 158 (41st);
Int.: 157; Ave.: 6.98; Rush: 494; Yds.: 2,282; Ave.: 4.6; TDs: 22;
Total TDs: 23; Pts.: 138

Denver Bronco receivers are never out of range when John Elway is quarterbacking; nobody in the NFL has a stronger arm than Elway's, an arm which has led the Denver Broncos to three Super Bowl appearances during the 1980s. Those three appearances provide the only knock against Elway — he hasn't won the big one yet; his Broncos have fallen short in each game.

But the pressure of a big game has never bothered Elway; he's led his team to 30 come-from-behind wins in his career. Entering the 1993 season, Elway's record as a starter is 89-52-1, a .626 lifetime winning percentage.

At 6-3, 215 pounds, Elway's an ideal size for a quarterback. He has an uncanny sense of where his receivers are, and has a knack for staying in or getting out of the pocket. Although he scrambles to buy time, not necessarily to run, but to hit an open receiver, Elway's the only player in NFL history to throw for 3,000 yards and rush for more than 200 in seven straight seasons.

As an All-American quarterback at Stanford, Elway was known for imprinting the "The Elway Cross" on receivers; after practice they'd show off the cross-like bruises where the nose of an Elway-launched football had drilled them. While at Stanford, Elway, a runner-up to Herschel Walker in the 1982 Heisman Trophy balloting, set five NCAA passing records, becoming the first quarterback to throw for 2,500 yards in three different seasons.

Elway also played collegiate baseball as an outfielder and was selected by the New York Yankees in the first round of the 1982 free agent draft. He spent that season with the single A Oneonta team before realizing most scouts rated him as only an average baseball player.

The Baltimore Colts made Elway the first pick in the NFL's 1983 draft, but when he refused to sign with the team, Denver traded Chris Hinton (the fourth pick overall), Mark Herrmann and a #1 pick in the 1984 draft for him. Elway then signed a five-year, $5-million contract, making him the highest paid player before he even played pro ball.

A Pro Bowler four times and the Associated Press Most Valuable Player in 1987, Elway, a tenacious, enthusiastic competitor, is well schooled in the fundamentals; his father was a collegiate coach. Elway's arm has been compared with Joe Namath's, while his mobility has been compared with Fran Tarkenton's.

Elway's card will never attain the values of Namath's (1965 Topps, $1,500) or Tarkenton's (1962 Topps, $325) rookie cards. Dan Marino has gotten all the ink for his individual records and moved up on the charts faster, but look who's been to the Super Bowl more times — Elway, three to one, and that's why he makes the big bucks. His card $23 1984 Topps rookie card is a steal compared to Marino's $70 rookie card from the same set.

John Elway Checklist

Year	Company	No.	Price
1984	Topps	63	23.00
1985	Topps	235	.35
1985	Topps	238	4.00
1986	Topps	112	1.50
1987	Topps	31	1.00
1988	Topps	23	.50
1989	Pro Set (Trade)	100	.35
1989	Topps	241	.30
1990	Action Packed	63	1.00
1990	Fleer	21	.20
1990	Pro Set	88	.20
1990	Score	25	.20
1990	Score	564 (Hot Guns)	.12
1990	Topps	37	.20
1991	Action Packed	63	.60
1991	Bowman	127	.20
1991	Fleer	45	.20
1991	Fleer Ultra	35	.20
1991	Pacific	115	.20

John Elway Checklist

Year	Company	No.	Price
1991	Pro Line Portraits	257	.20
1991	Pro Set	138	.20
1991	Score	410	.20
1991	Score Pinnacle	7	.40
1991	Topps	554	.20
1991	Topps Stadium Club	294	1.25
1991	Upper Deck	75 (checklist)	.20
1991	Upper Deck	124	.20
1991	Wild Card NFL	4	.20
1992	Action Packed	69	.60
1992	Collectors Edge	37	1.00
1992	Fleer	#94	20
1992	Fleer Ultra	97	.50
1992	GameDay	23	.50
1992	Pacific	75	.20
1992	Playoff	77	1.25
1992	Pro Line Portraits QB Gold	4	3.50
1992	Pro Line Profiles	226-234	.20 each
1992	Pro Set	25	.20
1992	Pro Set	155	.20
1992	Pro Set Power	7	.40
1992	Score Pinnacle	212	.50
1992	Score Pinnacle	353	.50
1992	SkyBox Impact	10	.20
1992	SkyBox PrimeTime	50	.50
1992	Topps	125	.20
1992	Topps Stadium Club	110	.50
1992	Upper Deck	200	.20
1992	Upper Deck	514	.10
1992	Wild Card Field Force	51	.25
1992	Wild Card Stat Smashers	SS4	2.50

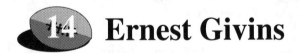 **Ernest Givins**

Ernest Givins: 1987 Topps #310, $3; 30 cents in July 1991.

Sept. 3, 1964; 5-9, 172; Northeastern Oklahoma A&M and the University of Louisville; Houston's second-round pick in 1986, 34th overall; wide receiver; active; seven seasons (all with Houston).

Career statistics entering the 1993 season

Rec.: 438; Yds.: 6,527; Ave.: 14.9; TDs.: 41; Rush.: 28; Yds.: 331; Ave.: 11.8; TDs.: 1; Total TDs.: 42; Pts.: 252.

Possessing great speed as a long-range receiver, Givins is an exciting big-play man in the Houston Oilers' run-and-shoot offense. Although he's relatively small, he's able to tack on a lot of yards after the catch.

138

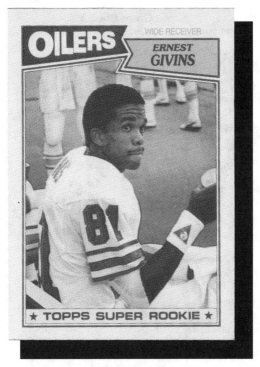

Ernest Givins

While in college at the University of Louisville, the speedy Givins ran the 40-yard dash in 4.36 seconds. In 1987 he participated in the NFL's Fastest Man Competition.

In Houston's run-and-shoot offense, led buy quarterback Warren Moon, Givins has played a slot position, teaming with Drew Hill, Curtis Duncan and Haywood Jeffires during the years. In his rookie season of 1986, when Givins was named an NFL First-Team All-Rookie, he and Hill became the 19th tandem in history to each gain 1,000 or more yards on receptions.

Givins has been sharing the ball with a lot of good receivers in Houston, but he's still averaging 62 catches a year. At 438 life-time receptions, he's only 73 away from breaking into the top 25 all-time, something he could do in 1993, in just his eighth season. He's young enough and on pace to make a run at Biletnikoff's and Carmichael's numbers.

This might be a wise $15 investment at this point; buy five cards and put them away for when Givins retires.

Ernest Givins Checklist

Year	Company	No.	Price
1987	Topps	310	3.00
1988	Topps	107	.75
1989	Pro Set	143	.25
1989	Score	194	.50
1989	Topps	103	.25
1990	Action Packed	92	.40
1990	Fleer	127	.15
1990	Pro Set	119	.15
1990	Score	352	.15
1990	Topps	228	.15
1991	Action Packed	92	.15
1991	Bowman	190	.10
1991	Fleer	61	.10
1991	Fleer Ultra	47	.10
1991	Pacific	173	.10
1991	Pro Line Portraits	38	.10
1991	Pro Set	164	.10
1991	Score	81	.10
1991	Score Pinnacle	145	.15
1991	Topps	224	.10
1991	Topps Stadium Club	389	.25
1991	Upper Deck	312	.10
1991	Wild Card NFL	19	.10
1992	Action Packed	92	.15
1992	Collectors Edge	61	.40
1992	Fleer Ultra	144	.15
1992	GameDay	264	.25
1992	Pacific	117	.10
1992	Playoff	8	.50
1992	Score Pinnacle	116	.15
1992	SkyBox Impact	165	.10
1992	SkyBox PrimeTime	169	.15
1992	Topps	187	.10
1992	Topps Stadium Club	451	.20
1992	Upper Deck	120	.10

15 Sterling Sharpe

Sterling Sharpe: 1989 Score Supplemental #333, $16; $2.50 in July 1991.

April 6, 1965; 5-11, 202; University of South Carolina; drafted in 1988 by Green Bay in the first round, seventh overall; wide receiver; active; five seasons (all with Green Bay).

Career statistics entering the 1993 season

Rec.: 389; Yds..: 5,741; Ave.: 14.7; TDs.: 36; Rush: 16; Yds..: 49; Ave.: 3.0; TDs: 0; Total TDs: 37; Pts.: 222.

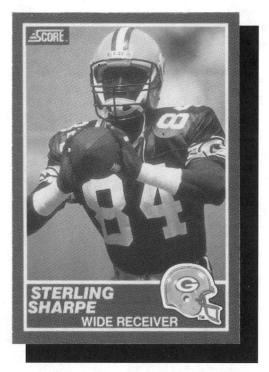

Sterling Sharpe

Green Bay's go-to receiver, despite often facing double coverage, Sharpe set an NFL record 108 receptions in 1992, with a league-leading 13 touchdowns and 1,461 yards. The Packers, who have lacked a second receiver to take the burden off Sharpe, head into the 1993 season with a possible solution; the team signed Miami's Mark Clayton, hoping he can still be productive.

Nevertheless, Green Bay's ball-control offense is geared toward getting the ball to Sharpe, who's as dangerous as any in the open field. Don't be surprised if he gets the ball 70 or 80 times in each of the next few seasons, hooking up with quarterback Brett Favre. Sharpe can conceivably hit the 90 mark again in receptions, as he's done in two of his five seasons, with at least 10 touchdowns.

Sharpe's averaged 73 catches per season so far. At that pace, if he plays 10 years, he'll sneak into third all-time, right ahead of another Packer receiver, James Lofton.

Sharpe, a two-time Pro Bowler, is compared favorably with San Francisco's future Hall of Famer, Jerry Rice, and is the heir apparent to take over Rice's spot as the top receiver in the NFL. Sharpe's rookie card will probably never surpass Rice's 1986 Topps card in total value, but his is scarcer, and should hit the $50 mark that Rice's rookie card is at.

Sterling Sharpe

Year	Company	No.	Price
1989	Score Supplemental	333	16.00
1989	Topps	379	3.50
1989	Pro Set	550	4.00
1990	Action Packed	90	2.50
1990	Pro Set	114	.60
1990	Pro Set	13 (Leaders)	.15
1990	Topps	140	.60
1990	Fleer	180	.60
1990	Score	245	.60
1990	Pro Set	415 (Pro Bowl)	.25
1990	Score	560 (Rocket Man)	.25
1990	Score	589 (All-Pro)	.60
1991	Score	Pinnacle 11	1.25
1991	Score	42	.30
1991	Topps Stadium Club	79	6.00
1991	Action Packed	88	1.25
1991	Wild Card NFL	119	.30
1991	Upper Deck	136	.30
1991	Pro Set	161	.30
1991	Pacific	166	.30
1991	Bowman	172	.30
1991	Fleer Ultra	178	.30
1991	Fleer	261	.30
1991	Topps	456	.30
1991	Upper Deck	459	.30
1991	Score	639	.30
1992	Action Packed	81	1.00
1992	Collectors Edge	51	2.50
1992	Fleer	135	.30
1992	Fleer Ultra	136	.75
1992	GameDay	272	1.00
1992	Pacific	104	.30
1992	Playoff	142	2.25
1992	Pro Line Profiles	73-81	.25 each
1992	Pro Line Portraits	338	.30
1992	Pro Set	176	.30
1992	Pro Set Power	286	.75
1992	Score Pinnacle	95	.75
1992	Score Pinnacle	343	.30
1992	SkyBox Impact	75	.35
1992	SkyBox PrimeTime	123	.75
1992	Topps	490	.30
1992	Topps Stadium Club	592	1.00
1992	Upper Deck	92	.15
1992	Upper Deck	252	.30

BASKETBALL

 ## Kevin McHale

Kevin McHale: 1981-82 Topps #75, $15; $17.50 in July 1991.

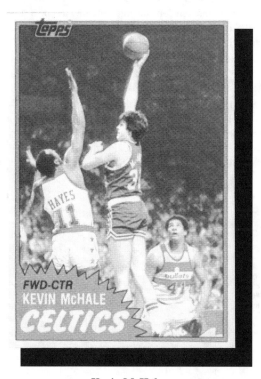

Kevin McHale

Dec. 19, 1957; 6-10, 225; University of Minnesota; Boston's first-round pick in 1980, third overall; forward/center; retired; 13 seasons (all with Boston).
G: 971 (30th); Min.: 30,118; FGA: 12,334; FGM: 6,830 (35th); Pct.: .553; FTA: 4,554; FTM: 3,665; Pct.: .804; OReb: 2,358; DReb: 4,764; TReb: 7,122 (44th); Ast.: 1,670; Stl.: 344; Blk.: 1,690 (14th); Pts: 17,335 (41st); Ave.: 17.8 ppg.

NBA All-Rookie Team 1980-81; NBA Sixth Man Award 1983-84, 1984-85; All-NBA First Team in 1986-87; NBA All-Defensive First Team 1985-86, 1986-87, 1987-88; NBA All-Defensive Second Team 1982-83, 1988-89, 1989-90; Led NBA in field goal percentage in 1986-87 (.604) and 1987-88 (.604); Played on NBA championship teams in 1980-81, 1983-84, 1985-86.

A sure two points, McHale is the only player in NBA history to shoot 60 percent (.604) from the field and 80 percent (.836) from the line in the same season (1986-87). He possessed a strong inside game, often posting up smaller forwards, but could hit the 18-footers, too. An average defensive rebounder who played finesse defense, McHale's 14th all-time in blocks. A gutsy player, the forward played with a broken foot for three months in one season. Selected to play in the All-Star game five times, McHale was flanked by Larry Bird and Robert Parish on three World Champion Celtics teams.

Although McHale's 1981-82 rookie card was in one of three 44-card sets distributed regionally throughout the country in addition to a main 66-card set, McHale's card, distributed in the East, is not too scarce.

In July 1991 the card, the major rookie in the set, was at $17.50. It sells for $15 now, but McHale will remain in the spotlight for the next five or six years. He'll be linked with Bird when he enters the Hall of Fame, then he'll be elected himself, and then he'll gain publicity again when Parish follows the two forwards into the Hall. His card value will rebound and pass $17.50 on its way to doubling.

Kevin McHale Checklist

Year	Company	No.	Price
1981-82	Topps	75	15.00
1983-84	Star Co.	34	55.00
1983-84	Star Co. All-Star Game	7	4.00
1983-84	Star Co. Awards Banquet	5	5.00
1984-85	Star Co.	9	12.00
1984-85	Star Co. 5x7 Court Kings	42	6.50
1985-86	Star Co.	98	10.00
1985-86	Star Co. Court Kings	22	4.25
1986-87	Fleer	73	4.50
1987-88	Fleer	74	1.75
1988-89	Fleer	11	1.00
1989-90	Fleer	11	.75
1989-90	NBA Hoops	156 (All-Star)	.10
1989-90	NBA Hoops	280	.15
1990-91	Fleer	12	.10
1990-91	NBA Hoops	6 (All-Star)	.25
1990-91	NBA Hoops	44	.10
1990-91	SkyBox	19	.20
1991-92	Fleer	13	.05
1991-92	NBA Hoops	14	.10
1991-92	NBA Hoops	255 (All-Star)	.10
1991-92	NBA Hoops	504 (Art)	.05
1991-92	SkyBox Mini	3	.50
1991-92	SkyBox	17	.10
1991-92	SkyBox	433	.10
1991-92	Upper Deck	62 (All-Star)	.07

Kevin McHale Checklist

Year	Company	No.	Price
1991-92	Upper Deck	225	.07
1992-93	Fleer	17	.15
1992-93	Fleer Ultra	14	.15
1992-93	NBA Hoops	16	.07
1992-93	SkyBox	16	.07
1992-93	Topps	57	.07
1992-93	Topps Gold	57	.50
1992-93	Topps Stadium Club	147	.25
1992-93	Upper Deck	183	.07

2 Walter Davis

Walter Davis: 1978-79 Topps #10, $6; $4 in July 1991.

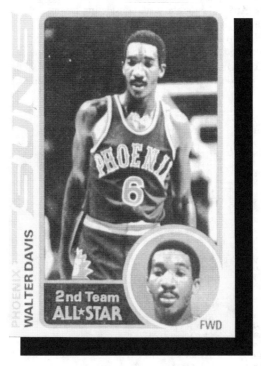

Walter Davis

Sept. 9, 1954; 6-6, 200; University of North Carolina; Phoenix's first-round pick in 1977, fifth overall; forward and guard; retired; 15 seasons (Phoenix 1977-88; Denver 1988-90; Denver/Portland 1990-91; Denver 1991-92).

G: 1,033 (22nd); Min.: 28,859; FGA: 15,871; FGM: 8,118 (15th); Pct.: .511; FTA: 3,676; FTM: 3,128; Pct.: .850; OReb: 889; DReb: 2,164; TReb: 3,053; Ast.: 3,878 (37th); Stl.: 1,280 (21st); Blk.: 133; Pts.: 19,521 (20th); Ave.: 18.8 ppg.

Member of the United States Olympic Team in 1976; NBA Rookie of the Year in 1977-78; NBA All-Rookie Team 1977-78; All-NBA Second Team in 1977-78, 1978-79.

A good shooter, especially with his jump shot, Davis ranks as one of the top per-minute scorers and is 20th all-time in points. The offensive-oriented guard was a good ball-handler who finished his career as one of the league's best sixth men. The classy playmaker was a member of the United States' gold medal-winning Olympic team in 1976. Nicknamed "Sweet D" and "Greyhound," Davis was the 1977-78 Rookie of the Year with Phoenix, scoring 24.2 ppg.

If you have the patience to wait five or six years, sit on your Walter Davis rookie cards. At $6, they are a steal, considering Dennis Johnson rookie cards from the same year are $9. Johnson is a potential Hall of Famer who, only within the last two seasons, has been knocked out of the top 50 all-time in scoring, but still ranks 16th all-time in steals and eighth all-time in rebounds by a guard. Davis is a future Hall of Famer based on his offensive merits, including six 20+ ppg. seasons, and his cards will rise in value accordingly.

Walter Davis Checklist

Year	Company	No.	Price
1978-79	Topps	10	6.00
1979-80	Topps	80	1.00
1980-81	Topps	4 (All-Star)	.75
1980-81	Topps	191	.50
1981-82	Topps	33	.25
1983-84	Star Co.	109	4.00
1983-84	Star Co. All-Star	17	1.50
1984-85	Star Co.	39	3.25
1985-86	Star Co.	36	3.00
1985-86	Star Co. Rookie of the Year	8	3.50
1986-87	Fleer	23	2.25
1987-88	Fleer	26	.75
1989-90	Fleer	39	.10
1989-90	NBA Hoops	61	.07
1990-91	Fleer	47	.07
1990-91	NBA Hoops	93	.05
1990-91	SkyBox	73	.07
1991-92	Fleer Update	274	.03
1991-92	NBA Hoops	173	.05
1991-92	NBA Hoops	356	.07
1991-92	NBA Hoops	557	.05
1991-92	SkyBox	236	.05
1991-92	SkyBox	623	.05
1991-92	Upper Deck	380	.05
1991-92	Upper Deck	422	.07
1992-93	SkyBox	58	.05

 # John Stockton

3) John Stockton: 1988-89 Fleer #115, $25; $12.50 in July 1991.

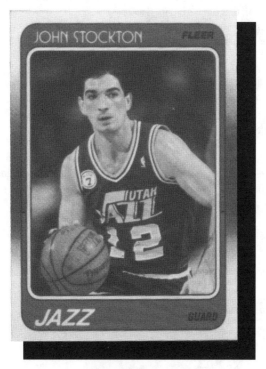

John Stockton

March 26, 1962; 6-1, 175; Gonzaga University; drafted by Utah in the first round in 1984, 16th overall; guard; active; 9 seasons (all with Utah).

Career statistics through 1992-93 season

G: 734; Min.: 23,179; FGA: 6,710; FGM: 3,425; Pct.: .510; FTA: 3,002; FTM: 2,473; Pct.: .823; OReb: 463; DReb: 1,407; TReb: 1,870; Ast.: 8,352 (4th); Stl.: 1,832 (3rd); Blk.: 142; Pts.: 9;634; Ave.: 13.2 ppg.

All-NBA Second Team 1987-88, 1988-89, 1989-90, 1991-92, 1992-93; All-

NBA Third Team 1990-91; NBA All-Defensive Second Team 1988-89, 1990-91, 1991-92; led NBA in assists 1987-88 (1,128), 1988-89 (1,118), 1989-90 (1,134), 1990-91 (1,164, a record), 1991-92 (1,126) and 1992-93 (987); led NBA in steals in 1988-89 (263) and 1991-92 (244); shares NBA playoff record for most assists in a game with 24, vs. Lakers in 1988, and holds record for the most in a seven-game playoff series (115) in 1988 vs. L.A.

Stockton, the NBA record-holder for most assists in one season, is the consummate playmaker. The unselfish team player passes more than he shoots; he's led the NBA in assists six straight seasons, falling short of the 1,000 mark for the first time in that run during the 1992-93 season. The five-time NBA All-Star was a member of the 1992 United States Dream Team. Stockton had 17 assists, 11 points and five assists in the 1989 All-Star Game, as a replacement for Magic Johnson, who he's gunning for as the NBA's all-time leader (9,921) in assists.

The durable catalyst, who has only missed four regular-season games during his entire career, could surpass Johnson in two years in assists. He's appeared in less than half as many playoff games as Magic, but if the Utah Jazz can find the one player to put them over the hump to win an NBA title, Stockton's 1988-89 Fleer rookie card value, a steal at $25, would benefit immediately, such as was the case for Scottie Pippen of the Chicago Bulls, who's 1988-89 Fleer rookie is already at $60. A definite lock for the Hall of Fame, it's just a matter of when Stockton decides to retire; then his card will make the gradual increases until he's elected. It's already doubled in the last two years.

John Stockton Checklist

Year	Company	No.	Price
1984-85	Star Co.	235	300.00
1985-86	Star Co.	144	100.00
1985-86	Star Co. Rookies	8	75.00
1986	Star Co. Best/Best	12	50.00
1988-89	Fleer	115	25.00
1988-89	Fleer	127	7.00
1989-90	Fleer	156	3.00
1989-90	Fleer	163 (All-Star)	.50
1989-90	NBA Hoops	140	.75
1989-90	NBA Hoops	297 (All-Star)	.25
1990-91	Fleer All-Stars	9	.50
1990-91	NBA Hoops	25 (All-Star)	.25
1990-91	NBA Hoops	294	.20
1990-91	SkyBox	285	.40
1990-91	Star Co. Slam	8	25.00
1990-91	Star Co. Court Kings	6	20.00
1990-91	Star Co. Nova	7	50.00
1990-91	Star Co. John Stockton (11) set		10.00
1991-92	Fleer	203	.20
1991-92	Fleer	217 (All-Star)	.25
1991-92	Fleer	221 (Leaders)	.10
1991-92	Fleer Update	397 (Leaders)	.10
1991-92	NBA Hoops	212	.20
1991-92	NBA Hoops	271 (All-Star)	.25
1991-92	NBA Hoops	500 (Supreme Court)	.15
1991-92	NBA Hoops	528 (Art)	.10

John Stockton Checklist

Year	Company	No.	Price
1991-92	NBA Hoops	584	.45
1991-92	SkyBox Mini	47	1.50
1991-92	SkyBox	285	.30
1991-92	SkyBox	539 (USA)	.50
1991-92	Upper Deck	32	.20
1991-92	Upper Deck	52 (All-Star)	.15
1991-92	Upper Deck	136	.20
1991-92	Upper Deck	470 (All-Star)	.15
1991-92	Upper Deck Holograms	3	1.00
1992-93	Fleer	227	.20
1992-93	Fleer	240 (Leaders)	.15
1992-93	Fleer All-Stars	22	3.00
1992-93	Fleer Sharpshooters (i)	11	2.50
1992-93	Fleer Total D	6	2.50
1992-93	Fleer Ultra	183	.85
1992-93	Fleer Ultra All-NBA	10	5.00
1992-93	Fleer Ultra Playmakers	9	4.00
1992-93	NBA Hoops	229	.15
1992-93	NBA Hoops	316 (All-Star)	.10
1992-93	NBA Hoops	347 (USA)	.15
1992-93	NBA Hoops	483	.15
1992-93	NBA Hoops Supreme Court (i)	8	1.25
1992-93	SkyBox	244	.20
1992-93	SkyBox	307	.10
1992-93	SkyBox Olympic Team	3	1.50
1992-93	SkyBox Thunder/Lightning	8	17.50
1992-93	Topps	101	.15
1992-93	Topps Gold	101	1.25
1992-93	Topps Stadium Club	200	1.00
1992-93	Topps Stadium Club Beam Team	11	25.00
1992-93	Upper Deck	66 (Scoring Threat)	.25
1992-93	Upper Deck	116	.15
1992-93	Upper Deck All-Division Team	14	2.50
1992-93	Upper Deck All-NBA Team	6	3.00
1992-93	Upper Deck Holograms	2	.75
1992-93	Upper Deck Team MVPs	27	2.50

 # Dominique Wilkins

Dominique Wilkins: 1986-87 Fleer #121, $70; $27.50 in July 1991.

Jan. 12, 1960; 6-8, 200; University of Georgia; Utah's first round pick in 1982 as an undergraduate, third pick overall; active; 11 seasons (all with Atlanta).

Career statistics through 1992-93 season
G: 833; Min.: 30,858; FGA: 17,747; FGM: 8,322 (13th); Pct.: .468; FTA: 6,184 (18th); FTM: 5,013 (16th); Pct.: .810; OReb: 2,412; DReb: 3,402; TReb: 5,814; Ast.: 2,207; Stl.: 1,182 (26th); Blk.: 566; Pts.: 22,096 (11th); Ave.: 26.5 ppg. (6th).

149

Dominique Wilkins

All-NBA First Team 1985-86; All-NBA Second Team 1986-87, 1987-88, 1990-91; All-NBA Third Team 1988-89; All-NBA Rookie Team 1982-83; led the NBA in scoring in 1985-86 (30.3).

Wilkins is nicknamed the "Human Highlight Film" for his fabulous air shows capped with flamboyant dunks. The dazzling winner of slam dunk titles in 1985 and 1990, Wilkins, the runner up in 1986 and 1988, and Michael Jordan are the only two-time winners. Although he's only won one NBA scoring title, "Nique" has scored 25+ or more ppg. in nine of his 11 seasons, giving him the NBA's sixth best all-time average, at 26.5 ppg. The flashy acrobatic superstar, who keeps moving up the all-time scoring list, is an eight-time All-Star selection who just keeps getting better with age. He should crack the top 10 in scoring in 1993-94.

If you want to make a big-time investment, pick up a 1986-87 Fleer wax box of 36 packs for $6,000. You should be able to assemble two or three complete 132-card sets, which means two Wilkins cards. Plus, the $1,350 set contains the first major-issue cards for Charles Barkley ($180), Clyde Drexler ($75), Joe Dumars ($70), Patrick Ewing ($90), Michael Jordan ($750), Karl Malone ($80), Chris Mullin ($60), Akeem Olajuwon ($70) and Isiah Thomas ($35).

If you want to make a smaller investment, pick up a few wax packs at $225 each, and just let them sit; don't open them. If that's still too high, and you want something for less than $100, how can you go wrong with a Wilkins card for $70? He's a sure Hall of Famer, and although his value might be behind some of the others in the Fleer set, due in part to the fact they've had more post-season exposure and wins, Wilkins will catch up to them eventually when he gets inducted. Then, many cards from the 1986-87 Fleer set, including Wilkins', will be in the $200-$300 range.

Dominique Wilkins Checklist

Year	Company	No.	Price
1983	Star Co. Rookies	8	35.00
1984	Star Co. Slam Dunk	9	27.50
1983-84	Star Co.	263	250.00
1984-85	Star Co. 5x7 Court Kings	12	12.00
1984-85	Star Co. Slam Dunk	8	20.00
1984-85	Star Co. Slam Dunk	10	15.00
1984-85	Star Co.	76	75.00
1984-85	Star Co. Gatorade	8	25.00
1985-86	Star Co.	42	75.00
1986	Star Co. Court Kings	32	20.00
1986-87	Fleer	121	70.00
1986	Star Co. Best/Best	14	35.00
1987-88	Fleer	118	15.00
1988-89	Fleer	5	4.00
1988-89	Fleer	125	2.00
1989-90	Fleer	7	1.25
1989-90	Fleer	165 (All-Star)	.25
1989-90	NBA Hoops	130	.40
1989-90	NBA Hoops	234 (All-Star)	.20
1990-91	Fleer	6	.25
1990-91	NBA Hoops	12 (All-Star)	.15
1990-91	NBA Hoops	36	.20
1990-91	NBA Hoops	355 (Art)	.15
1990-91	SkyBox	11	.30
1990-91	Star Co. Slam	9	20.00
1990-91	Star Co. Court Kings	8	15.00
1990-91	Star Co. Nova	9	50.00
1990-91	Star Co. Dominique Wilkins	(11) set	10.00
1991-92	Fleer	6	.20
1991-92	Fleer	212 (All-Star)	.15
1991-92	Fleer Dominique Wilkins	(12) set	9.00
1991-92	Fleer Update	372 (Leaders)	.07
1991-92	NBA Hoops	7	.20
1991-92	NBA Hoops	259 (All-Star)	.15
1991-92	NBA Hoops	449 (Supreme Court)	.10
1991-92	NBA Hoops Slam Dunk	2	.75
1991-92	SkyBox	10	.20
1991-92	SkyBox	326 (GQ)	.15
1991-92	SkyBox	588 (Skymaster)	.10
1991-92	Upper Deck	66 (All-Star)	.15
1991-92	Upper Deck	255	.30
1992-93	Fleer	8	.15
1992-93	Fleer Team Leaders	1	2.00

151

Dominique Wilkins Checklist

Year	Company	No.	Price
1992-93	Fleer Ultra	6	.60
1992-93	NBA Hoops	8	.15
1992-93	SkyBox	8	.20
1992-93	SkyBox	282	.10
1992-93	Topps	35	.15
1992-93	Topps	125	.15
1992-93	Topps Gold	35	1.25
1992-93	Topps Gold	125	1.25
1992-93	Topps Stadium Club Beam Team	2	20.00
1992-93	Upper Deck	148	.25
1992-93	Upper Deck All-Division Team	7	2.50
1992-93	Upper Deck Foreign Exchange	10	2.50
1992-93	Upper Deck Team MVPs	2	2.00
1992-93	Upper Deck 15,000 Point Club	1	3.00

Artis Gilmore

Artis Gilmore: 1972-73 Topps #180, $30; $17.50 in July 1991.

Sept. 21, 1949; 7-2, 265; Gardner-Webb Junior College and Jacksonville University; drafted by Chicago in seventh round of the 1971 draft, 117th overall, and by Kentucky of the ABA in first round in 1971; retired; 17 seasons (Kentucky 1971-76; Chicago 1976-82; San Antonio 1982-87; Chicago/Boston 1987-88).

ABA Stats:
G: 420; Min.: 17,449; FGA: 6,581; FGM: 3,669; Pct.: .557; FTA: 3,022; FTM: 2,018; Pct.: .667; Reb: 7,169; Ast.: 1,273; Pts.: 9,362; Ave.: 22.3 ppg.

NBA Stats:
G: 909 (46th); Min.: 29,685; FGA: 9,570; FGM: 5,732; Pct.: .598; FTA: 5,768 (23rd); FTM: 4,114 (34th); Pct.: .713; OReb: 2,639; DReb: 6,522; TReb: 9,161 (25th); Ast.: 1,777; Stl.: 470; Blk.: 1,747 (12th); Pts.: 15,579; Ave.: 17.1 ppg.

ABA MVP and Rookie of the Year in 1971-72; ABA All-Rookie Team in 1971-72; ABA All-Star First Team in 1971-72, 1972-73, 1973-74, 1974-75, 1975-76; ABA All-Defensive Team 1972-73, 1973-74, 1974-75, 1975-76; ABA All-Star Game MVP in 1974; ABA playoff MVP in 1975; member of 1975 ABA championship team; led ABA in rebounding 1971-72 (1,491), 1972-73 (1,476), 1973-74 (1,538), 1975-76 (1,303); led ABA in field goal percentage 1971-72 (.598), 1972-73 (.560); named to NBA All-Defensive Second Team in 1977-78; led NBA in field goal percentage in 1980-81 (.670), 1981-82 (.652), 1982-83 (.626), 1983-84 (.631); NBA all-time field goal percentage leader (.598).

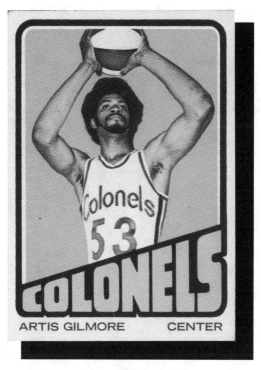

ARTIS GILMORE   CENTER

Artis Gilmore

As part of a Jacksonville front line that averaged 7 feet tall against UCLA in the 1971 NCAA Finals, Gilmore finished his collegiate career averaging 20 points and 20 rebounds per game at the university. He fit right into the ABA his first season, being named the league's Rookie of the Year and MVP and becoming only the fourth man in ABA history to score 2,000 points as a rookie. As the ABA's dominant center in the 1970s, Gilmore was a shot-blocker and rebounder for the San Antonio Spurs and later the NBA's Chicago Bulls.

If the Honors Committee considers Gilmore's ABA statistics, during which he was the league's first-team center five straight seasons, he would be a definite for the Hall of Fame. He'd rank 13th all-time in points, scoring 18.8 ppg., fourth in rebounds (16,330), and second in blocked shots (3,178). The franchise player holds ABA records for most blocks in a career (750) and season (287, in 1973-74), and most rebounds in a game (40), against New York in 1974.

Gilmore's career statistics are quite favorable when compared to those of former Kentucky Colonel teammate Dan Issel, a 1992 Hall-of-Fame inductee.

Issel's 1971-72 rookie card is at $45; Gilmore's 1972-73 rookie card, currently at $30, should hit that mark when the Hall of Fame beckons.

Artis Gilmore Checklist

Year	Company	No.	Price
1972-73	Topps	180	30.00
1972-73	Topps	251 (All-Star)	6.00
1972-73	Topps	260 (Leaders)	3.00
1972-73	Topps	263 (Leaders)	20.00
1973-74	Topps	235 (Leaders)	1.50
1973-74	Topps	238 (Leaders)	1.50
1973-74	Topps	250	6.00
1974-75	Topps	180	3.50
1974-75	Topps	211 (Leaders)	1.75
1974-75	Topps	224 (Leaders)	3.00
1975-76	Topps	222 (Leaders)	5.00
1975-76	Topps	225 (Leaders)	1.50
1975-76	Topps	250	3.00
1975-76	Topps	280 (Leaders)	2.00
1976-77	Topps	25	3.00
1977-78	Topps	115	2.00
1978-79	Topps	73	1.00
1979-80	Topps	25	.75
1980-81	Topps	44	.30
1980-81	Topps	259 (Slam Dunk)	.35
1981-82	Topps	7	.60
1981-82	Topps	46 (Leaders)	.30
1981-82	Topps	MW107 (Leaders)	.40
1983	Star Co. All-Stars	17	3.50
1983-84	Star Co.	244	5.00
1984	Star Co. Awards Banquet	14	2.00
1984-85	Star Co. 5x7 Court Kings	34	4.00
1984-85	Star Co.	64	5.00
1985-86	Star Co.	145	5.00
1986-87	Fleer	37	2.75
1987-88	Fleer	40	1.00

Gail Goodrich

Gail Goodrich: 1969-70 Topps #2, $25; $7.50 in July 1991.

April 23, 1943; 6-1, 175; UCLA; drafted by Los Angeles in the first round as a territorial choice in 1965; retired; 14 seasons (Los Angeles 1965-68; Phoenix 1968-70; Los Angeles 1970-76; New Orleans 1976-79).

G: 1,031 (24th); Min.: 33,527; FGA: 16,300; FGM: 7,431 (21st); Pct.: .455; FTA: 5,354 (35th); FTM: 4,319 (30th); Pct.: .806; TReb: 3,279; Ast.: 4,805 (22nd); Stl.: 545; Blk.: 72; Pts.: 19,181 (23rd); Ave.: 18.6 ppg.

Gail Goodrich

All-NBA First Team in 1974; Member of the 1972 NBA championship team.

Had he played anywhere else but in Los Angeles for nine of his 14 seasons, Goodrich, who's been unsuccessful in several elections, might have already been elected to the Hall of Fame. Although he had four of his six 20+ ppg. scoring seasons with the Lakers, and was often a leading scorer on a team which included Hall of Famers Jerry West and Wilt Chamberlain, the 6-1 guard could have been any other team's go-to guy. He was, however, able to work instinctively with West to get each other the ball for open shots and caught many touchdown passes from Chamberlain off the fast break.

Goodrich's quick movements and decisions made him successful, despite his lack of size; he's one of the smaller players to appear in the top 10 in scoring for a season. He ranks 23rd on the all-time scoring list with 19,181 points; the only guards who have scored more points are Oscar Robertson, George Gervin, Hal Greer, Michael Jordan, Walter Davis and West. Although Springfield has turned Goodrich away several times already, his rookie card, which was but

$7.50 two years ago, has tripled in value since then. Perhaps his card has peaked, and will only increase due to general appreciation. If not, and he falls from his on-the-fence status and lands in the Hall of Fame, you've got a bargain at $25.

Gail Goodrich Checklist

Year	Company	No.	Price
1969-70	Topps	2	25.00
1970-71	Topps	93	10.00
1971-72	Topps	121	4.00
1972-73	Topps	50	2.50
1972-73	Topps	174 (Leaders)	3.00
1973-74	Topps	55	3.00
1974-75	Topps	90 (Leaders)	1.50
1974-75	Topps	120	2.00
1975-76	Topps	110	1.50
1975-76	Topps	125 (Leaders)	1.50
1976-77	Topps	125	2.00
1977-78	Topps	77	1.50
1978-79	Topps	95	1.00
1979-80	Topps	32	.75

 **Alex English**

Alex English: 1979-80 Topps #31, $18; $16 in July 1991.

Jan. 5, 1954; 6-7, 190; University of South Carolina; Milwaukee's second-round pick in 1976, 23rd overall; forward; retired; 15 seasons (Milwaukee 1976-78; Indiana 1978-79; Indiana/Denver 1979-80; Denver 1980-90; Dallas 1990-91).

G: 1,193 (7th); Min.: 38,063; FGA: 21,036; FGM: 10,659 (4th); Pct.: .506; FTA: 5,141 (38th); FTM: 4,277 (32nd); Pct.: .831; OReb: 2,778; DReb: 3,760; TReb: 6,538 (52nd); Ast.: 4,351 (31st); Stl.: 1,067 (38th); Blk.: 833; Pts.: 25,613 (7th); Ave.: 21.5 ppg. (26th).

All-NBA Second Team 1981-82, 1982-83, 1985-86; led NBA in scoring in 1982-83 (28.4); holds NBA record for most consecutive seasons (8) with 2,000 or more points.

The NBA's seventh-leading scorer all-time did most of his scoring in Denver's run-and-gun offense. English was not known to drive much; many of his points came off floaters from the corner. Although he lacks an NBA championship ring, English was a point machine throughout his career, scoring 20+ ppg. nine straight seasons. The classy competitor is fourth all-time in most field goals made (10,659), and seventh in career points, which will land him in the Hall of Fame in five years. His impressive 21.5 ppg. scoring average ranks 26th all-time. English played in eight All-Star games, including four as a starter.

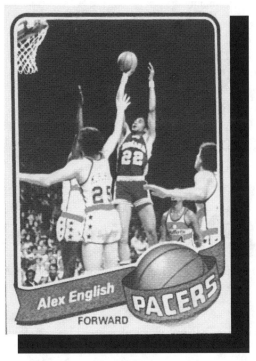

Alex English

The only forwards who have outscored English during their careers are Elvin Hayes and John Havlicek. Hayes' 1969-70 Topps rookie is at $70; Havlicek's 1969-70 rookie is at $175. Because English's rookie card is 10 years younger, it won't reach those heights for quite some time. But English is often overlooked, so stock up on his cards now. When he gets inducted into the Hall of Fame, his card should at least double in price, as Calvin Murphy's did after his induction.

Alex English Checklist

Year	Company	No.	Price
1979-80	Topps	31	18.00
1980-81	Topps	75	2.50
1981-82	Topps	W68	1.50
1983	Star Co. All-Stars	15	3.50
1983-84	Star Co.	186	7.50
1984	Star Co. All-Star Game	18	3.00
1984-85	Star Co. 5x7 Court Kings	22	5.00
1984-85	Star Co.	137	5.00
1985-86	Star Co.	50	5.00

Alex English Checklist

Year	Company	No.	Price
1986	Star Co. Court Kings	12	5.00
1986-87	Fleer	30	3.00
1987-88	Fleer	34	1.25
1988-89	Fleer	34	.50
1989-90	Fleer	40	.25
1989-90	NBA Hoops	120	.10
1989-90	NBA Hoops	133 (All-Star)	.07
1990-91	Fleer	48	.07
1990-91	Fleer Update	19	.10
1990-91	NBA Hoops	94	.10
1990-91	NBA Hoops	407	.07
1990-91	SkyBox	74	.15
1990-91	SkyBox	375	.07
1990-91	Star Co. Slam	2	15.00
1990-91	Star Co. Court Kings	2	14.00
1991-92	NBA Hoops	315 (Milestone)	.10

 # Maurice Cheeks

Maurice Cheeks: 1980-81 Topps #178 (with Magic Johnson All-Star/Ron Boone), $50; $20 in July 1991.

Sept. 8, 1956; 6-1, 180; West Texas State University; Philadelphia's second-round pick in 1978, 36th overall; guard; active; 15 seasons (Philadelphia 1978-89; San Antonio/New York 1989-90; New York 1990-91; Atlanta 1991-92, New Jersey 1992-93).

Career statistics through 1992-93 season

G: 1,101 (10th); Min.: 34,845; FGA: 9,374; FGM: 4,906; Pct.: .523; FTA: 2,938; FTM: 2,331; Pct.: .793; OReb: 713; DReb: 2,375; TReb: 3,088; Ast.: 7,392 (5th); Stl.: 2,308 (1st); Blk.: 294; Pts.: 12,195; Ave.: 11.0 ppg.

Named to NBA All-Defensive First Team 1982-83, 1983-84, 1984-85, 1985-86; All-Defensive Second Team 1986-87; member of 1983 NBA championship team; NBA all-time steals leader.

Cheeks is winding down his career having logged a lot of minutes; he's 10th all-time in games played. The NBA's all-time leader in steals has always been more defensive-minded than offensively geared, but ranks fifth all-time in assists, too. He's been a playmaker who owns a strong assist-to-turnover ratio and, as his high shooting percentage indicates, he's made his shots count. Although this guard with court savvy could beat you in many ways, and led the Philadelphia 76ers to a title in 1983, he's widely underrated, due in part to his lack of offensive production. Many have written him off as a Hall of Famer, but the defensive skills of this four-time NBA All-Defensive First Team selection are second to none.

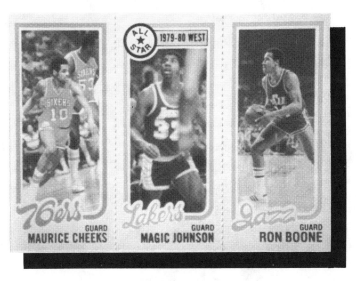

Maurice Cheeks

Cheeks' rookie card is on the three-player panels from the 1980-81 Topps set, and should be collected as an entire card, not perforated into individual parts. Because this set is so confusing (there are 264 different players on 176 panels of three) it isn't too popular among collectors. The panel with Cheeks/Magic Johnson All-Star/Ron Boone is at $50, but since it contains two future Hall of Famers on it, it will continue to rise. It's worth buying right now. The panel with Cheeks/George Gervin All-Star/Jim Chones is at $5 (it was $1.50 in July 1991); that's worth a five-spot, too, since Gervin is also headed to the Hall of Fame.

Maurice Cheeks Checklist

Year	Company	No.	Price
1980-81	Topps	66	50.00
1980-81	Topps	176 (Leaders)	.75
1980-81	Topps	178	5.00
1981-82	Topps	59 (Leaders)	1.50
1981-82	Topps	E90	1.50

159

Maurice Cheeks Checklist

Year	Company	No.	Price
1983	Star Co. All-Stars	3	2.00
1983-84	Star Co.	2	15.00
1984-85	Star Co. 5x7 Court Kings	29	2.50
1984-85	Star Co.	203	5.00
1985-86	Star Co.	1	3.50
1986	Star Co. Court Kings	7	2.50
1986-87	Fleer	16	2.25
1987-88	Fleer	20	.75
1988-89	Fleer	86	.25
1989-90	Fleer	115	.10
1989-90	NBA Hoops	65	.25
1989-90	NBA Hoops	320	.07
1990-91	Fleer	124	.05
1990-91	NBA Hoops	202	.05
1990-91	SkyBox	186	.07
1991-92	Fleer	135	.02
1991-92	Fleer Update	242	.03
1991-92	NBA Hoops	139	.05
1991-92	NBA Hoops	320 (Yearbook)	.05
1991-92	NBA Hoops	331	.05
1991-92	NBA Hoops	533 (Art)	.05
1991-92	SkyBox	188	.05
1991-92	SkyBox	615	.05
1991-92	Upper Deck	281	.05
1992-93	NBA Hoops	2	.05
1992-93	SkyBox	2	.05

Isiah Thomas

Isiah Thomas: 1986-87 Fleer #109, $35; $30 in July 1991.

April 30, 1961; 6-1, 185; Indiana University; Detroit's first pick as an undergraduate in 1981, second overall; active; 12 seasons (all with Detroit).

Career statistics through 1992-93 season

G: 921; Min.: 33,766; FGA: 15,141; FGM: 6,876 (32nd); Pct.: .454; FTA: 5,058 (40th); FTM: 3,855 (38th); Pct.: .762; OReb: 905; DReb: 2,414; TReb: 3,319; Ast.: 8,662 (3rd); Stl.: 1,793 (5th); Blk.: 243; Pts.: 17,966 (35th); Ave.: 19.5 ppg. (45th).

Named to the All-NBA First Team in 1983-84, 1984-85, 1985-86; All-NBA Second Team in 1982-83, 1986-87; NBA All-Rookie Team 1981-82; NBA All-Star Game MVP in 1983-84, 1985-86; member of NBA championship teams in 1988-89, 1989-90; NBA playoff MVP in 1990; led NBA in assists in 1984-85 (1,123); member of the 1981 NCAA championship team; 1980 United States Olympic Team member.

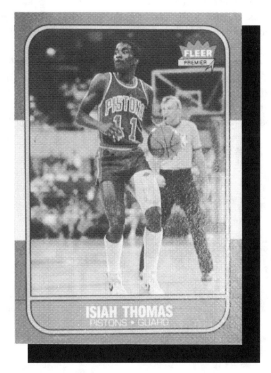

Isiah Thomas

Thomas is third all-time in assists, trailing only Magic Johnson and Oscar Robertson. The streak-shooting competitor, who once held the single-season assist record with 1,123 in 1984-85 before John Stockton topped it, could catch Johnson in three more seasons. His career assist average per game, at 9.4, is second all-time, while his 13.9 apg. in the 1984-85 season is an NBA record. He ranks 35th on the all-time scoring list, and, so mentally tough, is known for hitting the clutch shots and his lightning-fast moves to the hoop.

Thomas, who has made 11 straight All-Star game appearances, is the only player to start in his first five seasons. A seven-time starter, he's a two-time All-Star game MVP (1984 with 21 points, all in second half, plus 15 assists; 1986, with 30 points and 10 assists). He was the leader on Detroit's back-to-back championship teams, being named the MVP of the finals in 1990 when the team won its second title. The 1986-87 J. Walter Kennedy Citizenship Award winner, as voted by the Pro Basketball Writers Association of America, Thomas has also served as the president of the NBA Players Association.

The 1986-87 Fleer set, at $1,350, contains the big-ticket major-issue rookie cards for Clyde Drexler ($75), Charles Barkley ($180), Akeem Olajuwon ($70), Chris Mullin ($60), Karl Malone ($80), Patrick Ewing ($70), Michael Jordan ($750) and Dominique Wilkins ($70). Considering Thomas' first major-issue card is also in the set, it's a steal at $35, and it's a mystery as to why it's so low.

Thomas' career statistics are overall better than each of the others, except perhaps Wilkins, plus Thomas has two championship rings. He will definitely be elected to the Hall of Fame sooner than the others, who still need a few solid seasons added to their career numbers. When Thomas is inducted, his Fleer card's price will do some catching up to the other big-ticket cards in the Fleer set, and will probably even pass them.

Isiah Thomas Checklist

Year	Company	No.	Price
1983	Star Co. All-Star Game	11	30.00
1983-84	Star Co.	94	150.00
1984	Star Co. All-Star Game	11	8.00
1983-84	Star Co. Awards Banquet	12	7.50
1984-85	Star Co. 5x7 Court Kings	30	10.00
1984-85	Star Co. All-Stars	6	10.00
1984-85	Star Co.	261	50.00
1984-85	Star Co.	287	25.00
1985	Star Co. Crunch N Munch	6	10.00
1985-86	Star Co.	10	35.00
1986	Star Co. Court Kings	28	7.50
1986-87	Fleer	109	35.00
1986	Star Co. Best/Best	13	35.00
1987-88	Fleer	106	9.00
1988-89	Fleer	45	3.00
1989-90	Fleer	50	.60
1989-90	NBA Hoops	177 (All-Star)	.15
1989-90	NBA Hoops	250	.25
1990-91	Fleer	61	.30
1990-91	Fleer All-Stars	6	.40
1990-91	NBA Hoops	11 (All-Star)	.15
1990-91	NBA Hoops	111	.15
1990-91	NBA Hoops	389 (Don't Foul Out)	.20
1990-91	SkyBox	93	.25
1990-91	Star Co. Court Kings	7	17.50
1990-91	Star Co. Gold	10	20.00
1990-91	Star Co. Nova	8	45.00
1990-91	Star Co. Silver	10	20.00
1990-91	Star Co. Isiah Thomas	(11) set	9.00
1991-92	Fleer	64	.20
1991-92	Fleer Schoolyard Stars	2	.40
1991-92	NBA Hoops	66	.15
1991-92	NBA Hoops	464 (Supreme Court)	.10
1991-92	NBA Hoops	510 (Art)	.15
1991-92	NBA Hoops All-Star MVPs	7	.75
1991-92	SkyBox	88	.15
1991-92	Upper Deck	333	.20
1991-92	Upper Deck	451 (All-Star)	.15
1992-93	Fleer	69	.10
1992-93	Fleer	255 (Pro Visions)	.10
1992-93	Fleer All-Stars	11	1.25
1992-93	Fleer Team Leaders	8	1.50
1992-93	Fleer Ultra	59	.25

Isiah Thomas Checklist

Year	Company	No.	Price
1992-93	Fleer Ultra Playmakers	10	3.00
1992-93	NBA Hoops	68	.10
1992-93	NBA Hoops	303 (All-Star)	.07
1992-93	SkyBox	73	.15
1992-93	SkyBox	289	.07
1992-93	Topps	118	.15
1992-93	Topps Gold	118	1.25
1992-93	Topps Stadium Club	50	.50
1992-93	Upper Deck	263	.10
1992-93	Upper Deck Team MVPs	9	.75

Phil Jackson

10) Phil Jackson: 1972-73 Topps #32, $20; $1.50 in July 1991.

Phil Jackson

Sept. 17, 1945; 6-8, 230; University of North Dakota; drafted by the New York Knicks in the second round in 1967, 17th pick overall; forward; retired; 12 seasons (1967-78, New Jersey 1978-80); currently head coach of the Chicago Bulls.

G: 807; Min.: 14,201; FGA: 4,583; FGM: 2,076; Pct.: .452; FTA: 1,734; FTM: 1,276; Pct.: .735; TReb: 3,454; Ast.: 898; Stl.: 281; Blk.: 199; Pts.: 5,428; Ave.: 6.7 ppg.

Named to NBA All-Rookie Team in 1968; member of the Knicks' 1972-73 championship team.

Coaching record

Five seasons in the Continental Basketball Association (1982-87, all with Albany); CBA Coach of the Year in 1985 (34-14); lifetime record of 115-107 (.518); he was 21-18 in playoffs, including the league championship team in 1983-84 (25-19); assistant to the Chicago Bulls in 1987-88 and 1988-89; named head coach in 1989-90 and through 1992-93 has a lifetime record of 240-88 (.731); only the third coach ever to win three successive NBA Championships (1990-91, 1991-92, 1992-93).

Is there life after Michael Jordan? It seems Jackson's ultimate challenge, more so than winning three straight championships, will be rebuilding the Bulls after Jordan retires. Jackson's coaching ability, without the benefit of the greatest basketball player ever, will then become more apparent; fans will realize it was Jackson who provided Jordan his supporting cast — one which, well coached, blended together as the players performed their designated roles around Jordan. Jackson's teams have always been top-notch defensive teams, and, despite inevitably being labeled a one-man offensive team, Jackson has made concerted efforts to get everyone involved.

You don't win three straight championships without a total team concept. At $20, Jackson's 1972-73 card might seem like a risk, especially since it was just $1.50 in July 1991, but if he continues coaching at the same pace for another decade, he'll have compiled some Hall-of-Fame-caliber numbers, coupled with his three (or more) NBA Championship rings. His card's value, which will have increased through general appreciation anyway, will then rise even more. This might be a low-yield return on your investment, but you can't lose money on the card.

Phil Jackson Checklist

Year	Company	No.	Price
1972-73	Topps	32	20.00
1973-74	Topps	71	6.00
1974-75	Topps	132	5.00
1975-76	Topps	111	5.00
1976-77	Topps	77	3.50
1989-90	NBA Hoops	266 (Coaches)	.07
1990-91	NBA Hoops	308 (Coaches)	.05
1990-91	NBA Hoops	348 (Then/Now)	.07

Phil Jackson Checklist

Year	Company	No.	Price
1990-91	SkyBox	304 (Coaches)	.07
1991-92	Fleer	29 (Coaches)	.03
1991-92	NBA Hoops	224 (Coaches)	.07
1991-92	SkyBox	381 (Coaches)	.07
1992-93	Fleer	31 (Coaches)	.05
1992-93	NBA Hoops	242 (Coaches)	.07
1992-93	NBA Hoops	305 (All-Star Coach)	.05
1992-93	SkyBox	258 (Coaches)	.10

 **Adrian Dantley**

11) Adrian Dantley: 1977-78 Topps #56, $16; $12.50 in July 1991.

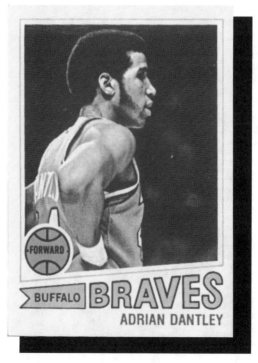

Adrian Dantley

Feb. 28, 1956; 6-5, 210; University of Notre Dame; drafted by Buffalo in the first round as an undergraduate in 1976, sixth pick overall; retired; 15 seasons (1976-77 Buffalo; Indiana 1977-78; Los Angeles 1977-79; Utah 1979-86; Detroit 1986-89; Dallas 1988-90; Milwaukee 1990-91).

G: 955 (36th); Min.: 34,151; FGA: 15,121; FGM: 8,169 (14th); Pct.: .540; FTA: 8,351 (6th); FTM: 6,832 (5th); Pct.: .818; OReb: 2,207; DReb: 3,248; TReb: 5,455; Ast.: 2,830; Stl.: 944; Blk.: 150; Pts.: 23,177 (9th); Ave.: 24.3 ppg. (12th).

NBA Rookie of the Year in 1976-77; NBA All-Rookie Team in 1976-77; All-NBA Second Team in 1980-81 and 1983-84; NBA Comeback Player of the Year 1983-84; member of the United States Olympic team in 1976; led NBA in scoring in 1980-81 (30.7) and 1983-84 (30.6).

Dantley, one of the game's most prolific scorers, had four straight seasons in which he scored 30+ ppg., twice leading the league. The forward's only drawback is that he never played on a championship team, something which favors Bob McAdoo's case for induction. When McAdoo goes in, Dantley, whose numbers are better than McAdoo's in every category except rebounds, should eventually follow. The best $33.50 deal you'll ever find would be for a Dantley rookie ($16), with a McAdoo 1973-74 Topps rookie, at $17.50, thrown in for good measure.

Adrian Dantley Checklist

Year	Company	No.	Price
1977-78	Topps	56	16.00
1978-79	Topps	132	4.00
1979-80	Topps	54	1.75
1980-81	Topps	6	.25
1980-81	Topps	234 (Leaders)	.25
1980-81	Topps	240	.40
1981-82	Topps	40	.75
1981-82	Topps	65 (Leaders)	.25
1983-84	Star Co.	133	5.00
1984	Star Co. All-Star Game	16	3.00
1984	Star Co. Awards Banquet	4	2.00
1984	Star Co. Awards Banquet	13	2.00
1984-85	Star Co. 5x7 Court Kings	36	5.00
1984-85	Star Co.	228	5.00
1984-85	Star Co. All-Stars	9	3.00
1984-85	Star Co. Crunch N Munch	8	3.00
1985-86	Star Co.	138	4.00
1986	Star Court Kings	9	2.00
1985-86	Star Co. Rookie of the Year	9	5.00
1986-87	Fleer	21	2.25
1987-88	Fleer	24	.75
1988-89	Fleer	39	.50
1989-90	Fleer	33	.15
1989-90	NBA Hoops	125	.15
1990-91	Fleer	39	.10
1990-91	NBA Hoops	83	.10
1990-91	SkyBox	61	.15

 # Robert Parish

Robert Parish: 1977-78 Topps #111, $60; $18 in July 1991.

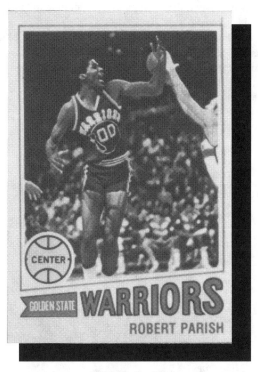

Robert Parish

Aug. 30, 1953; 7-0, 230; Centenary College; drafted by Golden State in the first round in 1976, eighth pick overall; active; 17 seasons (Golden State 1976-80; Boston 1980-93).

Career statistics through 1992-93 season
G: 1,339 (2nd); Min.: 40,873; FGA: 16,433; FGM: 8,909 (9th); Pct.: .542; FTA: 5,283 (36th); FTM: 3,810 (40th); Pct.: .721; OReb: 4,233; DReb: 9,198; TReb: 13,431 (9th); Ast.: 2,003; Stl.: 1,123 (33rd); Blk.: 2,156 (6th); Pts.: 21,628 (13th); Ave.: 16.1 ppg.

All-NBA Second Team in 1981-82; All-NBA Third Team in 1988-89; member of NBA championship teams in 1980-81, 1983-84, 1985-86.

Parish has played 17 illustrious years in the NBA and hasn't yet announced any plans to retire. He won't catch Kareem Abdul-Jabbar for games played, but needs just 134 points to pass former teammate Larry Bird for 12th all-time in scoring. Only three centers, using just NBA statistics, have scored more points — Kareem Abdul-Jabbar, Wilt Chamberlain and Moses Malone. Only those three centers, plus Bill Russell, have made more than Parish's eight All-Star game appearances. The "Chief" also ranks sixth all-time in blocked shots, and ninth all-time in rebounds.

But the most important line on Parish's resume is his three NBA title rings, won as a member of a legendary Boston Celtics front line which had two other future Hall of Famers — Bird and Kevin McHale. It won't be right if basketball's equivalent to baseball's Tinker-to-Evers-to-Chance Hall of Fame combo isn't enshrined as a unit into the NBA's Hall of Fame. At $60, Parish's rookie card might seem a bit steep, but it should reach $100, after he follows McHale and Bird into the Hall of Fame.

Robert Parish Checklist

Year	Company	No.	Price
1977-78	Topps	111	60.00
1978-79	Topps	86	12.00
1979-80	Topps	93	7.00
1980-81	Topps	92 (Leaders)	2.00
1980-81	Topps	93 (Leaders)	3.50
1980-81	Topps	97	4.00
1981-82	Topps	6	4.00
1981-82	Topps	E108 (Leaders)	2.00
1983	Star Co. All-Stars	9	5.00
1983-84	Star Co.	35	60.00
1984	Star Co. All-Star Game	9	5.00
1984-85	Star Co. 5x7 Court Kings	31	7.50
1984-85	Star Co.	10	15.00
1985-86	Star Co.	99	12.00
1986	Star Court Kings	26	7.00
1986-87	Fleer	84	5.00
1987-88	Fleer	81	3.00
1988-89	Fleer	12	1.25
1989-90	Fleer	12	.50
1989-90	NBA Hoops	185	.20
1990-91	Fleer	13	.15
1990-91	NBA Hoops	8 (All-Star)	.15
1990-91	NBA Hoops	45	.10
1990-91	SkyBox	20	.20
1991-92	Fleer	14	.05
1991-92	NBA Hoops	15	.07
1991-92	NBA Hoops	256 (All-Star)	.10
1991-92	NBA Hoops	305 (Inside Stuff)	.10
1991-92	NBA Hoops	324 (Yearbook)	.05
1991-92	NBA Hoops	452 (Supreme Court)	.07
1991-92	SkyBox Mini	4	.50
1991-92	SkyBox	18	.10
1991-92	SkyBox	575 (Salutes)	.05
1991-92	Upper Deck	72 (All-Star)	.07

Robert Parish Checklist

Year	Company	No.	Price
1991-92	Upper Deck	163	.10
1992-93	Fleer	18	.15
1992-93	Fleer Ultra	15	.10
1992-93	NBA Hoops	17	.07
1992-93	SkyBox	17	.07
1992-93	Topps	146	.07
1992-93	Topps Gold	146	.50
1992-93	Topps Stadium Club	63	.25
1992-93	Upper Deck	179	.07

 # Alonzo Mourning

Alonzo Mourning: 1992-93 Upper Deck #2, $4.

Alonzo Mourning

Feb. 8, 1970; 6-10, 240; Georgetown University, drafted in the first round by the Charlotte Hornets in 1992, the second pick overall; active; one season.

Career statistics through 1992-93 season

G: 78; Min.: 2,644; FGA: 1,119; FGM: 572; Pct.: .511; FTA: 634; FTM: 495; Pct.: .780; OReb: 263; DReb: 542; TReb: 805; Ast.: 76; Stl.: 27; Blk.: 271; Pts.: 1,639; Ave.: 21.0 ppg.

Member of the NBA All-Rookie Team 1992-93.

There's not much to say about Mourning yet; he hasn't been in the league long enough. But the NBA's runner-up for the 1992-93 Rookie of the Year Award compiled first-year statistics that are better than the rookie years of those whose footsteps he's following — Georgetown predecessors Patrick Ewing and Dikembe Mutombo. And Mourning will only get better. Charlotte made its first-ever appearance in the NBA playoffs in 1992-93; the young team is on the rise, and with a few more key ingredients and experience, will be primed to make a run at a title soon. Teammate Larry Johnson and Alonzo Mourning will be the dominant forward/center combo of the 1990s.

If you really want to invest, pick up three 1992-93 Upper Deck wax packs for $1.50 each. Just let them sit until Mourning's career is over. Perhaps there'll be a Mourning card inside, which is valued at $4. Or, maybe inside there'll be a Shaquille O'Neal ($18) or Christian Laettner ($3) card. The set is loaded with top rookie cards; if any of those players pans out, an unopened wax pack will bring considerably more than $1.50. If Mourning's worst year in the league is his first, and he averages his first-year statistics for 15 years, there won't be too many centers with better career statistics. His $4 card will pay huge dividends by then.

Alonzo Mourning Checklist

Year	Company	No.	Price
1992-93	Fleer	311	2.50
1992-93	Fleer Ultra	193	7.00
1992-93	Fleer Ultra All-Rookies	6	30.00
1992-93	Fleer Ultra Rejectors	1	25.00
1992-93	NBA Hoops	361	3.00
1992-93	NBA Hoops Lottery mail in	2	50.00
1992-93	NBA Hoops Magic's All-Rookie	2	60.00
1992-93	SkyBox Draft Picks	2	20.00
1992-93	SkyBox	332	3.00
1992-93	Upper Deck	2	4.00
1992-93	Upper Deck Rookie Standouts	2	25.00

 # Joe Dumars

14) Joe Dumars: 1986-87 Fleer #27, $30; $27.50 in July 1991.

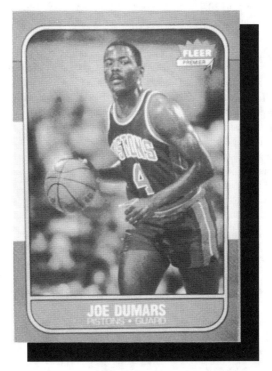

Joe Dumars

May 24, 1963; 6-3, 190; McNeese State University; drafted by Detroit in the first round in 1985, 18th overall; guard; active; eight seasons (all with Detroit).

Career statistics through 1992-93 season

G: 626; Min.: 21,446; FGA: 8,324; FGM: 3,959; Pct.: .475; FTA: 2,717; FTM: 2,308; Pct.: .849; OReb: 497; DReb: 896; TReb: 1,393; Ast.: 1,740; Stl.: 600; Blk.: 64; Pts.: 10,455; Ave.: 16.7 ppg.

171

All-NBA Second Team 1992-93; All-NBA Third Team 1989-90 and 1990-91; All-Defensive First Team 1988-89, 1989-90, 1992-93; All-Defensive Second Team 1990-91; 1988-89 and 1989-90 NBA championship team member; NBA playoff MVP 1988-89; NBA All-Rookie Team 1985-86.

Dumars has always been recognized as one of the top defenders in the league, oftentimes drawing the opponent's top player. Although he's been asked to concentrate on defense while with the Pistons, he can step it up on offense, too, as he did when needed while winning the MVP Award during the 1988-89 NBA Finals. Plus, his scoring average increased in each of his first six seasons too, from 9.4 ppg. to 20.4, then dropped a bit to 19.9 in 1991-92. In 1992-93 he increased his output again, to 23.5 ppg., and was selected to the All-NBA Second Team.

Although his card is at $30, it's perhaps a sleeper in the star-studded 1986-87 Fleer set. If Dumars remains in Detroit as his backcourt teammate, Isiah Thomas, closes in on retirement, Dumars will emerge from his teammate's shadow. If he plays for another six seasons or so at a 20 ppg. scoring clip, he would hit 20,000 career points, putting him in a select group in NBA history. If the Hall of Fame beckons, Dumars has two championship rings; that also puts him in an elite group among the Fleer 1986-87 class. This card might be a slow return on your investment, increasing only if Dumars compiles Hall-of-Fame-caliber numbers, but the card will at least retain its $30 value. If Dumars puts together another solid six seasons...

Joe Dumars Checklist

Year	Company	No.	Price
1986-87	Fleer	27	30.00
1987-88	Fleer	31	7.50
1988-89	Fleer	40	2.50
1989-90	Fleer	45	.50
1989-90	NBA Hoops	1	.30
1990-91	Fleer	55	.15
1990-91	NBA Hoops	3 (All-Star)	.10
1990-91	NBA Hoops	103	.15
1990-91	NBA Hoops	362 (Art)	.10
1990-91	SkyBox	84	.15
1990-91	SkyBox Mini	15	.50
1991-92	Fleer	59	.10
1991-92	Fleer Update	379 (Leaders)	.05
1991-92	NBA Hoops	60	.10
1991-92	NBA Hoops	250 (All-Star)	.10
1991-92	NBA Hoops	463 (Supreme Court)	.10
1991-92	SkyBox	81	.15
1991-92	SkyBox	565 (Magic of SkyBox)	.10
1991-92	Upper Deck	61 (All-Star)	.15
1991-92	Upper Deck	335	.15
1991-92	Upper Deck	459 (All-Star)	.15
1992-93	Fleer	63	.10
1992-93	Fleer All-Stars	4	1.25
1992-93	Fleer Ultra	56	.25
1992-93	NBA Hoops	64	.10
1992-93	NBA Hoops	296 (All-Star)	.07

 # Bernard King

15) Bernard King: 1978-79 Topps #75, $15; $15 in July 1991.

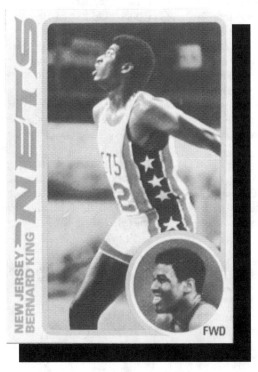

Bernard King

Dec. 4, 1956; 6-7, 205; University of Tennessee; drafted by New Jersey in first round as an undergraduate in 1977, seventh pick overall; active; 15 seasons

(New Jersey 1977-79; Utah 1979-80; Golden State 1980-82; New York 1982-87; Washington 1987-92; New Jersey 1992-93).

Career statistics through 1992-93 season

G: 874; Min.: 29,417; FGA: 15,109; FGM: 7,830 (20th); Pct. .518; FTA: 5,444 (32nd); FTM: 3,972 (35th); Pct.: .729; OReb: 1,704; DReb: 3,356; TReb: 5,060; Ast.: 2,863; Stl.: 866; Blk.: 230; Pts.: 19,655 (19th); Ave. 22.4 ppg. (17th).

All-NBA First Team in 1983-84, 1984-85; All-NBA Second Team in 1981-82; All-NBA Third Team in 1990-91; led NBA in scoring in 1984-85 (32.9); NBA All-Rookie Team in 1977-78; NBA Comeback Player of the Year in 1980-81, 1987-88.

King sustained a career-threatening knee injury in March 1985, missed the entire 1985-86 season, and was limited to just six games in 1986-87. After returning, he re-emerged as the dominant player he once was and his scoring average climbed from 20.7 ppg. in 1988-89 to 28.4 in 1990-91, when he was third in the league in scoring. The prolific scorer was also the NBA Comeback Player of the Year in 1980-81, having been limited to just 19 games in the 1979-80 season. Had he not missed 221 games during three seasons, King would have scored another 5,000 points, putting him in the top 10 all-time.

King, who became only the second player in NBA history to score at least 50 points on successive nights, scores quickly and effortlessly. A two-time comeback player of the year, he's overcome a serious knee injury and a drinking problem to recapture the skills which have made one of the game's best forwards.

Although King's card has held steady, $15 for the last two years, if you're banking on Adrian Dantley, Bob McAdoo and Alex English to make the Hall of Fame, you inevitably have to include Bernard King, too. You can buy any one of their rookie cards for less than $20, a real deal, considering their values will surely double if those players are in fact elected.

Bernard King Checklist

Year	Company	No.	Price
1978-79	Topps	75	15.00
1979-80	Topps	14	4.50
1981-82	Topps	W72	1.75
1983-84	Star Co.	61	12.00
1984	Star Co. All-Star Game	5	1.50
1984-85	Star Co. 5x7 Court Kings	23	5.00
1984-85	Star Co.	25	7.50
1984-85	Star Co.	284	5.00
1986	Star Court Kings	20	4.50
1986-87	Fleer	60	2.50
1988-89	Fleer	116	.75
1989-90	Fleer	159	.25
1989-90	NBA Hoops	240	.10
1990-91	Fleer	194	.10
1990-91	NBA Hoops	300	.07
1990-91	NBA Hoops	381	.07

Bernard King Checklist

Year	Company	No.	Price
1990-91	SkyBox	291	.10
1991-92	Fleer	208	.05
1991-92	NBA Hoops	218	.07
1991-92	NBA Hoops	254 (All-Star)	.10
1991-92	NBA Hoops	322 (Yearbook)	.05
1991-92	NBA Hoops	502 (Supreme Court)	.05
1991-92	SkyBox Mini	49	.35
1991-92	SkyBox	294	.10
1991-92	SkyBox	573 (Salutes)	.05
1991-92	Upper Deck	65	.07
1991-92	Upper Deck	365	.10
1992-93	SkyBox	252	.07
1992-93	Topps	11	.07
1992-93	Topps Gold	11	.50
1992-93	Topps Stadium Club	158	.20
1992-93	Upper Deck	286	.05

HOCKEY

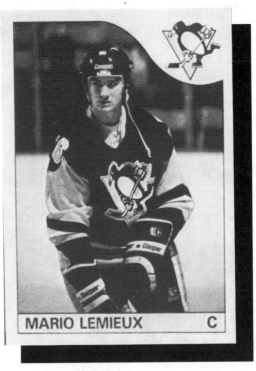

1 Mario Lemieux

Mario Lemieux: 1985-86 OPC #9, $375; $125 in July 1991.

Mario Lemieux

Oct. 5, 1965; 6-4, 210; the first choice in the 1984 entry draft, taken by Pittsburgh; center, shoots right; active; nine seasons (all with Pittsburgh).

Career statistics through the 1992-93 season
GP: 577; G: 477 (23rd); A: 697; TP: 1,174 (21st).

In French, "le mieux" means the best. "Super Mario" Lemieux is one of the great-est scorers in league history, reaching the 1,000-point milestone on March 24, 1992, his 513th career game. His goals-per-game average of .826 is the highest in National Hockey League history. He's a four-time Art Ross Trophy recipient for leading the NHL in scoring — in 1987-88 (70 goals/98 assists, 168 points), in 1988-89 (85 goals/114 assists, 199 points), in 1991-92 (44 goals/87 assists, 131 points, despite missing 16 games due to a bad back), and in 1992-93 (69 goals/91 assists, 160 points).

Although the superstar was diagnosed with Hodgkin's disease in 1993 and missed two months of the season, he captured his fourth scoring title in 1992-93 and capped the season by winning the Hart Memorial Trophy as the league's MVP. He also won the Masterton Trophy for his dedication to the sport.

Lemieux's 1984-85 rookie season was a sign of things to come. He was named MVP in the 1985 All-Star Game, tallying two goals and an assist in the Wales Conference's 6-4 win. At season's end he was awarded the Calder Trophy as the league's Rookie of the Year, becoming only the third rookie to score 100 points in a season, with 43 goals and 57 assists.

After winning his first Hart Memorial Trophy as the league's MVP in 1987-88, Lemieux ran off the second-longest point scoring streak in NHL history, notching at least one assist or goal in 46 straight games during the 1989-90 season. When the streak ended, he had recorded 39 goals and 64 assists for 103 points.

The Penguins' center, quick and mobile for his size, relies on his skating and passing skills. He threads his passes and possesses great anticipation. The record books are dotted with his single-season accomplishments — his 168 points in 1987-88 is the eighth highest total; his 85 goals in 1988-89 is fourth highest; his 114 assists in 1988-89 is tied for eighth; and his 13 shorthanded goals that season is a record. Lemieux has also scored eight points in a game twice.

But Lemieux, a second-team NHL All-Star in 1991-92 who has made the team five times, shines during games under the national spotlight, too. In front of his Pittsburgh fans during the 1990 All-Star Game, the hometown favorite scored four goals, leading the Wales Conference to a 12-7 win over the Campbell Conference. In doing so, he was named the game's MVP for the second consecutive time and third in his career.

Lemieux is also a two-time Conn Smythe winner as the playoff MVP, having led Pittsburgh to consecutive Stanley Cup titles. His 44 points in the 1991 playoffs were three shy of Wayne Gretzky's record. His 34 points, including five winning goals in 15 games (despite his missing five games with a broken hand) led the playoffs, too.

As Gretzky's career winds down, Lemieux, 27, has emerged as the fans' favorite. He's as popular as Gretzky, and, as his popularity has increased, his card value has skyrocketed, too, especially the last two years. He's two seasons away from cracking the top 10 in career scoring. If he can stay healthy, and he says his health is fine now, Lemieux could make a run at Marcel Dionne's third spot (1,850) with seven 100-point seasons.

Mario Lemieux Checklist

Year	Company	No.	Price
1985-86	O-Pee-Chee	9	375.00
1985-86	O-Pee-Chee	262	55.00
1985-86	Topps	9	175.00
1986-87	O-Pee-Chee/Topps	122	75.00/50.00
1987-88	O-Pee-Chee/Topps	15	35.00/25.00
1988-89	O-Pee-Chee/Topps	1	15.00/10.00
1989-90	O-Pee-Chee/Topps	1	1.50/2.50
1989-90	O-Pee-Chee	319 (Trophy)	.75
1989-90	O-Pee-Chee	327 (Highlight)	.75
1990-91	Bowman	204	.75
1990-91	O-Pee-Chee	175	1.00
1990-91	O-Pee-Chee Premier	63	6.00
1990-91	Pro Set	236	.50
1990-91	Pro Set	362 (All-Star)	.30
1990-91	Score American/Canadian	2	1.00/1.50
1990-91	Score American/Canadian	337 (Sniper)	.40/.50
1990-91	Score 100 Stars	34	.30
1990-91	Topps	175	.60
1990-91	Upper Deck English/French	59	.50/1.00
1990-91	Upper Deck English/French	144	2.50/3.50
1990-91	Upper Deck English/French	305 (Team)	.40/.75
1991-92	Bowman	87	.75
1991-92	Bowman	425 (Playoff MVP)	.30
1991-92	O-Pee-Chee	153	.75
1991-92	O-Pee-Chee	523 (Trophy)	.25
1991-92	O-Pee-Chee Premier	114	1.50
1991-92	Parkhurst English/French	137	1.75/2.25
1991-92	Pro Set English/French	194	.75
1991-92	Pro Set English/French	318 (Trophy)	.30
1991-92	Pro Set English/French	581 (Captain)	.15
1991-92	Pro Set Platinum	91	1.00
1991-92	Score American	200	1.00
1991-92	Score American	335 (Franchise)	.30
1991-92	Score American	426 (Trophy)	.30
1991-92	Score Canadian/Bilingual	200	1.00
1991-92	Score Canadian/Bilingual	316 (Trophy)	.50
1991-92	Score Canadian/Bilingual	365 (Franchise)	.50
1991-92	Score Pinnacle English/French	1	2.00
1991-92	Score Pinnacle English/French	380 (Technician)	.25
1991-92	Topps	153	.60
1991-92	Topps	523 (Trophy)	.25
1991-92	Topps Stadium Club	174	4.00
1991-92	Upper Deck English/French	45 (50/50 Club)	.75
1991-92	Upper Deck English/French	47 (White House)	.50
1991-92	Upper Deck English/French	156	1.00
1991-92	Upper Deck English/French	611 (All-Star)	.75
1992-93	Bowman	189	2.00
1992-93	Bowman	233	4.50
1992-93	Bowman	440 (Trophy)	4.00
1992-93	Fleer Ultra	165	1.75
1992-93	O-Pee-Chee	138	.75
1992-93	O-Pee-Chee	240	.50
1992-93	O-Pee-Chee	292	3.00
1992-93	Parkhurst	136	1.25
1992-93	Parkhurst	462 (All-Star)	.75
1992-93	Pro Set	1	.60
1992-93	Pro Set	139	.50
1992-93	Score Canadian/U.S.	390	.75
1992-93	Score Canadian/U.S.	413 (Leader)	.25
1992-93	Score Canadian/U.S.	433 (Franchise)	.25

Mario Lemieux Checklist

Year	Company	No.	Price
1992-93	Score Canadian/U.S.	448 (Highlight)	.25
1992-93	Score Canadian/U.S.	519 (Trophy)	.25
1992-93	Score Pinnacle	300	1.75
1992-93	Topps	212	.75
1992-93	Topps	265 (All-Star)	.50
1992-93	Topps Stadium Club	94	1.75
1992-93	Topps Stadium Club	251 (Members Only)	2.00
1992-93	Upper Deck	26	.90
1992-93	Upper Deck	433 (Award)	.50
1992-93	Upper Deck	436 (Award)	.50

 # Dale Hawerchuk

Dale Hawerchuk: 1982-83 OPC #380, $25; $10 in July 1991.

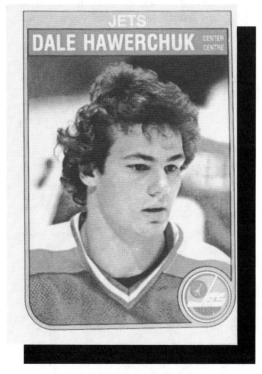

Dale Hawerchuk

April 4, 1963; 5-11, 190; Winnipeg's first choice in the 1981 entry draft, first overall; center, shoots left; active; 12 seasons (1981-90 Winnipeg, 1990-93 Buffalo).

Career statistics through the 1992-93 season
GP: 951; G: 449 (27th); A: 763 (17th); TP: 1,212 (16th).

Hawerchuk's rookie card is a steal at $25; it's probably the best buy in all of sports cards. The center, in his 13th NHL season, has scored more than 1,200 points in his career and is one of the top active scorers in the league. Although he notched his 1,000 career point against Chicago on March 8, 1991, the center has been overshadowed by Wayne Gretzky, Mario Lemieux and Mark Messier, plus he played for Winnipeg (the Houston Astros of the NHL) for his first nine seasons. Hawerchuk is another Hall-of-Famer in waiting.

Four times, Hawerchuk, an ironman, has tied for the league lead in games played in a season with 80, and has played in every game seven times in his career. His 75 assists in 1991-92 is a Buffalo record, and his five assists in a game against New Jersey on Jan. 15, 1992, tied the team record. The five-time team captain for Winnipeg also holds many career offensive records for the Jets, too.

A 1982 Calder Trophy Winner as the league's Rookie of the Year (45 goals/ 58 assists, for 103 points), Hawerchuk had a record five assists in one period against Los Angeles on March 6, 1984. He's 52 assists away from moving into the top 10 all-time.

Dale Hawerchuk Checklist

Year	Company	No.	Price
1982-83	O-Pee-Chee	3 (Record Breaker)	6.00
1982-83	O-Pee-Chee	374 (Team Leaders)	3.00
1982-83	O-Pee-Chee	380	25.00
1982-83	O-Pee-Chee	381 (In Action)	5.00
1983-84	O-Pee-Chee	377 (Team Leaders)	3.00
1983-84	O-Pee-Chee	385	5.00
1984-85	O-Pee-Chee	339	3.00
1984-85	O-Pee-Chee	393 (Record Breaker)	2.50
1984-85	Topps	152	1.50
1985-86	O-Pee-Chee/Topps	109	2.00/1.50
1986-87	O-Pee-Chee/Topps	74	1.50/.75
1987-88	O-Pee-Chee/Topps	149	1.20/1.00
1988-89	O-Pee-Chee/Topps	65	.75/.40
1989-90	O-Pee-Chee/Topps	122	.15/.12
1990-91	Bowman	129	.10
1990-91	O-Pee-Chee	141	.12
1990-91	O-Pee-Chee Premier	40	.12
1990-91	Pro Set	330	.10
1990-91	Pro Set	415	.10
1990-91	Score American/Canadian	50	.10/.12
1990-91	Score Traded	2	.10
1990-91	Topps	141	.10
1990-91	Upper Deck English/French	53	.10/.12
1990-91	Upper Deck English/French	443	.10/.12
1991-92	Bowman	31	.07

Dale Hawerchuk Checklist

Year	Company	No.	Price
1991-92	O-Pee-Chee	65	.07
1991-92	O-Pee-Chee Premier	1	.07
1991-92	Parkhurst English/French	18	.05/.07
1991-92	Parkhurst English/French	216 (1,000 pts.)	.10/.12
1991-92	Pro Set English/French	24	.05/.07
1991-92	Pro Set Platinum	11	.07
1991-92	Score American	259	.05
1991-92	Score American	376 (1,000 pts.)	.05
1991-92	Score Canadian	266 (1,000 pts.)	.10
1991-92	Score Canadian	479	.07
1991-92	Score Pinnacle English/French	80	.05/.07
1991-92	Topps	65	.05
1991-92	Topps Stadium Club	312	.05
1991-92	Upper Deck English/French	12 (Canada)	.05/.07
1991-92	Upper Deck English/French	79 (Team)	.05/.07
1991-92	Upper Deck English/French	126	.05/.07
1992-93	Bowman	308	.25
1992-93	Fleer Ultra	15	.15
1992-93	Parkhurst	11	.10
1992-93	Pro Set	12	.07
1992-93	Score Canadian/U.S.	272	.07
1992-93	Topps	296	.05
1992-93	Topps Stadium Club	419	.07
1992-93	Upper Deck	302	.10

3 Steve Yzerman

Steve Yzerman: 1984-85 OPC #67, $60; $40 in July 1991.

May 9, 1965; 5-11, 183; was the fourth player drafted overall in the 1983 draft, by Detroit; center, shoots right; active; 10 seasons (all with Detroit).

Career statistics through the 1992-93 season
GP: 757; G: 445 (29th); A: 595; TP: 1,040.

Yzerman, known as "Steve Wonder" by Red Wing Coach Jacques Demers, scored his 1,000th point during the 1991-92 season with Detroit. A 10-year veteran, he has played in seven straight All-Star games, but has yet to earn a first- or second-team all-star berth. His peers voted him the NHL's Most Outstanding Player in 1988-89, garnering him the Lester B. Pearson Award.

The exciting center is one of the league's most dangerous penalty killers; he led the NHL in shorthanded goals (8) in 1991-92 and led his team in scoring during the season, his sixth straight time in doing so. In 1988-89 the team captain set club records for most goals (65), assists (90) and points (155) for a season. He also holds the club record for most goals (37) and points (87) for a rookie, accomplished in 1983-84, when he led all NHL rookies in scoring. He was the runner-up in 1984 for the Calder Trophy as the league's Rookie of the Year.

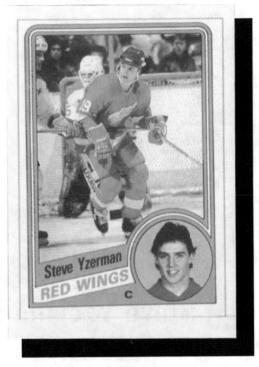

Steve Yzerman

Yzerman, who will enter the top 30 all-time in points in 1993-94, has the 13th highest total ever in a season — 155 points in 1988-89, on 65 goals and 90 assists. His 65 goals that season ranks 22nd. Yzerman's rookie card is only nine years old; there's plenty of room for it to continue increasing in value. Give it another 10 years or so, and then cash it in when it's surely more than $100.

Steve Yzerman Checklist

Year	Company	No.	Price
1984-85	O-Pee-Chee	67	60.00
1984-85	O-Pee-Chee	385 (Leaders)	8.50
1984-85	Topps	49	20.00
1985-86	O-Pee-Chee/Topps	29	20.00/15.00
1986-87	O-Pee-Chee/Topps	11	15.00/8.00
1987-88	O-Pee-Chee/Topps	56	6.50/3.50
1988-89	O-Pee-Chee/Topps	196	2.50/1.50
1989-90	O-Pee-Chee/Topps	83	.75/.50
1990-91	Bowman	233	.35
1990-91	O-Pee-Chee	222	.35
1990-91	O-Pee-Chee Premier	130	1.25
1990-91	Pro Set	79	.35

Steve Yzerman Checklist

Year	Company	No.	Price
1990-91	Pro Set	347 (All-Star)	.25
1990-91	Score American/Canadian	3	.30/.35
1990-91	Score American/Canadian	339 (Magician)	.10/.12
1990-91	Topps	222	.25
1990-91	Upper Deck English/French	56	.60/.75
1990-91	Upper Deck English/French	303 (Team)	.20/.25
1990-91	Upper Deck English/French	477 (All-Star)	.25/.35
1991-92	Bowman	41 (Hat Trick)	.10
1991-92	Bowman	42	.25
1991-92	O-Pee-Chee	424	.25
1991-92	O-Pee-Chee Premier	73	.60
1991-92	O-Pee-Chee Premier	142 (Team)	.05
1991-92	Parkhurst English/French	44	.40/.45
1991-92	Pro Set English/French	62	.25
1991-92	Pro Set English/French	281 (All-Star)	.10
1991-92	Pro Set English/French	571 (Captain)	.10
1991-92	Pro Set Platinum	32	.25
1991-92	Score American/Canadian	190	.25
1991-92	Score American	419 (Franchise)	.10
1991-92	Score Canadian	335 (Franchise)	.10
1991-92	Score Pinnacle English/French	75	.50/.60
1991-92	Topps	424	.25
1991-92	Topps Stadium Club	81	1.00
1991-92	Upper Deck English/French	146	.30/.45
1991-92	Upper Deck English	626 (All-Star)	.15
1992-93	Bowman	103	.75
1992-93	Bowman	220	3.00
1992-93	Fleer Ultra	55	.30
1992-93	O-Pee-Chee	61	.15
1992-93	O-Pee-Chee	321	.50
1992-93	Parkhurst	44	.25
1992-93	Parkhurst	456 (All-Star)	.20
1992-93	Pro Set	39	.15
1992-93	Pro Set	247	.10
1992-93	Score Canadian/U.S.	400	.15
1992-93	Score Canadian/U.S.	423 (Franchise)	.10
1992-93	Score Pinnacle	241	.30
1992-93	Score Pinnacle	258	.15
1992-93	Score Pinnacle	350	.25
1992-93	Topps	207	.15
1992-93	Topps Stadium Club	19	.30
1992-93	Topps Stadium Club	254 (Members Choice)	.25
1992-93	Upper Deck	155	.20

 Guy Lafleur

Guy Lafleur: 1971-72 OPC #148, $200; $150 in July 1991.

Sept. 20, 1951; 6-0; 185; drafted by Montreal as the first pick overall in the 1971 draft; right wing, shoots right; retired; 17 seasons (Montreal 1971-85, New York Rangers 1988-89, Quebec 1989-91); Hall of Fame 1988.

GP: 1,126; G: 560 (8th); A: 793 (13th); TP: 1,353 (8th).

He's not at the top of all the record lists, but Guy Lafleur holds one distinction that makes him an elitist among the 200 players in the Hockey Hall of Fame — he played NHL hockey after he was enshrined. Lafleur, the consummate talent, retired after the 1984-85 season and was elected to the Hall in 1988. But he returned to the ice in 1988-89 for one season with the New York Rangers and then two seasons with Quebec.

Guy Lafleur

The dazzling Montreal winger was a three-time scoring champion, two-time MVP, and six-time All-Star. He led the Canadians to four straight Stanley Cups from 1976-79 and played on five winners. When the Canadians swept the Boston Bruins for the Stanley Cup in 1977, Lafleur won the Conn Smythe Trophy as the MVP. His 134 points in 128 playoff games ranks 18th all-time.

The right winger was awarded the Hart Memorial Trophy as the league's MVP in 1976-77 (56 goals/80 assists, for a league-leading 136 points) and again in 1977-78 (60 goals/72 assists, for a league-leading 132 points). In addition to winning the Art Ross Trophy as the league's leading scorer those two seasons, he preceded them with a league-leading 125 points in 1975-76, on 56 goals and

69 assists. He's the first player in NHL history to have six straight 50-or-more-goal seasons, from 1975-80.

Lafleur, who relied on stickhandling and skating skills, consistently turned "situations" into victories. As one of the game's fastest skaters, he displayed a dazzling speed and agility and never let up. He transcends statistics and standings; the revered, graceful Hall of Famer made the game an art form when he played. He ranks with Mike Bossy and Lanny McDonald as one of the best right wingers ever, ranks with Reed Larson and Larry Robinson as having one of the best slapshots, and his stickhandling skills were comparable to those of Gilbert Perreault and Marcel Dionne. Lafleur had as much natural talent as Wayne Gretzky and Perreault, and as such, was one of the most exciting players of his era.

At $200, this card will take a long time to offer a healthy return on your initial investment. But the NHL's popularity continues to increase during the 1990s, 1970s cards will always be scarce, and Lafleur will always be considered the player of the 1970s. So get his card now, before the younger hockey fans, as they trace hockey history, with money in their hands for cards, realize Lafleur's importance and impact on the game.

Guy Lafleur Checklist

Year	Company	No.	Price
1971-72	O-Pee-Chee	148	200.00
1972-73	O-Pee-Chee	59	60.00
1972-73	Topps	79	50.00
1973-74	O-Pee-Chee/Topps	72	20.00
1974-75	O-Pee-Chee/Topps	232	20.00/15.00
1975-76	O-Pee-Chee/Topps	126	17.50/15.00
1975-76	O-Pee-Chee/Topps	208 (Leaders)	5.00/3.00
1975-76	O-Pee-Chee/Topps	290 (All-Star)	6.00/3.00
1975-76	O-Pee-Chee/Topps	322 (Team Leaders)	4.00/2.00
1976-77	O-Pee-Chee/Topps	1 (Leaders)	3.50/2.00
1976-77	O-Pee-Chee/Topps	3 (Leaders)	3.00/2.00
1976-77	O-Pee-Chee/Topps	5 (Leaders)	3.00/2.50
1976-77	O-Pee-Chee/Topps	163 (All-Star)	14.00/10.00
1976-77	O-Pee-Chee	388 (Team Leaders)	2.50
1977-78	O-Pee-Chee/Topps	1 (Leaders)	3.00/2.00
1977-78	O-Pee-Chee/Topps	2 (Leaders)	2.00/1.50
1977-78	O-Pee-Chee/Topps	3 (Leaders)	2.00/2.00
1977-78	O-Pee-Chee/Topps	7 (Leaders)	2.00/1.50
1977-78	O-Pee-Chee/Topps	200 (All-Star)	10.00/7.00
1977-78	O-Pee-Chee/Topps	214 (Record Breaker)	3.00/1.75
1977-78	O-Pee-Chee/Topps	216 (Record Breaker)	3.00/1.75
1977-78	O-Pee-Chee/Topps	218 (Record Breaker)	3.00/1.75
1978-79	O-Pee-Chee/Topps	3 (Record Breaker)	3.00/2.00
1978-79	O-Pee-Chee/Topps	63 (Leaders)	2.50/1.50
1978-79	O-Pee-Chee/Topps	64 (Leaders)	2.00/1.50
1978-79	O-Pee-Chee/Topps	65 (Leaders)	2.00/1.50
1978-79	O-Pee-Chee/Topps	69 (Leaders)	2.00/1.50
1978-79	O-Pee-Chee/Topps	90 (All-Star)	5.00/4.00
1978-79	O-Pee-Chee	326 (All-Star)	3.00
1979-80	O-Pee-Chee/Topps	1 (Leaders)	3.50/2.50
1979-80	O-Pee-Chee/Topps	2 (Leaders)	2.00/2.00
1979-80	O-Pee-Chee/Topps	3 (Leaders)	2.00/2.00

Guy Lafleur Checklist

Year	Company	No.	Price
1979-80	O-Pee-Chee/Topps	7 (Leaders)	2.00/2.00
1979-80	O-Pee-Chee/Topps	200 (All-Star)	4.50/3.50
1980-81	O-Pee-Chee/Topps	10	4.00/3.00
1980-81	O-Pee-Chee/Topps	82 (All-Star)	2.50/1.50
1980-81	O-Pee-Chee/Topps	162 (Leaders)	15.00/10.00
1980-81	O-Pee-Chee/Topps	163 (Leaders)	15.00/10.00
1980-81	O-Pee-Chee/Topps	216 (Team Leaders)	1.00/.75
1981-82	O-Pee-Chee	177	2.50
1981-82	O-Pee-Chee	195 (In Action)	1.00
1981-82	Topps	19	2.50
1982-83	O-Pee-Chee	186	2.00
1982-83	O-Pee-Chee	187 (In Action)	.75
1983-84	O-Pee-Chee	183 (In Action)	.50
1983-84	O-Pee-Chee	189	1.50
1984-85	O-Pee-Chee	264	.1.50
1984-85	O-Pee-Chee	360 (Team Leaders)	.50
1984-85	Topps	81	1.50
1989-90	O-Pee-Chee/Topps	189	.15/.25
1990-91	O-Pee-Chee/Topps	142	.10
1990-91	O-Pee-Chee Premier	55	.30
1990-91	Pro Set	250	.10
1990-91	Score American/Canadian	290	.10/.15
1990-91	Score 100 Stars	96	.12
1990-91	Upper Deck English/French	162	.15/.25
1991-92	O-Pee-Chee/Topps	1 (Tribute)	.10
1991-92	O-Pee-Chee/Topps	2 (Tribute)	.10
1991-92	O-Pee-Chee/Topps	3 (Tribute)	.10
1991-92	Pro Set English/French	317 (All-Star)	.15
1991-92	Score American	401 (Tribute)	.10
1991-92	Score American	402 (Tribute)	.10
1991-92	Score American	403 (Tribute)	.10
1991-92	Score Canadian	291 (Tribute)	.10
1991-92	Score Canadian	292 (Tribute)	.10
1991-92	Score Canadian	293 (Tribute)	.10
1991-92	Upper Deck French/English	219	.15/.10
1991-92	Upper Deck English	638 (Heroes)	.10

 # 5 Mike Bossy

Mike Bossy: 1978-79 OPC #115, $70; $40 in July 1991.

Jan. 22, 1957; 6-0, 186; drafted by the New York Islanders in the first round of the 1977 draft, 15th overall; right wing, shoots right; retired; 10 seasons (all with New York Islanders, 1977-87); Hall of Fame 1991.

GP: 752; G: 573 (7th); A: 553 TP: 1,126 (24th).

If you need a shooter, Bossy's the man. Ranking with Guy Lafleur and Lanny McDonald as one of the best right wingers ever, Bossy holds records for most assists by a right wing, 83, and most points, 147, in a season, accomplished in 1981-82.

The burly Islander was a machine who, possessing the quickest release in the game, could fire off hard, accurate shots with his wrists. The instinctive Bossy had a sixth sense around the net and could execute off of it. With his uncanny ability, the winger could package goals like no one else before; his first 100 goals came faster than anyone else's in history, and he never went more than six games without scoring a goal. He scored 50+ goals in each of his first nine seasons, a record.

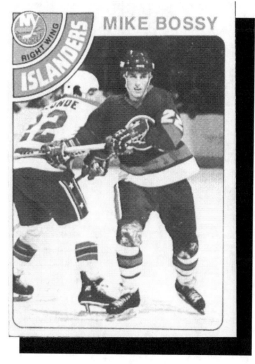

Mike Bossy

A key member of the famed New York Islanders team that won four consecutive Stanley Cup championships in the beginning of the 1980s, Bossy won the Conn Smythe Trophy in 1981-82 as the Stanley Cup MVP. He played in 129 playoff games, scoring 85 goals (4th) and adding 75 assists, for 160 points (8th).

Bossy, who was elected to the Hockey Hall of Fame in 1991, is seventh all-time in goals scored with 573. He posted the 17th-best offensive year ever in the NHL, scoring 147 points in 1981-82. His 69 goals in 1978-79 ranks 15th for a single season, while his 68 in 1980-81 (including a record nine hat-trick games) is tied for 17th, and his 64 in 1981-82 ranks 23rd.

In 1977-78, Bossy set a league record for most goals (53) by a rookie, including 25 power play goals, and added 38 assists for 91 points. He was named the NHL's Rookie of the Year that season, winning the Calder Trophy. The Hall of Famer is also a three-time winner of the Lady Byng Memorial Trophy for sportsmanship (1982-83, 1983-84, 1985-86).

Bossy, who played under the New York media for his entire career, has always been one of the game's most popular players; anyone who knows anything about hockey has heard of him. His rookie card is the key card in the 1978-79 O-Pee-Chee set and will always be its most valuable card.

Mike Bossy Checklist

Year	Company	No.	Price
1978-79	O-Pee-Chee/Topps	1 (Record Breaker)	10.00/8.00
1978-79	O-Pee-Chee/Topps	63 (Leaders)	2.50/1.50
1978-79	O-Pee-Chee/Topps	115	70.00/60.00
1979-80	O-Pee-Chee/Topps	1 (Leaders)	3.50/2.50
1979-80	O-Pee-Chee/Topps	5 (Leaders)	2.50/1.50
1979-80	O-Pee-Chee/Topps	7 (Leaders)	2.00/2.00
1979-80	O-Pee-Chee/Topps	161 (Record Breaker)	4.50/2.00
1979-80	O-Pee-Chee/Topps	230 (All-Star)	20.00/12.00
1980-81	O-Pee-Chee/Topps	25	8.00/6.00
1980-81	O-Pee-Chee/Topps	204 (Team Leaders)	3.00/2.00
1981-82	O-Pee-Chee	198	5.00
1981-82	O-Pee-Chee	208 (In Action)	1.50
1981-82	O-Pee-Chee	219 (Team Leaders)	.75
1981-82	O-Pee-Chee	382 (Leaders)	1.75
1981-82	O-Pee-Chee	386 (Leaders)	1.75
1981-82	O-Pee-Chee	388 (Leaders)	1.75
1981-82	O-Pee-Chee	390 (Record Breaker)	1.75
1981-82	Topps	4	3.00
1981-82	Topps	57 (Team Leaders)	.60
1981-82	Topps	East 125 (In Action)	1.50
1982-83	O-Pee-Chee	2 (Record Breaker)	1.75
1982-83	O-Pee-Chee	197 (Team Leaders)	1.00
1982-83	O-Pee-Chee	199	3.00
1983-84	O-Pee-Chee	1 (Team Leaders)	1.50
1983-84	O-Pee-Chee	3	2.00
1983-84	O-Pee-Chee	205 (Trophy)	1.50
1983-84	O-Pee-Chee	210 (Record Breaker)	4.00
1984-85	O-Pee-Chee	122	2.00
1984-85	O-Pee-Chee	209 (All-Star)	1.00
1984-85	O-Pee-Chee	362 (Team Leaders)	1.00
1984-85	O-Pee-Chee	376 (Trophy)	1.25
1984-85	Topps	91	1.50
1984-85	Topps	155 (All-Star)	.75
1985-86	O-Pee-Chee/Topps	130	1.75/1.50
1986-87	O-Pee-Chee/Topps	90	1.50/1.25
1987-88	O-Pee-Chee/Topps	105	1.00/1.00
1990-91	Pro Set	650	.15/.15

 # Larry Robinson

Larry Robinson: 1973-74 OPC #237, $75; $35 in July 1991.

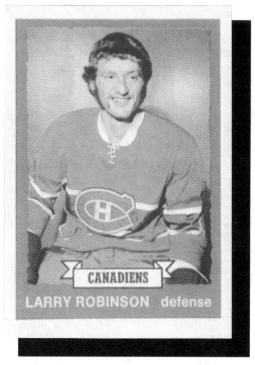

Larry Robinson

June 2, 1951; 6-4, 225; Montreal's fourth pick in the 1971 draft, 20th overall; defenseman, shoots left; retired; 20 seasons (Montreal 1972-89, Los Angeles 1989-92).

GP: 1,384 (9th); G: 208; A: 750 (19th); TP: 958.

Robinson can be considered one of the grand old men of hockey; he played for 21 years, mainly with the Montreal Canadians. One of the league's all-time best defenders, he compares favorably with Hall of Famer Doug Harvey, Montreal's pre-Bobby Orr consensus pick as all-time defenseman.

As the prototype for his position, Robinson 6-4, 225, was strong, tough and mobile. He used his size to his advantage; the hard-hitter could play a checking game, or wide open. The consummate defenseman, perhaps as complete a defenseman who has ever played the game, moved well without the puck, but could handle it well enough to play forward, too, leading the attack.

The two-time James Norris Memorial Trophy winner as the league's most outstanding defenseman (1976-77, 1979-80) is one of the all-time leaders for scoring by a defenseman with 958 total points, trailing only Denis Potvin's 1,052 and surpassing Bobby Orr and Brad Park. He also owns one of the game's best slapshots, along with Reed Larson and Guy Lafleur.

A three-time first-team All-Star, "Big Bird" was a leader on six Stanley Cup champion teams with the Canadians, winning the Conn Smythe Trophy in 1977-78 as the Stanley Cup MVP. His 227 playoff appearances is a record, while his 116 assists ranks third. His 144 playoff points is 14th.

Robinson's rookie card is 20 years old, so it's scarce. It's not going to sky-rocket in five or so years when Robinson enters the Hall of Fame, but it will be on its way to doubling in value, and will do so during the next 10 years, for sure.

Larry Robinson Checklist

Year	Company	No.	Price
1973-74	O-Pee-Chee	237	75.00
1974-75	O-Pee-Chee	280	25.00
1975-76	O-Pee-Chee/Topps	241	10.00/7.50
1976-77	O-Pee-Chee/Topps	151	7.00/5.00
1977-78	O-Pee-Chee/Topps	30 (All-Star)	5.00/3.50
1978-79	O-Pee-Chee/Topps	210	2.50/1.50
1978-79	O-Pee-Chee	329 (All-Star)	.75
1979-80	O-Pee-Chee/Topps	50 (All-Star)	1.25/1.00
1980-81	O-Pee-Chee/Topps	84 (All-Star)	1.00/.75
1980-81	O-Pee-Chee/Topps	230	1.25/1.00
1981-82	O-Pee-Chee	179	1.00
1981-82	O-Pee-Chee	196 (In Action)	.40
1981-82	Topps	31	.40
1982-83	O-Pee-Chee	191	.75
1983-84	O-Pee-Chee	195	.50
1984-85	O-Pee-Chee	270	.40
1984-85	Topps	82	.40
1985-86	O-Pee-Chee/Topps	147	.50/.40
1986-87	O-Pee-Chee/Topps	62	.40/.30
1987-88	O-Pee-Chee/Topps	192	.30/.30
1988-89	O-Pee-Chee	246	.15
1989-90	O-Pee-Chee	235	.10
1990-91	Bowman	150	.10
1990-91	O-Pee-Chee/Topps	261	.10/.10
1990-91	Pro Set	125	.15
1990-91	Score American/Canadian	260	.10/.10
1990-91	Upper Deck English/French	52	.20/.75
1991-92	Bowman	177	.10
1991-92	O-Pee-Chee	458	.10
1991-92	Parkhurst English/French	74	.10/.15
1991-92	Pro Set English/French	104	.10/.15
1991-92	Score American	291	.10
1991-92	Score Canadian	511	.10
1991-92	Score Pinnacle English/French	208	.12/.12

Larry Robinson Checklist

Year	Company	No.	Price
1991-92	Score Pinnacle English/French	403 (Sidelines)	.12/.12
1991-92	Topps	458	.10
1991-92	Topps Stadium Club	252	.15
1991-92	Upper Deck English/French	499	.15/.30
1992-93	Bowman	215	.30
1992-93	O-Pee-Chee	167	.25

 **Gilbert Perreault**

Gilbert Perreault: 1970-71 O-Pee-Chee #131, $85; $60 in July 1991.

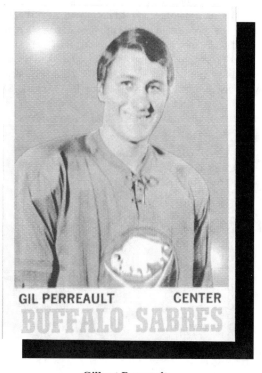

Gilbert Perreault

Nov. 13, 1950; 6-1, 195; drafted by Buffalo as the first player taken in the 1970 draft; center, shoots left; retired; 17 seasons (1970-87, all with Buffalo); Hall of Fame 1990.

GP: 1,191; G: 512 (15th); A: 814 (10th); TP: 1,326 (9th).

Looking for another Hall-of-Fame value? Perreault is one. One of the top 10 scorers in NHL history with 1,326 points, Perreault played his entire 17-year career with the Buffalo Sabres. He's the team's all-time leading scorer in every offensive category and is often overlooked among beginning collectors.

A superb skater and puckhandler, the Sabre scored 512 goals to rank 15th all-time. His 1,326 in 17 years with Buffalo ranks ninth. Elected to the Hall of Fame in 1990, Perreault is considered as good as Marcel Dionne and Guy Lafleur at stickhandling. His natural talent compares favorably with that of Wayne Gretzky and Lafleur, and his acceleration has been compared with Bobby Orr's.

The flashy, hard-working center won the Calder Trophy in 1971 as the league's Rookie of the Year, scoring 72 points on 38 goals (both records at the time) and 34 assists. He followed that award with the Lady Byng Memorial Trophy in 1972-73 for sportsmanship, and led his team to its first appearance in the Stanley Cup playoffs. Along with Rick Martin and Rene Robert, he formed part of Buffalo's "French Connection," a feared scoring line.

This card won't make any dramatic jumps in value, but Perreault is a Hall of Famer; that, coupled with the fact he's in a 1970-71 O-Pee-Chee set valued at $1,100 — with rookie cards for Brad Park ($60), Bobby Clark ($135) and Darryl Sittler ($100) — will keep his card in demand as one of the big-ticket cards from that set.

Gilbert Perreault Checklist

Year	Company	No.	Price
1970-71	O-Pee-Chee/Topps	131	85.00/65.00
1971-72	O-Pee-Chee/Topps	60	35.00/20.00
1971-72	O-Pee-Chee	246 (Trophy)	10.00
1972-73	O-Pee-Chee	136	20.00
1972-73	Topps	120	9.00
1973-74	O-Pee-Chee/Topps	70	9.00/5.00
1974-75	O-Pee-Chee/Topps	25	7.50/6.00
1975-76	O-Pee-Chee/Topps	10	5.00/3.00
1976-77	O-Pee-Chee/Topps	3 (Leaders)	3.00/2.00
1976-77	O-Pee-Chee/Topps	180 (All-Star)	3.00/2.00
1976-77	O-Pee-Chee/Topps	214 (French Connection)	3.50/2.50
1976-77	O-Pee-Chee/Topps	381 (Team Leaders)	1.75/1.00
1977-78	O-Pee-Chee/Topps	7 (Leaders)	2.00/1.50
1977-78	O-Pee-Chee/Topps	210 (All-Star)	5.00/2.00
1978-79	O-Pee-Chee/Topps	130	2.00/1.50
1979-8O	O-Pee-Chee/Topps	180	2.50/2.00
1980-81	O-Pee-Chee/Topps	80	2.25/1.50
1981-82	O-Pee-Chee	30	.75
1982-83	O-Pee-Chee	25 (Team Leaders)	.25
1982-83	O-Pee-Chee	30	.50
1983-84	O-Pee-Chee	67	.40
1984-85	O-Pee-Chee	24	.35
1984-85	Topps	19	.25

Gilbert Perreault Checklist

Year	Company	No.	Price
1985-86	O-Pee-Chee	160	.35
1985-86	Topps	160	.30
1986-87	O-Pee-Chee/Topps	79	.30/.25

 # Bob Gainey

Bob Gainey: 1974-75 OPC #388, $20; $5 in July 1991.

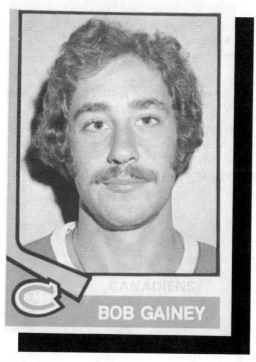

Bob Gainey

Dec. 13, 1953; 6-2, 200; eighth player taken in the 1973 draft; defenseman, shoots left; retired; 16 seasons (all with Montreal, from 1973-89); Hall of Fame 1992.

GP: 1,160; G: 239; A: 262; Pts: 501.

Do you want a Hall of Famer who you can get for $20? How about Bob Gainey? Elected to the Hall in 1992, Gainey was not known for his scoring as much as his defense and very physical play. No checker controlled the game as well as Gainey, one of the game's best technical, mechanically-perfect players, did. Gainey ranks with Bobby Clarke and Doug Risenbrough as one of the best fore-checkers in the game, and ranks with Clarke and Al MacAdam as one of the better back-checkers ever.

His play inspired the establishment of the Frank J. Selke Trophy for the NHL's best defensive forward, an award he's won four times. But he was never named to a post-season All-Star team.

Not many could catch Gainey, who was usually the one doing the catching. Gainey, along with Craig Ramsay and Don Luce, was one of the best penalty killers in the league, and controlled opponents with a straightjacket defense. He would often draw the top right wing guns for each team, but could score 30 goals in a season if his role had been changed.

Gainey, who appeared in 182 playoff games (fifth all-time), played on five Stanley Cup winners. He was the 1978-79 Conn Smythe Trophy winner as the Stanley Cup MVP.

The 1974-75 O-Pee-Chee set is at $500 and includes rookie cards for three Hall of Famers — Denis Potvin, Lanny McDonald and Gainey. Gainey's card, at $20, lags behind Potvin's ($55) and McDonald's ($45), but as their cards, and the set, appreciate, Gainey's will increase too; it has more room to do so than the other two's cards do. Thus, you can double your money faster with Gainey.

Bob Gainey Checklist

Year	Company	No.	Price
1974-75	O-Pee-Chee	388	20.00
1975-76	O-Pee-Chee/Topps	278	5.00/2.50
1976-77	O-Pee-Chee/Topps	44 1	.25/.75
1977-78	O-Pee-Chee/Topps	129	1.00/.75
1978-79	O-Pee-Chee/Topps	76	.75/.50
1979-80	O-Pee-Chee/Topps	170	.50/.40
1980-81	O-Pee-Chee/Topps	58	.50/.30
1981-82	O-Pee-Chee	176	.30
1981-82	O-Pee-Chee	194 (In Action)	.40
1981-82	Topps	13	.10
1982-83	O-Pee-Chee	181	.30
1983-84	O-Pee-Chee	187	.30
1984-85	O-Pee-Chee	261	.30
1985-86	O-Pee-Chee	169	.30
1986-87	O-Pee-Chee/Topps	96	.30/.15
1987-88	O-Pee-Chee	228	.25
1988-89	O-Pee-Chee	216	.15
1990-91	Pro Set	668 (Coach)	.10

9 Jari Kurri

Jari Kurri: 1981-82 OPC #107, $55; $17.50 in July 1991.

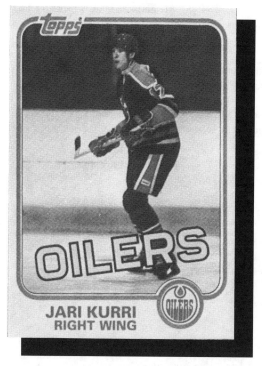

Jari Kurri

May 18, 1960; 6-1; 195; drafted 69th overall by Edmonton in 1980; center, shoots right; active; 12 seasons (1980-90 Edmonton, 1990-91 Milan, Italy; 1991-93 Los Angeles).

Career statistics through the 1992-93 season
GP: 909; G: 524 (13th); A: 666; TP: 1,190 (20th).

Like the others who were on the Edmonton Oiler teams of the 1980s, Kurri flourished under Wayne Gretzky's playmaking skills in Edmonton and Los Angeles, although he's often overlooked by hockey fans and collectors. Kurri is

13th all-time in NHL goals scored (524) and 20th overall in points (1,190). He's two seasons away from cracking the top 10.

A native Finlander, he played for Finland in the 1991 World Championships in Helsinki, his hometown. The "Fantastic Finn," one of the game's best defensive right wingers, took over for the injured Gretzky at center during the 1992-93 season. He's a seven-time All-Star who joined the Kings for the 1991-92 season after leaving Edmonton after the 1989-90 season to play in Milan, Italy in 1990-91.

The 1984-85 Lady Byng Memorial Trophy winner for his sportsmanship ranks 10th for most goals scored in a season (71 in 1984-85) and 17th (68 in 1985-86).

Kurri is one of most talented foreign players to ever play the game. His rookie card is in one of the better sets from the '80s. The set has rookie cards of many star players who may eventually be enshrined in the Hall of Fame, such as Paul Coffey ($110), Denis Savard ($40), Andy Moog ($32) and Peter Statsny ($25). The set, at $450, with this much potential down the line, can only go up; Kurri will ride on its coattails.

Jari Kurri Checklist

Year	Company	No.	Price
1981-82	O-Pee-Chee	107	55.00
1981-82	Topps	18	12.00
1982-83	O-Pee-Chee	111	10.00
1983-84	O-Pee-Chee	34	8.00
1984-85	O-Pee-Chee	215 (All-Star)	1.00
1984-85	O-Pee-Chee	249	5.00
1984-85	Topps	52	3.00
1984-85	Topps	161 (All-Star)	.50
1985-86	O-Pee-Chee/Topps	155	3.50/2.00
1986-87	O-Pee-Chee/Topps	108	2.00/1.25
1987-88	O-Pee-Chee/Topps	148	1.25/.75
1988-89	O-Pee-Chee/Topps	147	1.50/1.00
1989-90	O-Pee-Chee/Topps	43	.15/.12
1990-91	Bowman	191	.10
1990-91	O-Pee-Chee/Topps	5 (Highlight)	.10/.10
1990-91	O-Pee-Chee/Topps	108	.10/.10
1990-91	Pro Set	87	.15
1990-91	Pro Set	348 (All-Star)	.07
1990-91	Score American/Canadian	158	.10/.15
1990-91	Score American/Canadian	348 (Record Breaker)	.10/.15
1990-91	Upper Deck English/French	146	.15/.20
1991-92	O-Pee-Chee/Topps	295	.07/.07
1991-92	O-Pee-Chee Premier	111	.07
1991-92	Parkhurst English/French	72	.10/.15
1991-92	Parkhurst English/French	210 (1,000 pts)	.10/.15
1991-92	Parkhurst English/French	223 (All-Star)	.10/.15
1991-92	Pro Set English/French	93	.40/.50
1991-92	Pro Set Platinum	48	.20
1991-92	Score Traded	50	.10
1991-92	Score Canadian	600	.40
1991-92	Score Pinnacle English/French	48	.50/.50
1991-92	Upper Deck English/French	24 (Finland)	.15/.30
1991-92	Upper Deck English/French	366	.12/.25

 Marcel Dionne

Marcel Dionne: 1971-72 OPC #133, $145; $125 in July 1991.

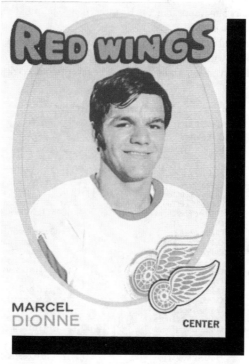

Marcel Dionne

Aug. 3, 1951; 5-8 185; drafted by Detroit in the first round in 1971, second player overall; center, shoots right; retired; 18 seasons (Detroit 1971-75, Los Angeles 1975-1986/1987, New York Rangers 1986/87-1989); Hall of Fame 1992.

GP: 1,348 (12th); G: 731 (3rd); A: 1,040 (3rd); TP: 1,771 (3rd).

In no other sport would the third all-time leading scorer's rookie card be less than $250, except in hockey. Dionne's is selling for $145. He has 1,771 career points in the NHL; only Gretzky and Gordie Howe have more. If you add in World Hockey Association totals, Bobby Hull pushes Dionne to the fourth spot, but you can't go wrong buying the Dionne card, especially with Gretzky's rookie card at $700, Howe's at $2,500 and Hull's at $2,000.

Dionne won the Art Ross Trophy in 1979-80 as the NHL's leading scorer with 137 points on 53 goals and 84 assists. He's won the Lady Byng Trophy twice (1974-75, 1976-77) for sportsmanship and the Lester Pearson Award twice, too (1979, 1980).

The two-time First-Team and two-time Second Team All-Star has made eight All-Star game appearances. He's the Kings' all-time leader in games, goals, assists and points.

The mercurial center, who was elected to the Hall of Fame in 1992, compares favorably with Bryan Trottier and Wayne Gretzky as hockey's best center and playmaker ever, and his hockey sense equals that of Gretzky.

Marcel Dionne Checklist

Year	Company	No.	Price
1971-72	O-Pee-Chee	133	145.00
1972-73	O-Pee-Chee	18	35.00
1972-73	Topps	8	3.00
1973-74	O-Pee-Chee/Topps	17	20.00/15.00
1974-75	O-Pee-Chee/Topps	72	17.00/10.00
1974-75	O-Pee-Chee/Topps	84 (Team Leaders)	2.50/1.50
1975-76	O-Pee-Chee/Topps	140	12.00/9.00
1975-76	O-Pee-Chee/Topps	210 (Leaders)	10.00/6.50
1975-76	O-Pee-Chee/Topps	318 (Team Leaders)	3.50/2.50
1976-77	O-Pee-Chee/Topps	91	9.50/7.00
1976-77	O-Pee-Chee	(Team Leaders)	1.75
1977-78	O-Pee-Chee/Topps	1 (Leaders)	3.00/2.00
1977-78	O-Pee-Chee/Topps	2 (Leaders)	2.00/1.50
1977-78	O-Pee-Chee/Topps	3 (Leaders)	2.00/2.00
1977-78	O-Pee-Chee/Topps	240 (All-Star)	7.00/5.00
1978-79	O-Pee-Chee/Topps	120	4.00/3.50
1979-80	O-Pee-Chee/Topps	1 (Leaders)	3.50/2.50
1979-80	O-Pee-Chee/Topps	2 (Leaders)	2.00/2.00
1979-80	O-Pee-Chee/Topps	3 (Leaders)	2.00/2.00
1979-80	O-Pee-Chee/Topps	5 (Leaders)	2.50/1.50
1979-80	O-Pee-Chee/Topps	160 (All-Star)	4.00/3.00
1980-81	O-Pee-Chee/Topps	20	3.00/2.00
1980-81	O-Pee-Chee/Topps	81 (All-Star)	1.50/1.00
1980-81	O-Pee-Chee/Topps	16 (Leaders)	15.00/10.00
1980-81	O-Pee-Chee/Topps	163 (Leaders)	15.00/10.00
1980-81	O-Pee-Chee/Topps	165 (Leaders)	2.00/1.50
1981-82	O-Pee-Chee	141	2.00

Marcel Dionne Checklist

Year	Company	No.	Price
1981-82	O-Pee-Chee	150 (In Action)	.75
1981-82	O-Pee-Chee	156 (Team Leaders)	.45
1981-82	O-Pee-Chee	391 (Record Breaker)	3.00
1981-82	Topps	9	1.50
1981-82	Topps	54 (Team Leaders)	.30
1981-82	Topps West	125 (In Action)	.60
1982-83	O-Pee-Chee	149 (Team Leaders)	.50
1982-83	O-Pee-Chee	152	1.50
1982-83	O-Pee-Chee	153 (In Action)	.50
1983-84	O-Pee-Chee	150 (Team Leaders)	.25
1983-84	O-Pee-Chee	151 (In Action)	.25
1983-84	O-Pee-Chee	152	.90
1983-84	O-Pee-Chee	211 (Record Breaker)	.25
1984-85	O-Pee-Chee	82	.75
1984-85	Topps	64	.40
1985-86	O-Pee-Chee/Topps	90	.65/.50
1986-87	O-Pee-Chee/Topps	30	.50/.40
1987-88	O-Pee-Chee/Topps	129	.35/.20
1988-89	O-Pee-Chee/Topps	13	.30/.25
1988-89	Topps	13	.25
1990-91	Pro Set	653	.15
1992-93	O-Pee-Chee	294	.40

 Dave Taylor

Dave Taylor: 1978-79 OPC #353, $25; $2.50 in July 1991.

Dec. 4, 1955; 6-0, 195; drafted in the 15th round, 210th overall, by Los Angeles in 1975; right wing, shoots right; active; 16 seasons (all with Los Angeles).

G: 1,078; G: 427 (33rd); A: 635; TP: 1,062 (29th).

This rookie card can be had for $25. A 1,000-point player, Taylor had a steady 15-year career in the NHL, spending almost his entire career with the Los Angeles Kings. He is often overlooked because of the Kings' horrible performance for most of his career, but wise hockey card fans and collectors know of his playing ability.

He was one of five players to reach the 1,000 games-played mark in 1991-92, when he did so with the Los Angeles Kings, his original team. As a right winger, Taylor played with Marcel Dionne and Charlie Simmer on the "Triple Crown" line, one of the most productive lines in NHL history when it scored 146 goals in 1979-80.

After the 1990-91 season, Taylor won the Bill Masterton Trophy for his dedication to the sport and the King Clancy Memorial Trophy for his humanitarianism and leadership.

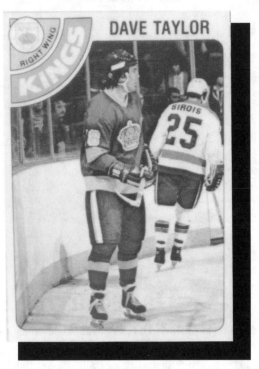

Dave Taylor

There's lots of room for this card to grow. Get in on the ground floor and buy it now at its low price. It'll be like money in the bank, accruing interest as it grows older.

Dave Taylor Checklist

Year	Company	No.	Price
1978-79	O-Pee-Chee	353	25.00
1979-80	O-Pee-Chee/Topps	232	6.00/5.00
1980-81	O-Pee-Chee/Topps	137	2.50/2.00
1981-82	O-Pee-Chee	143	1.00
1981-82	O-Pee-Chee	152 (In Action)	.50
1981-82	Topps	40	.45
1981-82	Topps	W132 (In Action)	.75
1982-83	O-Pee-Chee	161	.60
1983-84	O-Pee-Chee	163	.40
1984-85	O-Pee-Chee	92	.25
1985-86	O-Pee-Chee	214	.20
1986-87	O-Pee-Chee/Topps	63	.15/.10
1987-88	O-Pee-Chee/Topps	118	.10/.08

Dave Taylor Checklist

Year	Company	No.	Price
1988-89	O-Pee-Chee/Topps	46	.08/.05
1989-90	O-Pee-Chee/Topps	58	.05/.05
1990-91	Bowman	149	.10
1990-91	O-Pee-Chee/Topps	314	.05
1990-91	Pro Set	128	.05
1990-91	Score American/Canadian	166	.05/.07
1990-91	Upper Deck English/French	214	.05/.07
1991-92	Bowman	186	.05
1991-92	O-Pee-Chee/Topps	138	.05
1991-92	Parkhurst English/French	67	.05/.07
1991-92	Parkhurst English/French	214 (1,000 pts.)	.08/.10
1991-92	Pro Set English/French	103	.05
1991-92	Pro Set English/French	325 (Trophy)	.07/.10
1991-92	Score American/Canadian	214	.05
1991-92	Score Canadian	325 (Trophy)	.07
1991-92	Score Pinnacle English/French	249	.05/.07
1991-92	Score Pinnacle English/French	373 (Good Guy)	.07/.10
1991-92	Topps Stadium Club	232	.07
1991-92	Upper Deck English/French	270	.07/.10
1992-93	Bowman	37	.25
1992-93	Fleer Ultra	313	.10
1992-93	Parkhurst	307	.07
1992-93	Topps	446	.05
1992-93	Topps Stadium Club	234	.07

 **12 Bryan Trottier**

Bryan Trottier: 1976-77 OPC #115, $75; $55 in July 1991.

July 17, 1956; 5-11, 195; second pick overall by the New York Islanders in the 1974 draft; center, shoots left; active; 17 seasons (New York Islanders 1975-90, Pittsburgh 1990-92).

Career statistics through the 1992-93 season
GP: 1,238; G: 520 (14th); A: 890 (5th); TP: 1,410 (6th).

The sign in the stands was quite appropriate: "Jesus Saves & Trottier Scores." And he could score quickly, too; Trottier holds the record for the fastest goal from the start of a game, 5 seconds, against Boston in March of 1984. He once scored eight points (five goals, three assists) in a game against the New York Rangers in 1978; his six points in one period in that game is a record.

A top-notch passer and excellent playmaker, in his prime Trottier was as good as Gretzky, and could play with any man, any team, or in any era. The fierce, relentless checker formed a lethal offensive combination with Mike Bossy in New York, but he was a scorer who could play defense, too; he could neutralize other team's top gun.

Bryan Trottier

A sure-fire Hall of Famer, the modest Trottier started his career as the NHL's Rookie of the Year in 1976, winning the Calder Trophy for scoring a then-record 95 points (32 goals, 63 assists). He was the league's MVP in 1979, winning the Hart Memorial Trophy with 47 goals and 87 assists, for a league-leading 134 points and the Art Ross Trophy. During that season, the team's frontline of Trottier, Bossy and Clarke Gillies combined for an NHL record of 151 goals.

After having led the Islanders to four consecutive Stanley Cup championships from 1980-83, Trottier was released by the team in 1990. He signed as a free agent with Pittsburgh and helped the Penguins win back-to-back Stanley Cups in 1990-91 and 1991-92, giving him six coveted Stanley Cup rings, and a Conn Smythe Trophy as the 1979-80 Stanley Cup MVP. His 113 assists and 184 points in 209 playoff games each rank fourth all-time, while his 71 goals ranks eighth.

Trottier's efforts off the ice have been recognized, too. He won the 1988-89 King Clancy Memorial Trophy for his leadership and humanitarian efforts. He's served as president of the NHL Players' Association and in 1992-93 he held a front office job with the New York Islanders, but has been named an assistant coach for Pittsburgh for 1993-94.

Trottier has said he'll be a player coach, so he could pass Stan Mikita (1,467) in career points, but probably won't touch Phil Esposito (1,590) for fourth. He could also catch Mikita for fourth (926) in all-time assists. If he moves up on the scoring and assist lists, he'll stay in the spotlight and his card will remain in demand. His inevitable induction into the Hall of Fame will be delayed, but buy his card now and watch it gain momentum as the Hall draws closer.

Bryan Trottier Checklist

Year	Company	No.	Price
1976-77	O-Pee-Chee/Topps	67 (Record Breaker)	8.00/5.00
1976-77	O-Pee-Chee/Topps	115	75.00/50.00
1976-77	O-Pee-Chee/Topps	216 (Long Island Lightning)	5.00/2.50
1977-78	O-Pee-Chee/Topps	105	30.00/15.00
1978-79	O-Pee-Chee/Topps	10	15.00/10.00
1978-79	O-Pee-Chee/Topps	64 (Leaders)	2.00/1.50
1978-79	O-Pee-Chee/Topps	65 (Leaders)	2.00/1.50
1978-79	O-Pee-Chee	325 (All-Star)	3.00
1979-80	O-Pee-Chee/Topps	7 (Leaders)	2.00/2.00
1979-80	O-Pee-Chee/Topps	100 (All-Star)	4.00/3.00
1979-80	O-Pee-Chee/Topps	165 (Record Breaker)	.45/.30
1980-81	O-Pee-Chee/Topps	40	4.00/2.50
1981-82	O-Pee-Chee	200	2.00
1981-82	O-Pee-Chee	210 (In Action)	.75
1981-82	Topps	41	2.00
1981-82	Topps East	132 (In Action)	.65
1982-83	O-Pee-Chee	5 (Record Breaker)	.50
1982-83	O-Pee-Chee	214	1.50
1982-83	O-Pee-Chee	215 (In Action)	.50
1983-84	O-Pee-Chee	21	.75
1984-85	O-Pee-Chee	139	.65
1984-85	O-Pee-Chee	214 (All-Star)	.35
1984-85	Topps	104	.35
1984-85	Topps	160 (All-Star)	.20
1985-86	O-Pee-Chee/Topps	60	.50/.40
1986-87	O-Pee-Chee/Topps	155	.40/.30
1987-88	O-Pee-Chee/Topps	60	.35/.25
1988-89	O-Pee-Chee/Topps	97	.25/.15
1989-90	O-Pee-Chee/Topps	149	.20/.20
1990-91	O-Pee-Chee/Topps	6 (Highlight)	.10
1990-91	O-Pee-Chee/Topps	291	.15
1990-91	O-Pee-Chee Premier	121	.60
1990-91	Pro Set	511	.15
1990-91	Score American/Canadian	270	.15/.15
1990-91	Upper Deck English/French	137	.50/.60
1990-91	Upper Deck English/French	425	.50/.75
1991-92	Bowman	93	.15
1991-92	O-Pee-Chee	472	.10
1991-92	Parkhurst English/French	208 (1,000 pts.)	.10/.15
1991-92	Pro Set English/French	192	.12/.15
1991-92	Pro Set Platinum	216	.15
1991-92	Score American/Canadian	229	.15/.20
1991-92	Score Pinnacle English/French	241	.12/.15
1991-92	Topps	472	.07

Bryan Trottier Checklist

Year	Company	No.	Price
1991-92	Topps Stadium Club	91	.10
1991-92	Upper Deck English/French	329	.10/.15
1992-93	Bowman	152	.25
1992-93	Bowman	243	5.00
1992-93	O-Pee-Chee	107	.07
1992-93	Score Canadian/American	157	.07
1992-93	Topps	416	.07
1992-93	Topps Stadium Club	26	.20

 # Billy Smith

Billy Smith: 1973-74 OPC #142, $50; $45 in July 1991.

Dec. 12, 1950; 5-10, 185; goalie; retired; 18 seasons (Los Angeles 1971-72, New York Islanders 1972-89); Hall of Fame 1993.

GP: 680; W: 305 (8th); L: 233; T: 105; Pct.: .556;
GA: 2,031; ShO: 22; Ave.: 3.17.

Smith, who can be considered perhaps the best at the goalie position, just missed induction in 1992, but made it in in 1993. The former Islander was known for his fierce play between the nets.

He won the Vezina Trophy as the league's top goaltender in 1981-1982 (32-9-4, 2.97) and was runner up in 1976 and 1977. In 1982-83, he won the William M. Jennings Award for goalies, allowing the fewest goals.

At 88-36, with five shutouts and a 2.73 average, Smith is the all-time leader in Stanley Cup wins for a goalie. His 132 appearances also ranks first for a goalie. He's got rings for each finger, too, having played on the Islanders' four straight Stanley Cup winners (1980-83). For his play in the playoffs, in 1982-83 Smith added a Conn Smythe Trophy to his 1978 All-Star Game MVP Award.

Smith was perhaps hockey's equivalent of football's Conrad Dobler, but today's fans have taken to Quebec's goalie Ron Hextall's aggressive style of play, shades of Billy Smith in the nets. If Hextall has a Hall of Fame career, his predecessor's cards will surely take off in value, too. As younger collectors start going back in time from when they first started collecting, they'll find a lot of 1970s sets on dealers' shelves. When they start buying cards of some of hockey's early legends, Smith's value will hit the $100 range, which is where Bernie Parent's 1968-69 O-Pee-Chee card is at.

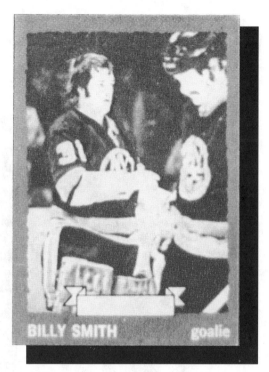

Billy Smith

Billy Smith Checklist

Year	Company	No.	Price
1973-74	O-Pee-Chee	142	50.00
1973-74	Topps	162	35.00
1974-75	O-Pee-Chee/Topps	82	11.00/9.00
1975-76	O-Pee-Chee	372	7.50
1976-77	O-Pee-Chee/Topps	46	4.00/2.50
1977-78	O-Pee-Chee/Topps	229	2.50/1.50
1978-79	O-Pee-Chee/Topps	62	2.00/1.50
1979-80	O-Pee-Chee/Topps	242	1.00/.75
1980-81	O-Pee-Chee/Topps	5 (Record Breaker)	.35/.25
1980-81	O-Pee-Chee/Topps	60	.75/.50
1981-82	O-Pee-Chee	207	.40
1981-82	Topps East	93	.30
1982-83	O-Pee-Chee	211	.25
1983-84	O-Pee-Chee	17	.20
1984-85	O-Pee-Chee	135	.20
1984-85	Topps	101	.15
1986-87	O-Pee-Chee	228	.15
1988-89	O-Pee-Chee/Topps	17	.15

14 Bernie Federko

Bernie Federko: 1978-79 OPC #143, $15; $2.50 in July 1991.

Bernie Federko

May 12, 1956; 6-0, 190; drafted by St. Louis in the first round in 1976, seventh overall; center, shoots left; retired; 14 seasons (1976-90, all with St. Louis).

GP: 1,000: G: 369; A: 761 (18th); TP: 1,130 (23rd).

Federko's card is another steal in the hockey card market. Federko holds the St. Louis Blues record for total points, goals and assists. In his 1,000 games played during a 14-year career, Federko has 1,130 total points (369 goals, 761 assists).

Federko will be eligible for induction in 1994; he's Hall-of-Fame caliber. Mike Bossy ($70) and Dave Taylor ($25) have rookie cards from the same set as

Federko. He ranks ahead of both of them on the all-time scoring list, and yet his rookie card can be had for less than $20. What a buy. His card should find a comfortable niche somewhere between Taylor's and Bossy's cards.

Bernie Federko Checklist

Year	Company	No.	Price
1978-79	O-Pee-Chee/Topps	143	15.00/10.00
1979-80	O-Pee-Chee/Topps	215	4.00/3.50
1980-81	O-Pee-Chee/Topps	71 (Team Leaders)	.30/.25
1980-81	O-Pee-Chee/Topps	136	2.25/1.50
1981-82	O-Pee-Chee	288	1.50
1981-82	O-Pee-Chee	300 (In Action)	.50
1981-82	O-Pee-Chee	304 (Team Leaders)	.30
1981-82	Topps	12	.40
1981-82	Topps	63 (Team Leaders)	.20
1981-82	Topps	West 127 (In Action)	.40
1982-83	O-Pee-Chee	302	.15
1982-83	O-Pee Chee	303 (In Action)	.15
1983-84	O-Pee-Chee	315	.15
1984-85	O-Pee-Chee	184	.15
1984-85	O-Pee-Chee	367 (Team Leaders)	.30
1984-85	Topps	131	.10
1985-86	O-Pee-Chee/Topps	104	.15/.10
1987-88	O-Pee-Chee/Topps	83	.10/.20
1988-89	O-Pee-Chee/Topps	81	.10/.15
1989-90	O-Pee-Chee/Topps	107	.08/.10
1990-91	Bowman	238	.10
1990-91	O-Pee-Chee/Topps	191	.10
1990-91	Pro Set	70	.10
1990-91	Score American/Canadian	252	.10/.12
1990-91	Upper Deck English/French	58	.15/.25
1991-92	Pro Set English/French	597 (Hall of Fame)	.10/.15

15 Borje Salming

Borje Salming: 1974-75 OPC #180, $17; $20 in July 1991.

April 17, 1951; 6-1, 193; defenseman, shoots left; retired; 17 seasons (1973-89 Toronto, Detroit 1989-90).

GP: 1,148; G: 150 A: 637 TP: 787.

Salming is the best defenseman in the history of the Toronto Maple Leafs and one of the NHL's all-time best. Playing in the shadows of other great defensemen such as Larry Robinson and Ray Bourque, he was the runner up for the Norris Trophy in 1977 and 1980. His offensive talents are comparable to those of Denis Potvin and Robinson.

Salming is still playing professionally overseas, so he hasn't been retired the mandatory three years before he can be nominated for induction. Compare the price of Salming's 20-year-old rookie card to those of Lanny McDonald ($45), Potvin ($55) and Bob Gainey ($20), from that same year, and you'll realize what a steal it is and where it's headed if he's inducted in with those Hall of Famers.

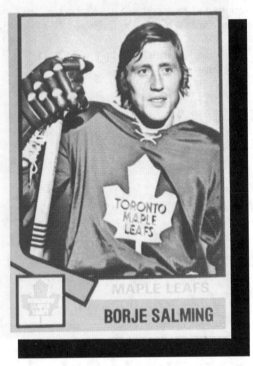

Borje Salming

Borje Salming Checklist

Year	Company	No.	Price
1974-75	O-Pee-Chee/Topps	180	17.00/10.00
1975-76	O-Pee-Chee/Topps	283	4.00/2.50
1975-76	O-Pee-Chee/Topps	294 (All-Star)	1.25/1.00
1976-77	O-Pee-Chee/Topps	22 (All-Star)	2.00/1.50
1977-78	O-Pee-Chee/Topps	140 (All-Star)	1.50/1.00
1978-79	O-Pee-Chee/Topps	240	1.00/.75
1978-79	O-Pee-Chee	328 (All-Star)	.75
1979-80	O-Pee-Chee/Topps	40 (All-Star)	.65/.50
1980-81	O-Pee-Chee/Topps	85 (All-Star)	.40/.30
1980-81	O-Pee-Chee/Topps	210	.50/.35
1981-82	O-Pee-Chee	307	.30
1981-82	Topps	33	.25
1982-83	O-Pee-Chee	332	.20
1983-84	O-Pee-Chee	341	.30
1984-85	O-Pee-Chee	311	.35
1985-86	O-Pee-Chee	248	.20
1986-87	O-Pee-Chee/Topps	169	.20/.20
1987-88	O-Pee-Chee	237	.15
1988-89	O-Pee-Chee	247	.10

SLEEPER CARD

 ## Wally Joyner

Wally Joyner: 1986 Donruss Rookies #1, $3; $3 in July 1991.

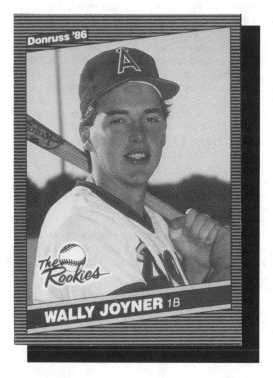

June 16, 1962; 6-2, 205; throws left, bats left; first baseman; active; seven seasons (California 1986-91; Kansas City 1992).

Career statistics entering the 1993 season
G: 995; AB: 3,780; R: 521; H: 1,079; 2B: 206; 3B: 13; HR: 123; TB: 1,680; RBI: 584; Ave.: .285; SB: 39.

Shares the major league record for the most home runs in the month of October (4, in 1987); led the A.L. in sacrifice flies in 1986 with 12; led A.L. first basemen in total chances in 1988 with 1,520 and in 1991 with 1,441; led A.L. first basemen with 148 double plays in 1988 and in 1992 with 138; hit three home runs in a game on Oct. 3, 1987.

Why does the name Robin Yount keep going through our minds when the name Wally Joyner comes up? Perhaps it's because Yount very quietly put together a Hall of Fame career. His 3,000 hits snuck up on everyone.

Joyner's career statistics are similar to or better than those Yount had compiled after seven seasons — 499 runs, 1,050 hits, 193 doubles, 38 triples, 57 home runs, 390 RBI, a .273 batting average and 98 stolen bases.

Joyner's career statistics average out to 74 runs, 154 hits, 29 doubles, two triples, 17 home runs, 83 RBI, a .285 batting average and five stolen bases annually. Compare those with Robin Yount's annual production of 82 runs, 159 hits, 29 doubles, six triples, 12 home runs, 71 RBI, a .287 batting average and 13 stolen bases.

If Joyner plays 19 seasons like Yount has played, and hits his average in every category, he's going to finish with around 1,400 runs, 2,900 hits, 550 doubles, 40 triples, 325 home runs, 1,575 RBI, a .285 batting average and 95 stolen bases. Now, go back and look at Yount's career statistics. They're quite similar.

Granted, Joyner, 31, is a first baseman, so his numbers should be compared to a first baseman's. Try those of Hall of Famer Johnny Mize— 2,011 hits, 367 doubles, 83 triples, 359 home runs, 1,337 RBI, a .312 batting average and 28 stolen bases. Joyner's drawback would be that he's got a lower career batting average than most of the 16 Hall of Fame first basemen. But only six would have hit more home runs at that position.

Joyner doesn't stand out among his peers, all good hitting first basemen. But he's quietly on his way to 3,000. Playing in Kansas City will help him too; he's always hit better on artificial turf.

Only one of 17 players in major league history to have 100 RBI in his first and second seasons, Joyner had a terrific sophomore season in 1987. He hit 34 home runs, with 117 RBI and a .285 batting average during the year. He hasn't equalled those numbers, but did hit .301 with 21 home runs and 96 RBI in 1991.

Wally Joyner Checklist

Year	Company	No.	Price
1986	Donruss Rookies	1	$3
1986	Fleer Update	U59	1.50
1986	Topps Traded	51T	1.00
1987	Donruss	1 Diamond King	.50
1987	Donruss	135	1.00
1987	Fleer	86	2.00
1987	Fleer	628	1.50
1987	Leaf	1 Diamond King	.80
1987	Leaf	252	3.00
1987	O-Pee-Chee	80	1.50
1987	Topps	80	.80
1988	Donruss	110	.30
1988	Fleer	493	.40
1988	Fleer	622	.35
1988	Leaf	50	.60
1988	O-Pee-Chee	168	.40
1988	Score	7	.35

Wally Joyner Checklist

Year	Company	No.	Price
1988	Topps	420	.25
1989	Bowman	47	.10
1989	Donruss	52	.20
1989	Fleer	481	.25
1989	O-Pee-Chee	270	.35
1989	Score	65	.20
1989	Topps	270	.20
1989	Upper Deck	573	.25
1989	Upper Deck	668	.08
1990	Bowman	299	.08
1990	Donruss	94	.15
1990	Fleer	136	.10
1990	Leaf	24	.40
1990	O-Pee-Chee	525	.20
1990	Score	120	.15
1990	Topps	525	.20
1990	Upper Deck	693	.15
1991	Bowman	195	.10
1991	Donruss	677	.12
1991	Fleer	317	.10
1991	Fleer Ultra	48	.15
1991	Leaf	31	.20
1991	Leaf Studio	26	.25
1991	O-Pee-Chee	195	.10
1991	Score	470	.12
1991	Score	873	.08
1991	Topps	195	.10
1991	Topps Stadium Club	2	.30
1991	Upper Deck	575	.10
1992	Donruss	333	.15
1992	Fleer	62	.10
1992	Fleer Ultra	373	.40
1992	Fleer Update	27	.12
1992	Leaf	439	.12
1992	Leaf Studio	185	.20
1992	Score	535	.08
1992	Score Pinnacle	284	.15
1992	Score Pinnacle	537	.20
1992	Score Traded	13	.08
1992	Topps	629	.10
1992	Topps Stadium Club	122	.20
1992	Topps Traded	59	.08
1992	Upper Deck	343	.10

Other Considerations
Basketball

1) Mark Aguirre 1986-87 Fleer #3, $4: He's on the fence as far as his chances for induction, but he's got two NBA championship rings and ranks 33rd all-time in scoring.

2) Bobby Jones 1975-76 Topps #298, $7: He's not going to be found among the all-time leaders in offensive categories; Jones will be inducted as one of the all-time best defensive forwards, with eight straight first team NBA All-Defensive selections and five All-Star selections.

3) Bob McAdoo 1973-74 Topps #135, $17.50: McAdoo ranks 26th all-time in scoring, won three straight scoring titles, a league MVP Award and two championship rings.

4) Sidney Moncrief 1980-81 Topps, panel, $5.50: Moncrief didn't play long enough to compile Hall of Fame statistics, but pick up the panel he shares with Kareem Abdul-Jabbar. Eventually, somebody will want this card from this goofy set.

5) Paul Westphal 1973-74 Topps #126, $15: He had five excellent All-Star seasons and seven mediocre ones, so he won't make the Hall of Fame based on his career statistics. But he'll keep his name in the limelight as he coaches Phoenix. A championship would spark his card's value.

6) Jack Sikma 1978-79 Topps #117, $6: Sikma ranks 39th all-time in scoring, 16th in rebounds and ninth in games played. Yet everyone forgets about him. Pick up a card or two now while it's under $10; Sikma's a probable Hall of Famer.

7) Hakeem Olajuwon 1986-87 Fleer #82, $70: The 1993 All-NBA First Team selection was the league's defensive player of the year, too. All that's missing from this projected Hall-of-Fame career is a championship ring.

Football

1) Mark Clayton 1985 Topps #308, $7.50: As Sterling Sharpe's partner, Clayton has a chance to help Green Bay to a Super Bowl, which would cap a Hall of Fame career.

2) Paul Gruber 1989 Score #77, 30 cents: If he played on any team other than Tampa Bay, he'd be a five-time All-Pro. This card is a gimme, a confidence builder, one to put in the win column. You'll eventually be able to sell it for more than the 30 cents you paid for it. A high percentage yield.

3) Paul Krause 1965 Philadelphia #189, $10: Only 11 defensive backs are in the Hall of Fame. Why isn't the all-time leader in interceptions enshrined?

4) Drew Hill 1982 Topps #379, $4.50: In Houston's run-and-shoot offense, he's always a threat and will keep adding to his 600 career receptions, which rank 10th all-time.

5) Bruce Matthews 1989 Score #109, 50 cents: Stay away from offensive linemen, except for the AFC's Offensive Lineman of the Year in 1992, who's made five straight Pro Bowl appearances. He's a definite Hall of Famer.

6) Jerry Kramer 1959 Topps #116, $25: Why hasn't the dominant offensive lineman of his era, who played on all those great Green Bay Packer teams, been elected to the Hall of Fame?

7) Reggie White 1985 Topps USFL #75, $27: This second-year card of the league's premiere defensive lineman is a key card in this set. He's headed for the Hall of Fame, too.

Hockey

1) Mark Messier 1980-81 O-Pee-Chee #289, $200: A driving force in Edmonton, the 1991-92 NHL MVP, and 12th all-time in NHL scoring — that says it all.

2) Paul Coffey 1981-82 O-Pee-Chee #111, $110: One of the league's best defensemen, shades of Hall of Famer Bobby Orr, Coffey's seventh all-time in assists.

3) Grant Fuhr 1982-83 O-Pee-Chee #105, $20: Lost in the shuffle with Wayne Gretzky, Paul Coffey and Mark Messier in Edmonton, Fuhr's one of the best goalies under pressure; he's got five Stanley Cup victories.

TOP SETS

This 609-card set marked the largest set up to that time for Topps. The card fronts feature large color pho-

1967 Topps Baseball	$5,000
	Near Mint
Common players 1-110	$1.00
Common players 111-370	$1.50
Common players 371-457	$1.25
Common players 458-533	$5.00
Common players 534-609	$12.00

tographs bordered by white. The player's name and position are printed at the top with the team at the bottom. Across the front of the cards are facsimile autographs, with the exception of card #254 (Milt Pappas). The backs are done vertically, although they contain the familiar biographical and statistical information. The only subsets are statistical leaders and World Series highlights. Rookie cards, featuring two players per card, are done by team or league. High-number cards (534-609) are quite scarce, and while it is known that some are even scarcer, by virtue of having been short-printed in relation to the rest of the series, there is no general agreement on which cards are involved. Rookie cards include Rod Carew and Tom Seaver.

The top 10 cards in the set by value are: #581 Mets Rookies (Tom Seaver, $1,200); #569 A.L. Rookies (Rod Carew, $500); #600 Brooks Robinson ($225); #150 Mickey Mantle ($200); #146 Steve Carlton ($125); #609 Tommy John ($125); #200 Willie Mays ($100); #250 Hank Aaron ($100); #475 Jim Palmer ($100); #604 Red Sox Team ($100).

This 352-card set was Topps' last to be issued in series form (1-132, 133-263, 264-351), with each series being scarcer than the

1972 Topps Football	$2,100
	Near Mint
Common card 1-132	.50
Common card 133-263	.70
Common card 264-351	$17
League Leaders	$1
Playoffs	$1.25
All-Pros	$19
Minor stars	.50-$2

one which preceded it. Since it's so difficult to complete a set, it is the most expensive Topps set of the 1970s. Subsets include statistical leaders, playoffs, All-Pros and In Action cards. Rookies include John Riggins, Archie Manning, Jim Plunkett, John Brockington, Ted Hendricks, L.C. Greenwood, Lyle Alzado, Dan Pastorini, Gene Upshaw, Roger Staubach, Charlie Joiner, Ron Yary, Larry Little and Steve Spurrier.

The top 11 cards in the set by value are: #343 Joe Namath In Action ($250); #200 Roger Staubach ($200); #294 Checklist ($60); #291 Steve Spurrier ($55); #272 Bob Griese All-Pro ($45); #348 George Blanda ($45); #341 Dick Butkus In Action ($42); #100 Joe Namath ($38); #150 Terry Bradshaw ($38); #280 Bob Lilly All-Pro ($38); #281 Ted Hendricks All-Pro ($38).

This 99-card set was the first major basketball card set issued since the 1961 Fleer

| 1969-70 Topps Basketball .... $2,000 |
| Near Mint |
| Common player .... $4 |
| Minor stars................................... $5-$10 |

set, so it contains several Hall of Famers who are featured on their first card. The cards are oversized (2 1/2-by-4 11/16) and feature a posed shot of a player in an oval with a white border containing generic basketball scenes. This set also marks the first and only time until the 1980s a "pre-rookie" card of any player was released by Topps; a card was issued for Lew Alcindor before he had even played an NBA game. The set did not have any subsets or All-Star designations. Rookie cards include Gail Goodrich, Cazzie Russell, Connie Hawkins, John Havlicek, Lew Alcindor, Walt Hazzard, Billy Cunningham, Bill Bradley, Jerry Lucas, Willis Reed, Paul Silas, Dave Bing, Wes Unseld, Bob Love, Earl Monroe, Don Nelson, Dave DeBusschere, Nate Thurmond and Walt Frazier.

The top 10 cards in the set by value are: #25 Lew Alcindor ($650); #99 Checklist ($300); #1 Wilt Chamberlain ($225); #20 John Havlicek ($175); #43 Bill Bradley ($150); #90 Jerry West ($100); #98 Walt Frazier ($85); #50 Oscar Robertson ($75); #75 Elvin Hayes ($70); #35 Elgin Baylor ($55).

This 132-card set was Fleer's first set since 1961 and is one

| 1986-87 Fleer Basketball.. $1,350 Mint |
| Common player .... $2 |
| Minor stars......................... $2.50-$4.50 |

of the most important sets ever issued. Cards were shown in alphabetical order on white cardboard stock. The fronts have a photo inside a red, white and blue frame with a "Premier" logo on it. The backs are in red and blue. Centering is a problem in this set, which contains one error — card #55 of Steve Jordan actually shows David Greenwood. Rookie cards include Mark Aguirre, Danny Ainge, Charles Barkley, Tom Chambers, Terry Cummings, Clyde Drexler, Joe

214

Dumars, Patrick Ewing, Michael Jordan, Jeff Malone, Karl Malone, Xavier McDaniel, Chris Mullin, Larry Nance, Akeem Olajuwon, Sam Perkins, Rickey Pierce, Isiah Thomas, Spud Webb, Dominique Wilkins, Kevin Willis and James Worthy.

The top 12 cards in the set by value are: #57 Michael Jordan ($750); #7 Charles Barkley ($180); #32 Patrick Ewing ($90); #68 Karl Malone ($80); #26 Clyde Drexler ($75); #82 Akeem Olajuwon ($70); #121 Dominique Wilkins ($70); #77 Chris Mullin ($60); #9 Larry Bird ($45); #53 Magic Johnson ($40); #109 Isiah Thomas ($35); #27 Joe Dumars ($30).

After years of 396-card sets, O-Pee-Chee dropped its card count to 264, eliminating such features as team leaders, action cards and high-lights. The main change between the Topps/OPC sets is on Pelle Lindbergh's card, #110, which carries a "1959-1985" notation above his name in the OPC series. Rookies in the set include Mario Lemieux (the highest-priced rookie card of the 1980s), Kirk Muller, Tomas Sandstrom and Brian Hayward.

1985-86 O-Pee-Chee Hockey	$500 Mint
Common player	.10
League Leaders	.15
Checklists	.40

The top 10 cards in the set by value are: #9 Mario Lemieux ($375); #237 (Al MacInnis ($55); #262 Rookie Scoring Leaders (Mario Lemieux, $55); #29 Steve Yzerman ($20); #120 Wayne Gretzky ($20); #123 Tomas Sandstrom; #84 Kirk Muller ($15); #137 Pat LaFontaine ($15); #210 Al Iafrate ($15); #228 Cam Neely ($15).

This 132-card set was Topps' first issue of United States Football League cards and is the company's most valuable set of the 1980s. Issued as a factory set, cards were printed on white stock. Bordered in red and red piping over white space with the USFL logo and "Premier Edition" at the top of a card, a team helmet appears at lower left with the team name in red and the player name in black over a yellow background below the photo. Cards are num-bered alphabetically by city name and the player's last name. Rookies include Jim Kelly, Herschel Walker, Reggie White, Anthony Carter, Bobby Hebert,

1984 Topps Football USFL	. $425 Mint
Common player	$1
Mint stars	$1.25-$2

Kelvin Bryant and Mike Rozier.

The top eight cards in the set by value are: #36 Jim Kelly ($180); #52 Steve Young ($110); #58 Reggie White ($75); #74 Herschel Walker ($75); #59 Anthony Carter ($24); #38 Ricky Sanders ($20), #42 Vaughan Johnson ($17); #62 Bobby Hebert ($16).

This set consists of 651 numbered cards, seven unnumbered checklists and two "Living Legends" cards (designated A and B). The A and B cards were issued only in wax packs and not available to hobby dealers purchasing vending sets. The card fronts differ in style from previous years, but feature the Donruss logo and year of issue. The card backs use black ink on green and white. The cards were issued with a 63-piece puzzle of Duke Snider. Subsets include the Diamond Kings and Rated Rookies. Diamond King cards have a variation. Those with backs which correctly say Perez-Steele are more valuable than those which say Perez-Steel. The price above does not include the variations. A limited print run has caused the set to escalate in price. Rookie cards include Tony Fernandez, Kevin McReynolds, Joe Carter, Sid Fernandez, Darryl Strawberry, Andy Van Slyke, Tom Henke, Don Mattingly, Ron Darling and Tom Candiotti.

1984 Donruss Baseball	$400 Mint
Common player	.12

The top 11 cards in the set by value are: #41 Joe Carter ($50); #68 Darryl Strawberry ($40); #248 Don Mattingly ($40); #60 Nolan Ryan ($25); #106 Cal Ripken ($25); #311 Ryne Sandberg ($25); #324 Tony Gwynn ($20); #151 Wade Boggs ($18); #183 Mike Schmidt ($15); #54 Rickey Henderson ($12); #83 Andy Van Slyke ($12).

The second straight WHA set for OPC was doubled in size to 132 cards, but was short-printed. Stars such as Gordie Howe, Frank Mahovlich, Gerry Cheevers, Jacques Plante and Bobby Hull and the relative scarcity of the set make this one of the decade's most sought-after sets. This is the most valuable of the four O-Pee-Chee World Hockey Association sets. First cards include Mark Howe and Marty Howe.

1975-76 O-Pee-Chee WHA	$400
	Near Mint
Common player	.35
All-Stars (62-72)	.50

The top seven cards in the set by value are: #1 Bobby Hull ($55); #100 Gordie Howe ($50); #60

Gordie Howe All-Star ($30); #7 Mark Howe ($27); #65 Bobby Hull All-Star ($25); #131 Checklist ($25); #34 Jacques Plante ($17).

This 792-card set doesn't have any form of "future stars" cards; Topps was saving them for its late-season "Traded" set. The card fronts have a large color photo with a smaller one alongside, similar in design to the 1963 set. Team colors frame the card. The player's name, position and team are at the bottom. The Topps logo is in the upper right-hand corner. The backs are horizontal and include personal information, statistics and 1982 highlights. Specialty cards include record break-

1983 Topps Baseball	.... $175 Mint
Common players	.08

ers, league leaders, All-Stars, checklists, "Team Leaders," and "Super Veteran" cards which have a current and a first-year picture of the honored player. Rookie cards include Ryne Sandberg, Tony Gwynn, Wade Boggs and Willie McGee.

The top 11 cards in the set by value are: #83 Ryne Sandberg ($40); #482 Tony Gwynn ($40); #498 Wade Boggs ($35); #163 Cal Ripken ($25); #360 Nolan Ryan ($10); #586 Frank Viola ($5); #49 Willie McGee ($4); #180 Rickey Henderson ($4); #350 Robin Yount ($4); #361 Super Veteran (Nolan Ryan, $4); #600 George Brett ($4).

This set is highly sought-after because of the excellent array of rookies in it and because it is one of the better-designed sets of the decade, too. The 396-card set is numbered alphabetically by city and by player name. AFC teams are listed first, followed by NFL leaders and the NFC teams. Team leader cards, which had for years shown team leaders in several categories, this year showed just one leader. Card fronts

1984 Topps Football	.... $120 Mint
Common card	.05
Record Breaker	.10
Playoffs	.10
Team Leaders	.10
League Leaders	.10
Checklists	.20
Instant Replay	.10
Minor stars	10-.35

show an angled photo, with the player's name above his photo and his team name and logo below. The Pro Bowl designation appears above the team name. Instant Replay cards in the set feature NFL stars in action poses. Rookies include Eric Dickerson, John Elway, Dan Marino, Curt Warner, Mark Duper, Willie Gault, Dave Krieg, Morten Andersen, Darrell Green, Howie Long and Roger Craig.

The top nine cards in the set by value are: #123 Dan Marino ($70); #63 John Elway ($23); #281 Eric Dickerson ($16); Dan Marino Instant Replay ($8); #380 Darrell Green ($5); #353 Roger Craig ($4.50); #111 Howie Long ($4); #195 Dave Krieg ($4); #358 Joe Montana ($4).

COUNTERFEITS

The second edition of the *Sports Collectors Digest Sportscard Counterfeit Detector* lists approximately 170 baseball, basketball, football and hockey cards which have been counterfeited and tells how the editor, Bob Lemke, determined the cards were counterfeit.

The book, which plans perpetual updating as new counterfeits are discovered, was created with contributions from many hobby professionals who provided definitive data in identifying the fakes.

However, there are undoubtedly counterfeit cards in the market which are not listed in this book. The final determination of whether a card is good or bad rests in your hands.

Most of the counterfeits in the book, which gives comparative close-up pictures of the areas in question, can be detected with a magnifying glass with a lens between 5X (producing an image five times actual size) and 10X.

The book lists major flaws in the counterfeits, but does not identify all of the incorrect characteristics; this was done to avoid letting the counterfeiters know of all the mistakes they have made.

Shading, intensity of color, ink coverage, clarity of the photo, texture of the cardboard stock and composition of the color printing dot structure are areas in which counterfeits can be detected.

The paper stock generally used for counterfeits is also a broad approximation of what was used for the real card; thus, the cardboard, when cut to size and imprinted, is significantly heavier or lighter, with a difference in weights seldom between 5-10 percent, and occasionally 20 percent or more.

However, these weight differences are only detectable with the very sensitive scales, those which can measure to one-tenth of a gram, so weights should only be considered as a relative measure.

Card companies, including Upper Deck, which first recognized the counterfeiting problem in 1989 with its counterfeit-proof hologram concept, Score and Donruss, have all promised to take measures during the 1990s to help curtail counterfeiting attempts.

The alteration of genuine cards to make them appear as valuable variations also exists. A classic example is an alteration which occurred on a T206 American Tobacco Co. card from the 1909-11 set.

Sherry Magee's card was originally misspelled as "MAGIE," but was quickly corrected; thus, a more valuable variation (MAGIE) exists. Due to that card's desirability and its value, the corrected Magee cards have been altered to MAGIE.

The following cards, which have been selected as being one of the top 101 sports card investments, are known to have been counterfeited:

Baseball 1): 1975 Topps Gary Carter #620
Baseball 3): 1978 Topps Lou Whitaker #704
Baseball 12): 1977 Topps Dale Murphy #476
Baseball 17): 1985 Donruss Kirby Puckett #438
Baseball 19): 1982 Topps Cal Ripken #21
Baseball 20): 1972 Topps Carlton Fisk #79
Baseball 23): 1987 Fleer Will Clark #269
Baseball 25): 1975 Topps George Brett #228
Baseball 26): 1975 Topps Robin Yount #223
Baseball 32): 1977 Topps Andre Dawson #473
Baseball 33): 1980 Topps Rickey Henderson #482
Baseball 39): 1985 Donruss Roger Clemens #273
Baseball 41): 1990 Leaf Frank Thomas #300
Baseball 43): 1984 Donruss Joe Carter #41
Baseball 49): 1973 Topps Mike Schmidt #615
Hockey 1): 1985-86 O-Pee-Chee Mario Lemieux #9
These players also have known counterfeit cards:

Baseball

1955 Topps Ernie Banks #28
1948 Bowman Yogi Berra #6
1976 Topps George Brett #19
1978 Topps George Brett #100
1976 Topps Gary Carter #441
1978 Topps Gary Carter #120
1984 Fleer Update Roger Clemens #U-27
1984 Fleer Update Dwight Gooden #U-43
1988 Cal Cards Ken Griffey Jr. (minor league) #34
1989 Donruss Ken Griffey Jr. #33
1989 Fleer Ken Griffey Jr. #548
1983 Fleer Tony Gwynn #360
1984 Donruss Tony Gwynn #324
1951 Bowman Mickey Mantle #253
1952 Bowman Mickey Mantle #101
1953 Topps Mickey Mantle #82
1969 Topps Mickey Mantle #500
1953 Topps Willie Mays #244
1972 Topps Willie Mays In Action #50
1973 Topps Willie Mays #305
1984 Fleer Update Kirby Puckett #U-93
1982 Fleer Cal Ripken Jr. #176
1984 Donruss Cal Ripken Jr. #106

1963 Topps Pete Rose #537
1966 Topps Pete Rose #30
1970 Topps Pete Rose #580
1971 Topps Pete Rose #100
1972 Topps Pete Rose #559
1973 Topps Pete Rose #130
1974 Topps Pete Rose #300
1975 Topps Pete Rose #320
1976 Topps Pete Rose #240
1977 Topps Pete Rose #450
1978 Topps Pete Rose #20
1979 Topps Pete Rose #650
1968 Topps Nolan Ryan #177
1972 Topps Nolan Ryan #595
1975 Topps Mini Nolan Ryan/Steve Carlton Strikeout Leaders #312
1983 Fleer Ryne Sandberg #507
1974 Topps Mike Schmidt #283
1975 Topps Mike Schmidt #70
1975 Topps Mini Mike Schmidt #70
1976 Topps Mike Schmidt #480
1977 Topps Mike Schmidt #140
1979 Topps Mike Schmidt #610
1959 Fleer Ted Williams #68
1976 Topps Robin Yount #316

Hockey

1986-87 O-Pee-Chee Mario Lemieux #122
1987-88 O-Pee-Chee Mario Lemieux #15
1988-89 O-Pee-Chee Mario Lemieux #1

These Top 10 sets have had cards counterfeited:
1967 Topps Baseball: Rod Carew #569, Tom Seaver #581, Brooks Robinson #600
1986-87 Fleer Basketball: Charles Barkley #7, Patrick Ewing #32, Michael Jordan #57, Karl Malone #68
1985-86 O-Pee-Chee Hockey: Mario Lemieux #9
1984 Topps Football USFL: Jim Kelly #36
1984 Donruss Baseball: Joe Carter #41, Tony Gwynn #324, Don Mattingly #248, Cal Ripken #106, Darryl Strawberry #68

HALL OF FAME
INDUCTEES

* indicates deceased members

National Baseball Hall of Fame & Museum

1st Basemen

Cap Anson * 1939
Jake Beckley * 1971
Jim Bottomley * 1974
Dan Brouthers * 1945
Frank Chance * 1946
Roger Connor * 1976

Jimmie Foxx * 1951
Lou Gehrig * 1939
Hank Greenberg * 1956
George Kelly * 1973
Harmon Killebrew 1984
Buck Leonard 1972

Willie McCovey 1986
Johnny Mize * 1981
George Sisler * 1939
Bill Terry * 1954

2nd Basemen

Rod Carew 1991
Eddie Collins * 1939
Bobby Doerr 1986
Johnny Evers * 1946
Frankie Frisch * 1947

Charlie Gehringer * 1949
Billy Herman * 1975
Rogers Hornsby * 1942
Nap Lajoie * 1937
Tony Lazzeri * 1991

Joe Morgan 1990
Jackie Robinson * 1962
Red Schoendienst 1989

Shortstops

Luis Aparicio 1984
Luke Appling * 1964
Dave Bancroft * 1971
Ernie Banks 1977
Lou Boudreau 1970
Joe Cronin * 1956

Travis Jackson * 1882
Hugh Jennings * 1945
Pop Lloyd * 1977
Rabbit Maranville * 1954
Pee Wee Reese 1984
Joe Sewell * 1977

Joe Tinker * 1946
Arky Vaughan * 1985
Honus Wagner * 1936
Bobby Wallace * 1953
Monte Ward * 1964

3rd Basemen

Frank Baker * 1955
Jimmy Collins * 1945
Ray Dandridge 1987

Judy Johnson * 1975
George Kell 1983
Fred Lindstrom * 1976

Eddie Mathews 1978
Brooks Robinson 1983
Pie Traynor * 1948

Outfielders

Hank Aaron 1982
Earl Averill * 1975
Cool Papa Bell * 1974
Lou Brock 1985
Jesse Burkett * 1946
Max Carey * 1961
Oscar Charleston * 1976
Fred Clarke * 1945
Roberto Clemente * 1973
Ty Cobb * 1936
Earle Combs * 1970
Sam Crawford * 1957
Kiki Cuyler * 1968
Ed Delahanty * 1945
Joe DiMaggio 1955
Hugh Duffy * 1945
Elmer Flick * 1963
Goose Goslin * 1968
Chick Hafey * 1971
Billy Hamilton * 1961

Harry Heilmann * 1952
Harry Hooper * 1971
Monte Irvin 1973
Reggie Jackson 1993
Al Kaline 1980
Willie Keeler * 1939
Joe Kelley * 1971
King Kelly * 1945
Ralph Kiner 1975
Chuck Klein * 1980
Mickey Mantle 1974
Heinie Manush * 1964
Willie Mays 1979
Tommy McCarthy * 1946
Joe Medwick * 1968
Stan Musial 1969
Jim O'Rourke * 1945
Mel Ott * 1951
Sam Rice * 1963
Frank Robinson 1982

Edd Roush * 1962
Babe Ruth * 1936
Al Simmons * 1953
Enos Slaughter 1985
Duke Snider 1980
Tris Speaker * 1937
Willie Stargell 1988
Sam Thompson * 1974
Lloyd Waner * 1967
Paul Waner * 1952
Zack Wheat * 1959
Billy Williams 1987
Ted Williams 1966
Hack Wilson * 1979
Carl Yastrzemski 1989
Ross Youngs * 1972

Catchers

Johnny Bench............................1989
Yogi Berra.................................1972
Roger Breshnahan *.................1945
Roy Campanella *.....................1969

Mickey Cochrane *.................1947
Bill Dickey..............................1954
Buck Ewing *..........................1939
Rick Ferrell.............................1984

Josh Gibson *...........................1972
Gabby Hartnett *.....................1955
Ernie Lombardi *.....................1986
Ray Schalk *............................1955

Pitchers

Grover Alexander *.................1938
Chief Bender *.........................1953
Mordecai Brown *...................1949
Jack Chesbro *.........................1946
John Clarkson *.......................1963
Stan Coveleski *......................1969
Dizzy Dean *...........................1953
Martin Dihigo *.......................1977
Don Drysdale *........................1984
Red Faber *..............................1964
Bob Feller...............................1962
Rollie Fingers..........................1992
Whitey Ford............................1974
Rube Foster *...........................1981
Pud Galvin *............................1965
Bob Gibson.............................1981
Lefty Gomez *.........................1972
Burleigh Grimes *...................1964
Lefty Grove *...........................1947

Jess Haines *............................1970
Waite Hoyt *............................1969
Carl Hubbell *..........................1947
Catfish Hunter.........................1987
Ferguson Jenkins.....................1991
Walter Johnson *......................1936
Addie Joss *.............................1978
Tim Keefe *.............................1964
Sandy Koufax..........................1972
Bob Lemon..............................1976
Ted Lyons *.............................1955
Juan Marichal..........................1983
Rube Marquard *......................1971
Christy Mathewson *...............1936
Joe McGinnity *.......................1946
Hal Newhouser.........................1992
Kid Nichols *...........................1949
Satchel Paige *.........................1971
Jim Palmer...............................1990

Herb Pennock *.......................1948
Gaylord Perry...........................1991
Eddie Plank *...........................1946
Old Hoss Radbourne *.............1939
Eppa Rixey *............................1963
Robin Roberts...........................1976
Red Ruffing *...........................1967
Amos Rusie *...........................1977
Tom Seaver...............................1992
Warren Spahn...........................1973
Dazzy Vance *..........................1955
Rube Waddell *........................1946
Ed Walsh *...............................1946
Mickey Welch *........................1973
Hoyt Wilhelm...........................1985
Early Wynn...............................1972
Cy Young *...............................1937

Managers

Walter Alston *.........................1983
Bucky Harris *.........................1975
Miller Huggins *......................1964
Al Lopez..................................1977

Connie Mack *.........................1937
Joe McCarthy *........................1957
John McGraw *.........................1937
Bill McKechnie *.....................1962

Wilbert Robinson *.................1945
Casey Stengel *........................1966

Naismith Memorial Basketball Hall of Fame

Nate Archibald.........................1991
Paul Arizin...............................1977
Thomas Barlow *......................1980
Rick Barry................................1987
Elgin Baylor.............................1976
John Beckman *.......................1972
Walt Bellamy...........................1993
Sergei Belov.............................1992
Dave Bing................................1990
Benny Borgmann *...................1961
Bill Bradley..............................1982
Joe Brennan *...........................1974
Al Cervi...................................1984
Wilt Chamberlain.....................1978
Charles Cooper *......................1976
Bob Cousy...............................1970
Dave Cowens...........................1991
Billy Cunningham.....................1986
Bob Davies *............................1969
Forrest DeBernardi *................1961
Dave DeBusschere....................1982
Dutch Dehnert *.......................1968
Paul Endacott...........................1971
Julius Erving............................1993
Bud Foster...............................1964
Walt Frazier.............................1987
Marty Friedman *.....................1971
Joe Fulks *...............................1977
Laddie Gale.............................1976
Harry Gallatin..........................1991
William Gates..........................1989

Tom Gola.................................1975
Hal Greer.................................1981
Robert Gruenig *......................1963
Cliff Hagen..............................1977
Victor Hanson *.......................1960
John Havlicek...........................1983
Connie Hawkins.......................1992
Elvin Hayes.............................1990
Tom Heinsohn..........................1986
Nat Holman..............................1964
Bob Houbregs...........................1987
Chuck Hyatt *..........................1959
Dan Issel.................................1993
Bill Johnson *..........................1976
Neil Johnston *........................1990
K.C. Jones...............................1989
Sam Jones................................1983
Edward Krause.........................1975
Bob Kurland.............................1961
Bob Lanier...............................1992
Joe Lapchick *.........................1966
Clyde Lovellette.......................1988
Jerry Lucas..............................1979
Hank Luisetti...........................1959
Ed Macauley............................1960
Pete Maravich *.......................1987
Slater Martin............................1981
Branch McCracken *................1960
Jack McCracken *....................1962
Bobby McDermott....................1988
George Mikan...........................1959

Earl Monroe.............................1990
Calvin Murphy.........................1993
Charles Murphy........................1960
Harlan Page *...........................1962
Bob Pettit................................1970
Andy Phillip.............................1961
Jim Pollard *............................1977
Frank Ramsey...........................1981
Willis Reed.............................1981
Oscar Robertson.......................1979
John Roosma *.........................1961
John Russell *..........................1964
Bill Russell.............................1974
Dolph Schayes..........................1972
Ernest Schmidt *......................1973
John Schommer *.....................1959
Barney Sedran *.......................1962
Bill Sharman...........................1975
Christian Steinmetz *...............1961
John Thompson *......................1962
Nate Thurmond.........................1984
Jack Twyman............................1982
Wes Unseld..............................1988
Robert Vandivier *...................1974
Ed Wachter *...........................1961
Bill Walton..............................1993
Bobby Wanzer..........................1987
Jerry West................................1979
Lenny Wilkens..........................1989
John Wooden............................1960

Pro Football Hall of Fame

Quarterbacks

Sammy Baugh 1963
George Blanda 1981
Terry Bradshaw 1989
Dutch Clark * 1963
Jimmy Conzelman * 1964
Len Dawson 1987
Paddy Driscoll * 1965
Dan Fouts 1993

Otto Graham 1965
Bob Griese 1990
Arnie Herber * 1966
Sonny Jurgensen 1983
Bobby Layne * 1967
Sid Luckman 1965
Joe Namath 1985
Clarence Parker 1972

Bart Starr 1977
Roger Staubach 1985
Fran Tarkenton 1986
Y.A. Tittle 1971
Johnny Unitas 1979
Norm Van Brocklin * 1971
Bob Waterfield * 1965

Running Backs

Cliff Battles * 1968
Jim Brown 1971
Earl Campbell 1991
Tony Canadeo 1974
Larry Csonka 1987
Bill Dudley 1966
Frank Gifford 1977
Red Grange * 1977
Joe Guyon * 1966
Franco Harris 1990
Clarke Hinkle * 1964
Paul Hornung 1986

John Henry Johnson 1987
Tuffy Leemans * 1978
Ollie Matson 1972
George McAfee 1966
Hugh McElhenny 1970
Johnny McNally 1963
Lenny Moore 1975
Marion Motley 1968
Bronko Nagurski * 1963
Ernie Nevers * 1963
Walter Payton 1993
Joe Perry 1969

John Riggins 1992
Gale Sayers 1977
O.J. Simpson 1985
Ken Strong * 1967
Jim Taylor 1976
Jim Thorpe * 1963
Charley Trippi 1968
Steve Van Buren 1965
Doak Walker 1986

Ends and Receivers

Lance Alworth 1978
Red Badgro 1981
Raymond Berry 1973
Fred Biletnikoff 1988
Guy Chamberlin * 1965
Mike Ditka 1988

Tom Fears 1970
Bill Hewitt * 1971
Elroy Hirsch 1968
Don Hutson 1963
Dante Lavelli 1975
John Mackey 1992

Don Maynard 1987
Wayne Millner * 1968
Bobby Mitchell 1983
Pete Pihos 1970
Charley Taylor 1984
Paul Warfield 1983

Offensive Linemen

Chuck Bednarik 1967
Roosevelt Brown...................... 1975
Turk Edwards * 1969
Dan Fortmann 1985
Frank Gatski 1985
Forrest Gregg 1977
Lou Groza 1974
John Hannah 1991
Ed Healey * 1964
Mel Hein * 1963
Pete Henry * 1963

Cal Hubbard * 1963
Stan Jones 1991
Walt Kiesling 1966
Bruiser Kinard * 1971
Jim Langer 1987
Larry Little 1993
Link Lyman * 1964
Mike McCormack...................... 1984
Mike Michalske 1964
Ron Mix 1979
George Musso 1982

Jim Otto 1980
Jim Parker............................... 1973
Jim Ringo 1981
Bob St. Clair 1990
Art Shell 1989
Joe Stydahar * 1967
George Trafton * 1964
Bulldog Turner 1966
Gene Upshaw 1987
Alex Wojciechowicz * 1968

Defensive Linemen

Doug Atkins............................. 1982
Buck Buchanan * 1990
Willie Davis 1981
Art Donovan 1968
Len Ford * 1976
Joe Greene............................... 1987

Deacon Jones 1980
Bob Lilly................................. 1980
Gino Marchetti......................... 1972
Leo Nomellini.......................... 1969
Merlin Olsen 1982
Alan Page................................ 1988

Andy Robustelli 1971
Ernie Stautner.......................... 1969
Arnie Weinmeister.................... 1984
Bill Willis 1977

Linebackers

Bobby Bell 1983
Dick Butkus 1979
George Connor.......................... 1975
Bill George * 1974

Jack Ham 1988
Ted Hendricks 1990
Sam Huff.................................. 1982
Jack Lambert 1990

Willie Lanier............................ 1986
Ray Nitschke 1978
Joe Schmidt 1973

Defensive Backs

Herb Adderley.......................... 1980
Lem Barney.............................. 1992
Mel Blount 1989
Willie Brown............................ 1984

Jack Christiansen * 1970
Ken Houston 1986
Dick Lane 1974
Lary Yale 1979

Emlen Tunnell * 1967
Larry Wilson............................ 1978
Willie Wood............................. 1989

Placekicker

Jan Stenerud............................. 1991

Hockey Hall of Fame

Forwards

Sid Abel 1969
Jack Adams * 1959
Syl Apps 1961
George Armstrong 1975
Ace Bailey * 1975
Dan Bain * 1945
Hobey Baker 1945
Bill Barber 1990
Marty Barry * 1965
Andy Bathgate 1978
Jean Beliveau 1972
Doug Bentley * 1964
Max Bentley 1966
Toe Blake 1966
Mike Bossy 1991
Frank Boucher * 1958
Dubbie Bowie * 1945
Punch Broadbent * 1962
John Bucyk 1981
Billy Burch 1974
Bobby Clarke 1987
Neil Colville 1967
Charlie Conacher 1961
Bill Cook * 1952
Yvan Cournoyer 1982
Bill Cowley 1968
Rusty Crawford * 1962
Jack Darragh * 1962
Scotty Davidson * 1950
Hap Day 1961
Alex Delvecchio 1977
Cy Denneny * 1959
Marcel Dionne 1992
Gordie Drillon * 1975
Graham Drinkwater * 1950
Woody Dumart 1992
Tommy Dunderdale * 1974
Babe Dye * 1970
Phil Esposito 1984
Arthur Farrell * 1965
Frank Foyston * 1958

Frank Frederickson * 1958
Bob Gainey 1992
Jimmy Gardner * 1962
Bernie Geoffrion 1972
Eddie Gerard * 1945
Rod Gilbert 1982
Billy Gilmour * 1962
Si Griffis * 1950
George Hay * 1958
Bryan Hextall * 1969
Tom Hooper * 1962
Gordie Howe * 1972
Syd Howe * 1965
Bobby Hull 1983
Harry Hyland * 1962
Dick Irvin * 1958
Busher Jackson * 1971
Aurel Joliat * 1947
Duke Keats * 1958
Ted Kennedy 1966
Dave Keon 1986
Elmer Lach 1966
Guy Lafleur 1988
Newsy Lalonde * 1950
Jacques Lemaire 1984
Herbie Lewis * 1989
Ted Lindsay 1966
Mickey MacKay * 1952
Frank Mahovlich 1981
Joe Malone * 1950
Jack Marshall * 1965
Fred Maxwell * 1962
Lanny McDonald 1992
Frank McGee * 1945
Billy McGimsie * 1962
Stan Mikita 1983
Dickie Moore 1974
Howie Morenz * 1945
Bill Mosienko * 1965
Frank Nighbor * 1947
Reg Noble * 1962

Buddy O'Connor * 1988
Harry Oliver * 1967
Bert Olmstead 1985
Lynn Patrick * 1980
Gilbert Perreault 1990
Tom Phillips * 1945
Joe Primeau * 1963
Bob Pulford 1991
Frank Rankin * 1961
Jean Ratelle 1985
Henri Richard 1979
Maurice Richard..................... 1961
George Richardson * 1950
Gordie Roberts * 1971
Blair Russel * 1965
Jack Ruttan * 1962
Fred Scanlan * 1965
Milt Schmidt........................... 1961
Sweeney Schriner * 1962
Oliver Seibert * 1961
Babe Siebert * 1964
Darryl Sittler......................... 1989
Alf Smith * 1962
Clint Smith 1991
Hooley Smith * 1972
Tommy Smith * 1973
Barney Stanley * 1962
Nels Stewart * 1962
Bruce Stuart * 1961
Fred Taylor * 1947
Harry Trihey * 1950
Norm Ullman 1982
Jack Walker * 1960
Marty Walsh * 1962
Harry Watson * 1962
Cooney Weiland * 1971
Harry Westwick * 1962
Fred Whitcroft * 1962

Defensemen

Leo Boivin 1986
Dickie Boon * 1952
Butch Bouchard 1966
George Boucher * 1960
Harry Cameron * 1962
King Clancy * 1958
Dit Clapper * 1947
Sprague Cleghorn * 1958
Art Coulter 1974
Red Dutton * 1958
Fernie Flaman 1990
Bill Gadsby 1970
Herb Gardiner * 1958
F.X. Goheen * 1952
Ebbie Goodfellow * 1963
Mike Grant * 1950
Wilf Green * 1962

Joe Hall * 1961
Doug Harvey 1973
Red Horner 1965
Tom Horton * 1977
Harry Howell 1979
Ching Johnson * 1958
Ernie Johnson * 1952
Tom Johnson 1970
Red Kelly................................ 1969
Jack Laviollette * 1962
Jacques Leperrier 1987
Sylvio Mantha * 1960
George McNamara * 1958
Bobby Orr............................... 1979
Lester Patrick * 1947
Pierre Pilote 1975
Didier Pitre * 1962

Denis Potvin........................... 1991
Babe Pratt * 1966
Marcel Pronovost 1978
Harvey Pulford * 1945
Bill Quackenbush 1976
Kenny Reardon 1966
Art Ross 1945
Serge Savard 1986
Earl Seibert............................ 1963
Eddie Shore * 1947
Joe Simpson * 1962
Allan Stanley.......................... 1981
Jack Stewart * 1964
Hod Stuart * 1945
Gordon Wilson * 1962

Goaltenders

Clint Benedict * 1965
Johnny Bower 1976
Frankie Brimsek...................... 1966
Turk Broda * 1967
Gerry Cheevers 1985
Alex Connell * 1958
Ken Dryden............................. 1983
Bill Durnan * 1964
Tony Esposito 1988
Chuck Gardiner * 1945

Eddie Giacomin 1987
George Hainsworth * 1961
Glenn Hall 1975
Riley Hern * 1962
Hap Holmes * 1972
J.B. Hutton * 1962
Hughie Lehman * 1958
Percy LeSueur * 1961
Harry Lumley 1980
Paddy Moran * 1958

Bernie Parent........................... 1984
Jacques Plante * 1978
Chuck Rayner 1973
Terry Sawchuck * 1971
Billy Smith 1993
Tiny Thompson * 1959
Vladislav Tretiak 1989
Georges Vezina * 1945
Gump Worsley 1980
Roy Worters............................ 1969